DOC

HEROIC STORIES OF MEDICS, CORPSMEN, AND SURGEONS IN COMBAT

DOC

HEROIC STORIES OF MEDICS, CORPSMEN, AND SURGEONS IN COMBAT

MARK R. LITTLETON AND CHARLES "CHUCK" WRIGHT

ZENITH
PRESS

First published in 2005 by Zenith Press, an imprint of MBI Publishing Company, Galtier Plaza, Suite 200, 380 Jackson Street, St. Paul, MN 55101-3885 USA

Zenith Press titles are also available at discounts in bulk quantity for industrial or sales-promotional use. For details write to Special Sales Manager at MBI Publishing Company, Galtier Plaza, Suite 200, 380 Jackson Street, St. Paul, MN 55101-3885 USA.

ISBN-13: 0-978-0-7603-2119-5
ISBN-10: 0-7603-2119-1

Printed in the United States of America

ON THE FRONT COVER: The advancing infantry was lightly engaged during D-day operations at Gloucester, and casualties were light. Here, three corpsmen working in a small front-line aid station treat a marine who has been shot in his left arm, December 1943. *Official USMC Photo*

ON THE BACK COVER: Medics from the 10th Mountain Division treat a German P.O.W., World War II. *U.S. Army Medical Department Museum*

CONTENTS

Contents

INTRODUCTION

This is not a history book as most histories go, starting at the beginning of some project, mission, or person's life, and going to the end. Rather, it's a compendium of shorter stories, many written by the people involved, that usually focus on a single incident. The stories are compelling, even disturbing. Some of the stories are funny in their own way. It is a strength of the men and women who write here that they can still see the humor in what they did, even if much of it was harrowing and heart-breaking.

The medical people in this book are from all the services (except the Air Force), and all major American conflicts from World War I through the 2003 war in Iraq. They helped save many lives, but most of the soldiers they helped they never saw again, or even knew what became of them. In a few cases, a wounded soldier has been reunited with the medic or corpsman who helped him, but this is only a few. Most of the cases are virtually anonymous. No one will ever completely know how many people were saved by the medical personnel serving on the battlefield.

These people also watched many badly wounded men die on the battlefield or the stretcher, witnessing horrific wounds which they had no hope of suturing, taping, or doping enough to save the victims. They do not enjoy remembering the losses, yet many of them are mentioned here, and some of those stories have forever marked the men and women involved.

All these stories, regardless of outcome, memorialize a group of people who are not always remembered when the shelling is over, yet they are the first to be called when someone is wounded—first to administer aid in the middle of a firestorm, first to see the ravages of a bullet or a grenade. They don't flinch. They never complain. "I'm no hero," many of these people say of their service during the horrific agonies of war. "I was just doing my job."

But to the rest of us—especially to the soldiers they served—they are heroes.

These are their stories, unembellished. The straight stuff.

We hope you enjoy them.

Mark Littleton

PROLOGUE: THE MOST DECORATED SOLDIER IN WORLD WAR I

Russ Dodge

October 1918

The most decorated soldier in World War I was not Sergeant Alvin York, as many believe, but rather a stretcher bearer named Charles Denver Barger.

Charles Denver Barger grew up in Stott City, Missouri. His father died when Barger was six, and his mother gave the children to an orphanage. He was adopted, and did not see his mother again until 1923 in Waco, Missouri. His mother's remarried name was Mrs. Charles A. Rolleg.

Barger served in the U.S. Army during World War I as a private first class in Company L, 354th Infantry, 89th Division. He was awarded the Medal of Honor for his bravery near Bois-de-Bantheville, France, on October 31, 1918. His citation reads: "Learning that two daylight patrols had been caught out in No Man's Land and were unable to return, Pfc. Barger and another stretcher bearer, upon their own initiative, made two trips 500 yards beyond our lines, under constant machine gun fire, and rescued two wounded officers." His medal was presented to him in 1919.

Barger married Ruth Bailey. They had three children: Charles D. Barger Jr., born in 1923; Joseph Ehner Barger, born in 1924; and Dan-Mable Louise Barger, born in 1927.

The medals Barger was awarded for his service in World War I:
Medal of Honor (U.S.)
Purple Heart with nine clusters (U.S.)
Bronze Star (U.S.)
Distinguished Service Cross (U.S.)
Medallion Militaire (French army)
Croix de Guerre (French military)
Croix de Guerre with one Palm (French government)
Croix de Guerre with two Palms (French minister of war)
Croix de Guerre (Government of Montenegro)
Croce di Guerra (Italian government)
Victory Cross, a.k.a. "Baby Vic" (Great Britain)
Legion of Honor (King of Belgium)
Medaille di Milituerre (Luxembourg)
Overseas Service Medal, USA Medical Service Medal, USA
Medical Corps, Stretcher Bearer Medal, USA
Life Saver Award, International Societies of the Red Cross
Life Savers Medal (American Red Cross)
Life Savers Medal (French Red Cross)
Life Savers Medal (British Red Cross)
Award of Valor (Red Lion Society)

PART I: WORLD WAR II

TO THE CORPSMAN
SECRETARY OF THE NAVY JAMES FORRESTAL

Marines of World War II will never forget the corpsman, the man with the awful needle and wonderful plasma. Many an individual marine wounded in battle has thanked for his aid many an individual corpsman, who himself at the moment was in imminent danger of being hit. Secretary Forrestal has, in an official commendation, expressed the gratitude of the navy and the nation for the unparalleled life-saving performance of the Hospital Corps.

Commendation:

Out of every 100 men of the United States Navy and Marine Corps who were wounded in World War II, 97 recovered.

That is a record not equaled anywhere, any time.

Every individual who was thus saved from death, owes an everlasting debt to the Navy's Hospital Corps. The Navy is indebted to the Corps. The entire nation is its debtor, for thousands of citizens are living normal, constructive, happy and productive lives who, but for the skill and toil of the Hospital Corps, might be dead or disheartened by crippling invalidism.

So, to the 200,000 men and women of the Hospital Corps, I say in behalf of the United States Navy: "Well done. Well done, indeed!"

Without your service, the Navy's Medical Corps could not have achieved the life-saving record and the mind-saving record its physicians and surgeons and psychiatrists achieved. That others might live, your fellow corpsmen have given their lives; 889 of them were killed or mortally wounded. Others died as heroically from diseases they were trying to combat. In all, the Corps' casualty list contains 1,724 names, an honor roll of special distinction because none among them bore arms.

The Hospital Corpsmen saved lives on all the beaches that the Marines stormed. Corpsmen were at the foremost of every invasion, in all the actions at sea, on all carrier decks. You were on your own in submarines and the small ships of the fleet, performing emergency surgery at times when you had to take the fearsome responsibility of trying to save a life by heroic means or see the patient die. Your presence at every post of danger gave immeasurable confidence to your comrades under arms. Their bravery was fortified by the knowledge that the Corpsmen, the sailors of solace, were literally at their sides with the skills and means to stanch wounds, allay pain and to carry them back, if need be, to safe shelter and the ministrations of the finest medical talent in the world.

You corpsmen performed fox-hole surgery while shell fragments clipped your clothing, shattered the plasma bottles from which you poured new life into the wounded, and sniper's bullets were aimed at the brassards on your arms. On Iwo Jima, for example, the percentage of casualties among your Corps was greater than the proportion of losses among the Marines. Two of your colleagues who gave their lives in that history battle were posthumously cited for the Medal of Honor. One of the citations reads: "by his great personal valor in saving others at the sacrifice of his own life (he) inspired his companions, although terrifically outnumbered, to launch a fiercely determined attack and repulse the enemy forces." All that he had in his hands were the tools of mercy, yet he won a memorable victory at the cost of his life.

No wonder men and women are proud to wear the emblem of the Hospital Corps! It is a badge of mercy and valor, a token of unselfish service in the highest calling—the saving of life in the service of your country.

Your Corps' men and women toiled, often as dangerously, never less vitally, in areas remote from battle: In hospitals, on hospital ships, in airplanes, in laboratories and pharmacies and dispensaries. They helped, and are helping (for the task is far from over) in the salvage of men's broken bodies and minds that is the grim product and perennial aftermath of war. Some of you contributed toward new techniques in research and practice. Some used particular skills in dental technology, some engaged in pest control to diminish unfamiliar diseases, others taught natives of distant lands the benefits of modern hygiene, even to midwifery and everyday sanitation.

Scores of Corpsmen, made prisoners of war, used their skill and strength to retain life and hope in their fellow captives through long years of imprisonment and deprivation.

Whatever their duty, wherever they were, the men and women of the Hospital Corps served the Navy and served humanity, with exemplary courage, sagacity and effort. The performance of their duty has been "in keeping with the highest traditions of the United States Naval Service." That, to a Navy man or woman, is the highest of praise. The Corps has earned it, and continues to earn it.

For, as I said, the task is not yet competed. Thousands of the war's casualties will long need the ministrations of physicians, nurses and the Hospital Corps before they can return to normal, peacetime pursuits. Hundreds may have to be cared for as long as they live; that these unfortunates are so few is in large measure due to the prompt, skillful aid accorded our wounded and stricken, by your Corps.

Illness and accident will add to these numbers, of course. There will always be the sick and the injured, and there will always be need for trained personnel to help restore them. The Navy's busy laboratories are forever engaging in research to combat disease, to speed the healing of torn flesh and broken bones, to devise new aids for the maimed to lead a normal life. And so I am impelled to address this message not only to the men and women of the Corps who have completed their service to the Navy, but to those who are presently in the Corps, and, also to those who are joining—or rejoining—in that inspiring career.

It is no easy profession, even in peacetime. There is danger in the test tubes and culture racks as menacing as the guns of an unvanquished enemy. The Hospital Corps is never at peace. It is forever on the firing line in the ceaseless war against disease and premature death. That is why the Corps' emblem is truly "the red badge of courage," a designation to all the world that the person who wears it has been self-dedicated to the service of humanity.

Customarily the "Well-done" signal is reserved for the closing phrase of a message of congratulation, but I placed it in the forefront where, in this instance, it most fittingly belongs. I repeat it, here, with the postscript that in earning its "Well done," the Hospital Corps is assured no other unit in the Navy did better in the degree of essential duty inspiringly performed.

ATTACK ON THE USS *UTAH*
PHARMACIST'S MATE SECOND CLASS LEE SOUCY
Pearl Harbor, December 7, 1941

I had just had breakfast and was looking out a porthole in sick bay when someone said, "What the hell are all those planes doing up there on a Sunday?" Someone else said, "It must be those crazy marines. They'd be the only ones out maneuvering on a Sunday." When I looked up in the sky, I saw five or six planes starting their descent. Then, when the first bombs dropped on the hangars at Ford Island, I thought, "Those guys are missing us by a mile." Inasmuch as practice bombing was a daily occurrence to us, it was not too unusual for planes to drop bombs, but the time and place were quite out of line. We could not imagine bombing practice in port. It occurred to me and to most of the others that someone had really goofed this time and put live bombs on those planes by mistake.

In any event, even after I saw a huge fireball and cloud of black smoke rise from the hangers on Ford Island and heard explosions, it did not occur to me that these were enemy planes. It was too incredible—simply beyond imagination! "What a SNAFU," I moaned.

As I watched the explosions on Ford Island in amazement and disbelief, I felt the ship lurch. We didn't know it then, but we were being bombed and torpedoed by planes approaching from the opposite (port) side.

The bugler and bosun's mate were on the fantail ready to raise the colors at eight o'clock. In a matter of seconds, the bugler sounded "General Quarters." I grabbed my first aid bag and headed for my battle station amidships.

A number of the ship's tremors are vaguely imprinted in my mind, but I remember one jolt quite vividly. As I was running down the passageway toward my battle station, another torpedo or bomb hit and shook the ship severely. I was knocked off balance and through the log room door. I got up a little dazed and immediately darted down the ladder below the armored deck. I forgot my first aid kit.

By then the ship was already listing. There were a few men down below who looked dumbfounded and wondered out loud, "What's going on?" I felt around my shoulder in great alarm. No first aid kit! Being out of uniform is one thing, but being at a battle station without proper equipment is more than embarrassing.

After a minute or two below the armored deck, we heard another bugle call, then the bosun's whistle followed by the boatswain's chant, "Abandon ship . . . Abandon ship."

We scampered up the ladder. As I raced toward the open side of the deck, an officer stood by a stack of life preservers and tossed the jackets at us as we ran by. When I reached the open deck, the ship was listing precipitously. I thought about the huge amount of ammunition we had on board and that it would surely blow up soon. I wanted to get away from the ship fast, so I discarded my life jacket. I didn't want a Mae West slowing me down.

The day previous, I had been part of a fire and rescue party dispatched to fight a small fire on Ford Island. The fire was out by the time we got there, but I remembered distinctly the rugged beach, so I tied double knots in my shoes whereas just about everyone else kicked theirs off.

I was tensely poised for a running dive off the partially exposed hull when the ship lunged again and threw me off balance. I ended up with my bottom sliding across and down the barnacle-encrusted bottom of the ship.

When the ship had jolted, I thought we had been hit by another bomb or torpedo, but later it was determined that the mooring lines snapped, which caused the twenty-one-thousand-ton ship to jerk violently as she keeled over.

Nevertheless, after I bobbed up to the surface of the water to get my bearings, I spotted a motor launch with a coxswain fishing men out of the water with his boot hook. I started to swim toward the launch. After a few strokes, a hail of bullets hit the water a few feet in front of me in line with the launch. As the strafer banked, I noticed the big red insignias on his wing tips. Until then, I really had not known who attacked us. At some point, I had heard someone shout, "Where did those Germans come from?" I quickly decided that a boat full of men would be a more likely strafing target than a lone swimmer, so I changed course and hightailed it for Ford Island.

I reached the beach exhausted, and as I tried to catch my breath, another pharmacist's mate, Gordon Sumner from the *Utah*, stumbled out of the water. I remember how elated I was to see him. There is no doubt in my mind that bewilderment, if not misery, loves company. I remember I felt guilty that I had not made any effort to recover my first aid kit. Sumner had his wrapped around his shoulders.

While we both tried to get our wind back, a jeep came speeding by and came to a screeching halt. One of the two officers in the vehicle had spotted our Red Cross brassards and hailed us aboard. They took us to a two- or three-story concrete bachelor officer's quarters (BOQ) facing Battleship Row to set up an emergency treatment station for several oil-covered casualties strewn across the concrete floor. Most of them were from the capsized or flaming battleships. It did not take long to exhaust the supplies in Sumner's bag.

A line officer came by to inquire how we were getting along. We told him that we had run out of everything and were in urgent need of bandages and some kind of solvent or alcohol to cleanse wounds. He ordered someone to strip the beds and make rolls of bandages with the sheets, then turned to us. "Alcohol? Alcohol?" he said. "Will whiskey do?"

Before we could mull it over, he took off, and in a few minutes he returned and plunked a case of Scotch at our feet. Another person who accompanied him had an armful of bottles—a variety of liquors. I am sure denatured alcohol could not have served our purpose better for washing off the sticky oil, as well as providing some antiseptic effect for a variety of wounds and burns.

Despite the confusion, pain, and suffering, there was some gutsy humor amidst the pathos and chaos. At one point, an exhausted swimmer, covered with a gooey film of black oil, saw me walking around with a washcloth in one hand and a bottle of booze in the other. He hollered, "Hey, Doc, could I have a shot of that medicine?" I handed him the bottle of whichever medicine I had at the time. He took a hefty swig. He had no sooner swallowed the "medicine" than he spewed it out along with black mucoidal globs of oil. He lay back a minute after he stopped vomiting, then said, "Doc, I lost that medicine. How about another dose?"

Perhaps my internal as well as external application of booze was not accepted medical practice, but it sure made me popular with the old salts. Actually, it probably was a good medical procedure if it induced vomiting. Retaining contaminated water and oil in one's stomach was not good for one's health.

I remember another incident. A low-flying enemy pilot was strafing toward our concrete haven while I was on my knees trying to determine what to do for a prostrate casualty. Although the sailor, or marine, was in bad shape, he raised his head feebly when he saw the plane approach and shouted, "Open the doors and let the sonofabitch in."

Events which occurred in seconds take minutes to recount. During the lull, regular medical personnel from Ford Island Dispensary arrived with proper supplies and equipment and released Sumner and me so we could rejoin other *Utah* survivors for reassignment.

When the supplies ran out at our first aid station, I suggested to Sumner that he volunteer to go to the naval dispensary for some more. When he returned, he mentioned that he had a close call. A bomb landed in the patio while he was at the dispensary. He didn't mention any injury, so I shrugged it off. After all, under the circumstances, what was one bomb more or less? That afternoon, while we were both walking along a lanai (screened porch) at the dispensary, he pointed to a crater in the patio. "That's where the bomb hit I told you about." "Where were you?" I asked. He pointed to a spot not far away. I said, "Come on, if you had been that close, you'd have been killed." To which he replied, "Oh, it didn't go off. I fled the area in a hurry."

Sometime after dark, a squadron of six scout planes from the carrier *Enterprise* (two hundred or so miles out at sea), their fuel nearly depleted, came in for a landing on Ford Island. All hell broke loose and the sky lit up from tracer bullets from numerous antiaircraft guns. As the *Enterprise* planes approached, some understandably trigger-happy gunners opened fire; then all gunners followed suit and shot down all but one of our planes. At least, that's what I was told. Earlier that evening, many of the *Utah* survivors had been taken to the USS *Argonne* (AP-4), a transport. Gunners manning .50-caliber machine guns on the partially submerged USS *California* directly across from the *Argonne* hit the ship while shooting at the planes. A stray, armor-piercing bullet penetrated *Argonne's* thin bulkhead, went through a *Utah* survivor's arm, and spent itself in another sailor's heart. He died instantly.

The name Price has been stored in my memory bank for a long time as this fatality, but, at a recent reunion of *Utah* survivors, another ex-shipmate, Gilbert Meyer, insisted that Price was not the one killed. I didn't argue too long because I recalled meeting two men at the Pearl Harbor Naval Hospital several weeks after the raid who walked around with their own obituaries in their wallets—clippings from hometown newspapers.

THE REAL THING
LIEUTENANT RUTH ERICKSON
Pearl Harbor, December 7, 1941

Lieutenant Ruth Erickson of the Nurse Corps, U.S. Navy, was assigned to the hospital ship Relief (AH-1) in the late 1930s. In the following excerpt from an oral history interview with Lieutenant Erickson provided by the historian, Bureau of Medicine and Surgery, her narrative begins two years before the Pearl Harbor attack, in her home port of San Pedro, California, where she has just received orders for a new assignment.

In late summer of 1939 we learned that spring 1940 fleet maneuvers would be in Hawaii, off the coast of Maui. Further, I would be detached to report to the Naval Hospital, Pearl Harbor, Territory of Hawaii, when maneuvers were completed. The orders were effective on May 8, 1940.

Tropical duty was another segment in my life's adventure! On this same date I reported to the hospital command in which Captain Reynolds Hayden was the commanding officer. Miss Myrtle Kinsey was the chief of nursing services with a staff of eight nurses. I was also pleased to meet up with Miss Winnie Gibson once again, the operating room supervisor.

We nurses had regular ward assignments and went on duty at 8 a.m. Each had a nice room in the nurses' quarters. We were a bit spoiled; along with iced tea, fresh pineapple was always available.

We were off at noon each day while one nurse covered units until relieved at 3 p.m. In turn, the p.m. nurse was relieved at 10 p.m. The night nurse's hours were 10 p.m. to 8 a.m.

One month I'd have a medical ward, and the next month I rotated to a surgical ward. Again, I didn't have any operating room duties here. The fleet population was relatively young and healthy. We did have quite an outbreak of "catarrhal fever" with flulike symptoms. This was the only pressure period we had until the war started.

What was off-duty like?

Cars were few and far between, but two nurses had them. Many aviators were attached to Ford Island. Thus, there was dating. We had the tennis courts, swimming at the beach, and picnics. The large hotel at Waikiki was the Royal Hawaiian, where we enjoyed an occasional beautiful evening and dancing under starlit skies to lovely Hawaiian melodies.

And then it all ended rather quickly.

Yes, it did. A big dry dock to be built in the area was destined to go right through the area where the nurses' quarters stood. We had vacated the nurses' quarters about one week prior to the attack. We lived in temporary quarters directly across the street from the hospital, a one-story building in the shape of an "E." The permanent nurses' quarters had been stripped, and the shell of the building was to be razed in the next few days.

By now, the nursing staff had been increased to thirty and an appropriate number of doctors and corpsmen had been added. The Pacific Fleet had moved its base of operations from San Diego to Pearl Harbor. With this massive expansion, there went our tropical hours! The hospital now operated at full capacity.

Were you and your colleagues beginning to feel that war was coming?

No. We didn't know what to think. I had worked the afternoon duty on Saturday, December 6, from 3 p.m. until 10 p.m., with Sunday to be my day off.

Two or three of us were sitting in the dining room Sunday morning having a late breakfast and talking over coffee. Suddenly we heard planes roaring overhead and we said, "The 'flyboys' are really busy at Ford Island this morning." The island was directly across the channel from the hospital. We didn't think too much about it, since the reserves were often there for weekend training. We no sooner got those words out when we started to hear noises that were foreign to us.

I leaped out of my chair and dashed to the nearest window in the corridor. Right then, there was a plane flying directly over the top of our quarters, a one-story structure. The rising sun under the wing of the plane denoted the enemy. Had I known the pilot, one could almost see his features around his goggles. He was obviously saving his ammunition for the ships. Just down the row, all the ships were sitting there—the battleships *California* (BB-44), *Arizona* (BB-39), *Oklahoma* (BB-37), and others.

My heart was racing, the telephone was ringing, the chief nurse, Gertrude Arnest, was saying, "Girls, get into your uniforms at once. This is the real thing!"

I was in my room by that time changing into uniform. It was getting dusky, almost like evening. Smoke was rising from burning ships.

I dashed across the street, through a shrapnel shower, got into the lanai and just stood still for a second, as did a couple of doctors. I felt like I was frozen to the ground, but it was only a split second. I ran to the orthopedic dressing room but it was locked. A corpsmen ran to the officer of the day's desk for the keys. It seemed like an eternity before he returned and the room was opened. We drew water into every container we could find and set up the instrument boiler. Fortunately, we still had electricity and water. Commander Dr. Clyde

W. Brunson, the chief of medicine, was making sick call when the bombing started. When he was finished, he was to play golf . . .

The first patient came into our dressing room at 8:25 a.m. with a large opening in his abdomen and bleeding profusely. They started an intravenous and transfusion. I can still see the tremor of Dr. Brunson's hand as he picked up the needle. Everyone was terrified. The patient died within the hour.

Then the burned patients streamed in. The USS *Nevada* (BB-36) had managed some steam and attempted to get out of the channel. They were unable to make it and went aground on Hospital Point right near the hospital. There was heavy oil on the water, and the men dived off the ship and swam through these waters to Hospital Point, not too great a distance, but when one is burned . . . How they ever managed, I'll never know.

The tropical dress at the time was white t-shirts and shorts. The burns began where the pants ended. Personnel retrieved a supply of Flit guns—hand-pumped atomizers—from stock. We filled these with tannic acid to spray burned bodies. Then we gave these gravely injured patients sedatives for their intense pain.

Orthopedic patients were eased out of their beds with no time for linen changes as an unending stream of burn patients continued until midafternoon. A doctor, who several days before had renal surgery and was still convalescing, got out of his bed and began to assist the other doctors.

Do you recall the Japanese plane that was shot down and crashed into the tennis court?

Yes, the laboratory was next to the tennis court. The plane sheared off a corner of the laboratory and a number of the laboratory animals, rats and guinea pigs, were destroyed. Dr. Shaver [Lieutenant j.g. John S. Shaver, the chief pathologist] was very upset.

About noon, the galley personnel came around with sandwiches and cold drinks; we ate on the run. About two o'clock the chief nurse was making rounds to check on all the units and arrange relief schedules.

I was relieved around 4 p.m. and went over to the nurses' quarters, where everything was intact. I freshened up, had something to eat, and went back on duty at 8 p.m. I was scheduled to report to a surgical unit. By now it was dark and we worked with flashlights. The maintenance people and anyone else who could manage a hammer and nails were putting up black drapes or black paper to seal the crevices against any light that might stream to the outside.

About 10 or 11 p.m., there were planes overhead. I really hadn't felt frightened until this particular time. My knees were knocking together, and the patients were calling, "Nurse, nurse!" The other nurse and I went to them, held their hands a few moments, and then went on to others.

The priest was a very busy man. The noise ended very quickly and the word got around that these were our own planes.

What do you remember when daylight came?

I worked until midnight on that ward and then was directed to go down to the basement level in the main hospital building. Here the dependents—the women and children—the families of the doctors and other staff officers were placed for the night. There were ample blankets and pillows. We lay body by body along the walls of the basement. The children were frightened and the adults tense. It was not a very restful night for anyone.

Everyone was relieved to see daylight. At 6 a.m. I returned to the quarters, showered, had breakfast, and reported to a medical ward. There were more burn cases and I spent a week there.

What could you see when you looked over toward Ford Island?

I really couldn't see too much from the hospital because of the heavy smoke. Perhaps at a higher level one could have had a better view.

On the evening of December 17, the chief nurse told me I was being ordered to temporary duty and I was to go to the quarters, pack a bag, and be ready to leave at noon. When I asked where I was going, she said she had no idea. The commanding officer ordered her to obtain three nurses and they were to be in uniform. In that era we had no outdoor uniforms. Thus it would be the regular white ward uniforms.

And so in our ward uniforms, capes, blue felt hats, and blue sweaters, Lauretta Eno, Catherine Richardson, and I waited for a car and driver to pick us up at the quarters. When he arrived and inquired of our destination, we still had no idea! The OD's desk had our priority orders to go to one of the piers in Honolulu. We were to go aboard the SS steamship *President Coolidge* and prepare to receive patients. We calculated supplies for a ten-day period.

We three nurses and a number of corpsmen from the hospital were assigned to the SS *Coolidge*.

Eight volunteer nurses from the Queen's Hospital in Honolulu were attached to the army transport at the next pier, U.S. Army transport *Scott*, a smaller ship.

The naval hospital brought our supplies the following day, the eighteenth, and we worked late into the evening. We received our patients from the hospital on the nineteenth, the *Coolidge* with 125 patients and the *Scott* with 55.

Were these the most critically injured patients?

The command decided that patients who would need more than three-months' treatment should be transferred. Some were very bad and probably should not have been moved. There were many passengers already aboard the ship, missionaries and countless others who had been picked up in the Orient. Two navy doctors on the passenger list from the Philippines were placed on temporary duty, and they were pleased to be of help.

Catherine Richardson worked 8 a.m. to 4 p.m. I had the 4 p.m. to midnight, and Lauretta Eno worked midnight to 8 a.m. Everyone was very apprehensive. The ship traveled without exterior lights, but there was ample light inside.

You left at night?

Yes, we left in the late afternoon of the nineteenth. There were eight or ten ships in the convoy. It was quite chilly the next day; I later learned that we had gone fairly far north instead of directly across. The rumors were rampant that a submarine was seen out this porthole in some other direction. I never get seasick and enjoy a bit of heavy seas, but this was different! Ventilation was limited by reason of sealed ports and only added to gastric misery. I was squared about very soon.

The night before we got into port, we lost a patient, an older man, perhaps a chief. He had been badly burned. He was losing intravenous fluids faster than they could be replaced. Our destination became San Francisco with 124 patients and one deceased.

We arrived at 8 a.m. on Christmas Day! Two ferries were waiting there for us with cots aboard and ambulances from the naval hospital at Mare Island and nearby civilian hospitals. The Red Cross was a cheerful sight with donuts and coffee.

Our arrival was kept very quiet. Heretofore, all ship's movements were published in the daily paper, but since the war had started, this had ceased. I don't recall that other ships in the convoy came in with us except for the *Scott*. We and the *Scott* were the only ships to enter the port. The convoy probably slipped away.

The patients were very happy to be home and so were we all. The ambulances went on ahead to Mare Island. By the time we had everyone settled on the two ferries, it was close to noon. We arrived at Mare Island at 4:30 p.m. and helped get the patients into the respective wards.

While at Mare Island, a doctor said to me, "For God's sake, Ruth, what's happened out there? We don't know a thing." He had been on the USS *Arizona* (BB-39) and was detached only a few months prior to the attack. We stayed in the nurses' quarters that night.

ABOARD THE *YORKTOWN*
Lieutenant Joseph P. Pollard
Battle of Midway, June 4, 1942

On December 15, 1941, I was detached from the U.S. Naval School of Aviation Medicine, Pensacola, Florida, destined to eventually join the crew of the USS *Yorktown*. After a short cruise in the USS *Hornet* and her plane guard, the USS *Noa* (DD-343), in the Atlantic, I drove across country by auto to San Diego and served briefly in Aircraft Scouting Force Pacific, Transition Training Squadron. After sailing in the USS *Fulton* (AS-11) to Pearl Harbor, I served briefly while attached to the 14th Naval District in the Old Naval School Dispensary, Honolulu. When the USS *Yorktown* arrived in Pearl Harbor from the Coral Sea, my orders to her were after this long time to be carried out.

On May 27, 1942, I was detached from Commander, 14th Naval District, and at 2000 reported on board the USS *Yorktown* for duty. She was alongside Pier B-16 in Pearl Harbor.

On May 30, the USS *Yorktown* put to sea at 0800 and took a course said to be toward Midway at a speed of about fifteen knots. Morale was excellent. I had the flight deck duty station when we took on board our aircraft. One of our lieutenant commanders was killed at this time in a very unfortunate accident. A fighter drifted over the arresting cables, over the barriers, and sat down on the back of his plane. The propeller of the fighter split his headrest, causing a compound skull fracture; the next blade pushed in the rim of the cockpit, crushing his jaw, face, and neck and severing the great vessels of his neck. Obviously, there was nothing I or anyone could do for him.

On May 31, we spent a busy but uneventful day at sea. The aircraft landings were better and we had no crashes. Our escorts were the *Portland*, *Astoria*, *Hammann*, *Hughes*, *Russell*, and *Balch*. The ship's company was informed that when this mission was completed, the ship was scheduled for a complete overhaul. This would mean perhaps a month's leave. Since the crew had just returned from the Coral Sea and had spent 102 days without liberty, this was welcomed news. We felt somewhat uneasy at going into battle in our condition, as the watertight integrity of the ship was said to be considerably reduced as a result of damage received in the Battle of the Coral Sea.

On June 1, we spent a very busy day making preparations for battle. Antiflash clothing, gas masks, and steel helmets were issued to all hands. We had the ship fitter repair the large overhead water tank in Battle Dressing Station Number 1 and fill it with water. We broke out and rechecked our emergency medical equipment.

On June 2, our scouting aircraft were out morning and afternoon. Excitement was running high in the ship and morale was excellent. We were told that our submarines had reported a Jap invasion force (battleships, cruisers, destroyers, and transports) off Midway Island. We rendezvoused with the *Hornet* and *Enterprise* and their escorts in late afternoon and remained with them overnight.

On June 3, scuttlebutt was thick. We heard that land-based aircraft had picked up the Jap invasion force and bombed them and also that our submarines were active. A Japanese carrier force was reported northwest of Midway consisting of three carriers and their screen. We were said to be heading toward them.

On June 4, I had the duty and Doctor Dobos assumed flight quarters in the morning while I took eye, ear, nose, and throat (EENT) sick call. Our scouting aircraft were dispatched. One returned about 0930 and dropped a message on our flight deck. The Jap task force of three carriers and their screen was reported to be two-hundred miles ahead, closing in on us at twenty-five knots. I was called to the flight deck to relieve Doctor Dobos, and sick call was suspended. All of our aircraft came aboard uneventfully and were gassed. Our bombers were loaded with thousand-pounders, the TBDs [Douglas "Devastator" torpedo-bombers] with torpedoes, and planes spotted for takeoff—fighters, then bombers, and lastly the TBDs. Everywhere there was an undercurrent of excitement. At any moment the word might be passed to begin our attack. At any moment we might be attacked.

Meanwhile, the *Hornet* had sent off her planes, the *Enterprise* sent hers off. We could see them on the horizon like a swarm of bees—then they were gone. A report came in from Midway Island that the Japs were attacking. We hoped that our planes would make their attack on the enemy carriers while their planes were over Midway. After a while a report came in that the *Enterprise* group was hitting the Jap carrier force at will. Apparently, the Japanese had hit Midway with everything they had and had not expected to be attacked themselves. The *Enterprise*'s attack was completed and word came over the bull horn, "Pilots, man your planes." We put off our bombers, torpedo planes, and a half-dozen fighters for their protection. Then we put up more fighters for our protection. We sat tight with no news for a while. There was a great deal of tension. There were small groups of people everywhere, talking in low tones. Everyone was wearing antiflash clothing and steel helmets. All was quiet—too quiet. Battle Dressing Station Number 1, my duty station, was manned and ready. The morning wore itself away and the afternoon began. I became hungry and went down to the wardroom for a sandwich.

About 1400 our planes began returning. They had been out a long time and were low on gas. A couple of well-shot-up SBDs [Douglas "Dauntless" dive-bombers] made their crash landings. Then the fighters started coming aboard. Many were riddled with holes. We landed about five and then one came in too hot and too high. He began to float over the deck and it looked like trouble. The pilot recognized that he was in trouble and made a dive for the deck. He somersaulted and skidded away on the deck. I made a quick dive under the wreckage but the pilot was unhurt and got out of the wreckage before I could get to him. I began to run across the flight deck to my station but before I arrived there general quarters sounded, and Jap planes were upon us. I dived down the ladder for Battle Dressing Station Number 1 and on my way saw one of our fighters fall on one wing and like a shooting star hit the drink. There was a puff of black smoke and that was all. Upon arriving at Number 1, I lay flat on the deck and hoped that we would not get a bomb in the crowded dressing room or anywhere for that matter. By this time our AA [antiaircraft guns] was in full bloom. I had never before heard such a roar—first the 5-inchers, then the 1.1-inchers and 20mms, the .50-calibers, and finally the hastily set up .30-caliber machine guns along the rail. I knew then they were upon us. Then all hell broke loose. I saw a burst of fire, heard a terrific explosion and in less then ten seconds was overwhelmed by a mass of men descending from the gun mounts and flight deck into the Dressing Station. An instantaneous five-hundred-pound bomb had struck just aft of the starboard side of the middle elevator, and shrapnel had wiped out nearly all of the men from AA mounts 3 and 4 (1.1-inchers) and also my corpsman, who stood on the aft island ladder platform where I usually stood. Another corpsman was injured who was standing in the gear locker doorway.

I was overwhelmed with work. Wounded were everywhere. Some men had one foot or leg off, others had both off; some were dying, some were dead. Everywhere there was need for morphine, tourniquets, blankets, and first aid. Battle Dressing Station Number 1 rapidly overflowed into the passageway, into the parachute loft, and into all other available spaces. I called for stretcher bearers to get the more seriously wounded to the sick bay, where they could receive plasma, etc., but the passageways had been blocked off due to the bomb hits. So we gave more morphine, covered the patients with blankets, and did the best we could. Many patients went rapidly into shock. All topside lights were out, and I never realized that flashlights gave such miserably poor light. There was no smoke in Battle Dressing Station Number 1, which was fortunate. Water hoses were dragged into the passageway in an attempt to control a fire some-where forward in the island. The hose had been perforated by shrapnel and sprayed water all over the deck and on some of my wounded, who were lying in the passageway. Our water tank was very useful to us, as there was a great need for drinking water and none was otherwise obtainable.

I went up to the flight deck. The first thing that I noticed was Mount Number 4. A pair of legs attached to the hips sat in the trainer's seat. A stub of spinal column was hanging over backward—there was nothing else remaining of the trainer. The steel splinter shield was full of men—or rather, portions of men, many of whom were not identifiable. Blood was everywhere. I turned forward and saw great billows of smoke rising from our stack region. We were dead in the water and it suddenly dawned on me how helpless we were lying there. A repair party was rebuilding a portion of the flight deck. Then I was called aft where there were several casualties from shrapnel, which came from a near miss off the fantail. There were wounded also along the catwalk along the starboard side.

Doctors A. M. French, N. E. Dobos, Lough, and Jackson came up—later, Captain W. D. Davis of the Medical Corps. We arranged to have our topside casualties lowered to the sick bay on the forward bomb elevator, and this was begun.

The fire by this time was discovered to be in the rag locker and was under control. This stopped the billowing column of smoke, which gave away our position and made us so susceptible to a sec-ond attack. Suddenly, there was a great burst of steam from our stack, then another, and amid cheers from all hands we got under way. Meanwhile, the admiral and his staff had gone over to the *Astoria* and it was said that we had orders to proceed to the States at the best speed we could make. We seemed to be doing all right and began getting the ship in shape. We were really beginning to have some hope that the Japs would not return, but alas and alack.

About 1600 our radar picked up enemy planes at forty to sixty miles coming in fast. We had just begun to gas five F4 Grumman "Wildcat" fighters that we had succeeded in landing just before the previous attack. Some had only twenty-five gallons aboard. Nevertheless, they took off post haste. We were just hitting twenty-two knots but they took a long run and made it off. Just as the last one left the deck I made a dive for Battle Dressing Station Number 1 and again the AAs began as before. By the time I could find an unoccupied place on the deck, there was a sickening thud and rumble throughout the ship and the deck rose under me, trembled, and fell away. One torpedo hit had occurred. My thought was that we could take this one and get away with it perhaps but not any more. Then another sickening thud and the good ship shuddered and rapidly listed hard to port. I knew we were completely helpless but did not want to admit it. Just then word came over the speaker, "Prepare to abandon ship." I was dumbfounded. It was incomprehensible.

A man lying beside me with one foot shot away and a severe chest wound turned his head toward me and asked, "What does this mean for us?" and turned his head away. He knew that he would have no chance in the water. This man was later seen in the Naval Hospital in Pearl Harbor, on the way to recovery. We listed more and more to port until it was almost impossible to stand on the slick deck. We searched frantically for life preservers for the wounded, taking some from the dead. Our stretchers had gone below to the sick bay, and we had difficulty finding enough for our wounded. All who could possibly walk did so. I went up on the flight deck and walked along the starboard edge, being very careful not to slip and skid the width of the ship and off the port side. The ship rolled slowly with the swells, but the water was not rough, and after each roll she returned to her former position. I thought a big wave might possibly capsize her. A bulkhead giving way below might also let her go over. Our list was about thirty degrees. The speakers were dead, and when word was passed to abandon ship, it did not get to me. Several life rafts were in the water, but the lines over the side were not long enough to reach the water. Lieutenant Wilson and I tied some lines together and lowered some wounded. Meanwhile, the sick bay wounded were being lowered from the hangar deck. Captain Elliott Buckmaster, commanding officer of the *Yorktown*, came up and said to abandon ship.

Captain Buckmaster approached me as I was on the verge of going over the side at a place we had lowered some wounded on the starboard side aft of the island structure. There were several life rafts of wounded floating below me. He asked what I was waiting for. I told him I was waiting to get off all the wounded and that we had searched the topside structure and the catwalks, and I was sure that we had every man that was alive from this area on the life rafts. He said something to the effect that, "They said the captain should be the last to leave the ship. I'm ready to go now. Would you leave?"

I chose a big line and went over the side. I stopped at the armor belt, a thick band of armor above and below the waterline, for a rest. It was at least seventy-five feet from the deck to the water and I still had some twenty feet to go. I worked along the armor belt to a spot which was immediately above a life raft. The line there was a small one, and soon after I started down, a corner of my life jacket got inside my grip and I began slipping. The fingers of both my hands were rather badly burned before I realized it. Then I released the line and dropped the remainder of the way into the water and swam through the oil to the raft. We took on board several wounded who were close by until the raft was overflowing and the few of us with life preservers had to get out and swim or hold on with one hand. As each wave broke over our heads, the oil burned our eyes and noses like liquid fire. It was impossible to keep from swallowing some of it.

Someone would swim alongside and say, "Hold me up a minute, please," and proceed to vomit the oil and then swim on. We had nine stretcher cases and about twenty-five men on or hanging on to our raft. We tried to flutter kick and paddle our raft away from the side of the ship, but each wave seemed to bring us back against her side. If she capsized we would be carried down by suction and not have a chance. Finally, someone got the bright idea of paddling aft along the side of the ship, and we began to make some headway. By doing this we finally got free of her stern.

Meanwhile, our destroyers were weaving back and forth about three-hundred yards away picking up survivors. Captain Buckmaster swam alongside the raft that I was holding onto but would not come aboard as we were so overcrowded. Instead he swam to a nearby raft and hung onto it. A passing motor whaleboat threw his raft a line and was towing it to the *Russell* but with too much speed, and a mess attendant was pulled off. Instead of treading water, he began screaming and wearing himself out. Captain Buckmaster turned loose of his raft and swam to the mess attendant. They were both about gone when a man from our raft swam out and helped keep both of them afloat. We took the mess attendant aboard but the captain preferred to swim.

About this time the *Hughes* threw us a line—two or three of them. All were short, and as enemy planes were reported coming in, our chances seemed to be at an all time low; but the *Hammann* finally came alongside and got us. She was a wonderful ship. We had been in the water 2 1/2 hours (picked up at 1930 hours). Just as we hit the deck of the *Hammann*, there was another general quarters alarm (enemy planes) and she went to full speed, but the planes proved to be friendly. Fortunately, the Japs seemed unaware of our predicament.

APPENDECTOMY ON THE USS *SEADRAGON*
Pharmacist's Mate Wheeler B. Lipes
September 1942

One of the most dramatic stories to come out of World War II recounted the emergency operation performed by a twenty-three-year-old corpsman as his submarine, USS Seadragon *(SS-194), cruised submerged in enemy waters. Related in a 1942 newspaper article, the story brought a Pulitzer Prize to journalist George Weller and fame to Pharmacist's Mate Wheeler B. Lipes. It also gave a much-needed dose of inspiration to the home front when good news about the war was hard to come by.*

Over the years the episode became legend, providing drama for such Hollywood productions as Destination Tokyo *and* Run Silent, Run Deep.

I joined the Navy in 1936. I was in a long time before the war broke out. I had been on the battleship USS *Texas* (BB-35) before I went to the Naval Hospital in Philadelphia. From there I went to Canacao near Manila. In October of 1941 I went into submarines.

How did that happen?

One day I just decided I wanted submarines. The personnel officer thought that I had a hole in my head. There weren't any subs available then, but I went looking for one and eventually got aboard the USS *Sealion* (SS-195). The *Sealion* and the USS *Seadragon* (SS-194) were sister ships. The *Sealion* was almost finished with its overhaul and the two subs were tied alongside one another at the Cavite Navy Yard. When the bombers came at noon on December 10, 1941, they just leisurely wiped out the yard. One bomb went right down the after engine room hatch. The shrapnel from that one killed some people on the *Seadragon's* conning tower and punched holes in her pressure hull. I was in the water for a while and was picked up on the perimeter of the navy yard late that night, with the yard burning and exploding. The *Seadragon's* pharmacist's mate was slightly wounded in the arm by shrapnel and he transferred himself off the sub, which left a vacancy. I was the logical choice to replace him. My escape from the Philippines was made possible by that event.

How many patrols did you participate in?

About five as I recall. Formosa, Camranh Bay. We were in the blockade of New Britain, New Ireland, Java, Java Sea, and in on all the initial efforts to hold back the Japanese and keep our finger in the dike until reinforcements arrived. As part of a squadron of submarines that was feeding Bataan, we would leave our torpedoes, except those in the tubes, in Cebu, take on forty to sixty tons of food, and run it into Corregidor. As Bataan was being overrun, we were taking people off Corregidor.

What actually happened on Seadragon *in September 1942?*

I had been up on the watch and when I came down to the after battery section of the submarine—the crew's compartment—I found Darrell Rector. It was his nineteenth birthday. He said to me, "Hey Doc, I don't feel very good." I told him to get into his bunk and rest a bit and kept him under observation. His temperature was rising. He had the classic symptoms of appendicitis. The abdominal muscles were getting that washboard rigidity. He then began to flex his right leg up on his abdomen to get some relief. He worsened and I went to the commanding officer (CO) to report his condition. The skipper went back and talked to Rector, explaining that there were no doctors around. Rector then said, "Whatever Lipes wants to do is OK with me." The CO and I had a long talk, and he asked me what I was going to do. "Nothing," I replied. He lectured me about the fact that we were there to do the best we could. "I fire torpedoes every day and some of them miss," he reminded me. I told him that I could not fire this torpedo and miss. He asked me if I could do the surgery and I said yes. He then ordered me to do it.

When I got to the appendix, it wasn't there. I thought, "Oh my God! Is this guy reversed?" There are people like that with organs opposite where they should be. I slipped my finger down under the cecum—the blind gut—and felt it there. Suddenly I understood why it hadn't popped up where I could see it. I turned the cecum over. The appendix, which was five inches long, was adhered, buried at the distal tip, and looked gangrenous two-thirds of the way. What luck, I thought. My first one couldn't be easy. I detached the appendix, tied it off in two places, and then removed it, after which I cauterized the stump with phenol. I then neutralized the phenol with torpedo alcohol. There was no penicillin in those days. When you think of what we have in the armamentarium today to prevent infection, I marvel.

You did have sulfa, didn't you?

We had some tablets that I ground into a powder and then put in the oven to kill any spores. This was all I had. I had given this kid a three-inch incision, yet he healed well and was back on duty in a few days. In fact, the ship's cook said, "Doc, you must have sewed him up with rubber bands, the way he eats."

Obviously, this was not the first time you had seen such an operation.

Oh, no. I assisted many times in the OR. In fact, the day I was to leave the Naval Hospital at Canacao, a doctor I had worked with, Carey Smith, came over to me and said, "You never know what's going to happen in a submarine. One of the things you may face is appendicitis. Never use a purse-string closure." I remembered that advice.

What was the general reaction to your successful surgery?

After we submitted our report, there was a great deal of consternation in the Bureau of Medicine and Surgery. Everyone did then exactly what they would probably do now. They reacted to a situation they knew absolutely nothing about. There was an old warrant officer I knew back at BUMED [the U.S. Navy Bureau of Medicine and Surgery] who was on duty the night the message came in about the operation. He told me later how much trouble I had caused him. There were many doctors back there who were very upset about what I had done. I guess they were afraid that because I had performed an appendectomy everyone in the fleet would be running around looking for the first opportunity to do one. They forgot there were commanding officers and you had supervisory chains that would preclude this.

Were you ever officially recognized for having performed the operation?

The day I returned I got one of those canned retirement letters signed by the surgeon general. It gave me credit for bravery in action during the sinking of the submarine *Sealion*. Yet neither it nor any document I ever received mentioned the appendectomy. Not that that incident in itself was so important. What was important was that I did my job and saved the guy's life. It was my job to do anything I could to preserve life and, really, I didn't deserve special credit or recognition for doing that. However, since the incident had gone so far to give the navy good publicity and to present to the public the fact that navy men were well trained and dedicated, the omission was that much more evident.

I think the whole point of the operation was not that I did it. It was the fact that those hospital corpsmen on independent duty had been so well trained. It was proof that the navy's training program was tested and found to be effective. There was a hardcore group of hospital corpsmen and pharmacist's mates in those days who worked very closely with doctors who themselves spent a lot of time teaching us. And those on independent duty demonstrated that whether it was in the field with the marines or aboard surface ships, or wherever, we could do the job.

When did you get back home?

I returned to the States in January 1943 and reported to the Naval Hospital in Philadelphia, where I was promoted to warrant officer. I then represented the navy in war bond drives and visits to war plants.

How long were you on the speaking circuit?

About eight or nine months. I would go from plant to plant, making speeches and trying to increase production and sell bonds. This was in addition to my regular duty at the hospital.

How did George Weller come to write the original article?

[The interviewer is referring to an article Weller, a reporter for the *Chicago Daily News*, wrote on the appendectomy incident; he received the 1943 Pulitzer Journalism Prize in Reporting for this article.]

When I got back from that patrol, our report—"One Merchant Ship, One Oil Tanker, and One Successful Appendectomy"—had already caused a stir. I was told I was wanted in the wardroom of the submarine tender USS *Holland* (AS-3). When I arrived, there was Admiral Charles A. Lockwood commander submarines, southwest Pacific. He and I had a conversation and then Weller came in. He and I talked at some length and then he wrote the story.

In the last forty-four years not a month has gone by that I'm not reminded of that incident. Weller's story has even appeared in high school literature books. When my grandson was in the seventh grade in New Mexico, he found it in one of his books. In fact, he proudly told the teacher that this was his grandfather. The teacher said something like, "Go away, little boy, don't tell stories." It's also been the subject of movies and TV programs. There was a series in the 1950s called *The Silent Service*, in which the incident was portrayed in an episode called "Operation *Seadragon*."

I was on an airplane recently and the man next to me was reading a magazine containing one of those "Ripley's Believe It or Nots." It told of a submarine sailor who removed the appendix of a shipmate. This guy turned to me and said, "Can you believe that?" I read it, shook my head, and said, "Don't you believe a word of it."

Wheeler B. Lipes retired from the Medical Service Corps in 1962. He then became chief executive officer of the thousand-bed Memphis hospital, which serves as the teaching facility for the University of Tennessee and, subsequently, president of Memorial Medical Center in Corpus Christi, Texas.

Darrell Dean Rector, Lipes' patient, did not survive the war. He died October 24, 1944, in the tragic sinking of USS Tang *(SS-306). On her fifth war patrol,* Tang *launched a surface attack against a Japanese transport. One torpedo ran true; the other turned sharply left, circled, and hit the submarine in the stern. The wound was fatal. There were but nine survivors. All spent the rest of the war as POWs. Her skipper, Commander R. H. O'Kane, survived the war and received the Medal of Honor.*

There were two other successful appendectomies performed by submarine corpsmen during the war, one aboard USS *Grayback* (SS-208), the other aboard USS *Silversides* (SS-236).

BATTLE OF GUADALCANAL
Pharmacist's Mate First Class Louis Ortega
1942–1943

Ortega was with the 7th Marine Regiment in 1942. The follow-ing interview picks up just before Ortega's arrival on Guadal-canal. [Oral history provided courtesy of Historian, Bureau of Medicine and Surgery.]

As a corpsman, I lugged around a Unit 3 medical bag and Form 782 field equipment pack, poncho, blankets, cartridge belt, hel-met, pack, etc. This was the old pack. Today they have the knapsacks. Some of us had the old puttee World War I–style wrap-around leg-gings. Later on we got the regular lace-up leggings. We had the old tin hat. The Unit 3 was like a horse harness you put over your head and it had two bags full of first aid equipment. And that was it.

So there we were in early April 1942 on the transport USS *Fuller* (AP-14). On our way overseas with the 7th Marine Regiment. Thirty days later, May 10, 1942, we pulled into a pier at Samoa, and that's where they dropped us off. In the meantime, the 1st and 5th Marines were being formed at New River, now Camp Lejeune, North Carolina. They were calling in all the guards from the navy yards, the recruiters, all the outposts, from the islands of Puerto Rico. All the veterans were in the 7th Regiment. The 4th Marines had all been captured in the fall of the Philippines. And of course I would get Chesty Puller [Lieutenant Colonel Lewis B. "Chesty" Puller, USMC], commanding officer of 1st Battalion, 7th Marine Regiment at Guadalcanal. He thought he would be in on the first action. When they dropped us in Samoa, it nearly broke his heart.

By then there was nothing between the Japs and Australia. Everything had fallen. When we got to Samoa, there was nothing there. We worked day and night building defenses. When the word came that the 1st Marine Division had landed at Guadalcanal, I thought Chesty was going to kill himself. We were all broken-hearted. And then we started to get the bad news. We lost five cruisers in one night—Savo Island.

Toward the end of August, we got the word. We were needed. We were hot to trot. On September 15, we landed at Lunga Beach. We went up on the transport USS *Crescent City* (AP-40). Again, it was one of these over-the-side transports, and the landing craft didn't have ramps. They went in so far and then you jumped out in to the water and everything had to be passed by hand. We went down the cargo nets into the Higgins boats [wooden thirty-six-foot infantry landing craft]. When we got on the beach we had to take our gear off, lay it on the beach, and form a line to pass supplies.

Was there any opposition?

No. Not at that time. That night everything was piled up on the beach. I was with a marine driver because the medical companies, the stretcher bearers, were all musicians. They used musicians to help with the stretcher bearing. I was sitting with this corporal on top of these boxes. It was my turn to be on watch—twelve to four in the morning. So I was sitting with this corporal on top of these boxes. He said, "I wonder what the hell we're sitting on?" He pries open a box, sticks in his bayonet. "Hey, peaches!" He just passed one over to me when *kaboom*! I went flying on my ass. A spotlight came on from the sea and the shells started coming and the trees were falling. It was a mess. A shell cut off the top of a palm tree, which fell on me.

It was a Jap submarine that came up and threw in a couple of shells. Then it disappeared. One guy was wounded.

Then we marched into the bush and were assigned positions. I dug a little slit trench, put my foot in it and thought, "That's deep enough." Then put a piece of tin over it, then some palm trees. A few days went by while we were getting organized. We weren't moving anywhere. Then came the first air raid. Everyone just sat out there and watched. "Wow, look at that one over there." Suddenly shrapnel from the antiaircraft started falling. I got into my trench. I learned two things. When you build a foxhole, build it deep. And secondly, never go into it alone. When you're by yourself, you think, and your mind starts doing all kinds of weird things. You hear the swish of a bomb, which sounds like shaking tinfoil. Then the ground shakes, and then you wait for the next one. And the ground shakes again. By that time you really want some company. With two people in there you learn one thing. Look at that sonofabitch, he's scared as hell. And he's looking at you and saying the same thing. Oh, I'm not scared, he's scared. With someone else there, you're able to compensate for the fear, but when you're alone, you sweat. You knew when an air raid was coming. Every fly, bird, every insect seemed to head for a foxhole. And sure enough, soon the bombs started falling. I don't know how the insects knew it.

There were always flies all over the place. The coconut groves had been unattended for years. The coconuts were rotting. There was a difference to the smell of the jungle. The rot, the dampness. Some places the sun never shined.

The following day there was another raid and a bomb hit close by. The edge of the crater was three yards from my foxhole and caved it in. I saw that and I began digging deeper. We dug it so deep that you could stand up in it and still be underground. And being Americans, we liked our comfort so we put matting around it. We put two stools inside. We put logs over it and sandbags on top of those and ponchos to make it waterproof and then poured dirt on top of that. What we had was a pillbox.

After being on the line almost a month, we pulled back to Henderson Field [airfield on Guadalcanal, captured by marines and named for a deceased marine pilot] for some rest. It started about 11 p.m. on October 13, 1942. We were lying down in our pillbox. A whistling noise and then boom! "What the hell was that?" And then another one. For the next four hours we were bombarded by four battleships and two cruisers. Let me tell you something. You can get a dozen air raids a day, but they come and they're gone. A battleship can sit there for hour after hour and throw fourteen-inch shells. I will never forget those four hours. The next morning when they stopped shelling, there was a haze over the whole area. Five miles of coconut groves were gone! Where the day before you had miles and miles of coconut trees, now five square miles were wiped clean. Every tree was gone. The airfield was destroyed.

And over on Point Cruz you could see six Japanese transport ships merrily unloading troops. The next day after they unloaded, in comes a U.S. transport ship. We hadn't seen a transport in over a month since we landed. It brought the 164th Army Infantry Regiment with the new Garand rifles [.30-caliber M1]. That helped a lot later on. We had the old Springfield '03 [.30-caliber M-1903] with the bolt action. When the next battle took place and threw the 164th into the line, the Japs would charge and wait for the five shots the '03 had. But this time the army would let them have it with two extra shots, actually three—the M1 rifle had an eight-round clip. They hadn't seen a semiautomatic rifle because theirs were bolt actions, too. We marines stayed with the Springfield right up to the end of that campaign. It was when we got to Australia that we got M1s.

And, while we were at Guadalcanal we got rid of the old World War I–style steel helmet and adopted the pot helmets.

After the battleships worked you over, did you have any casualties to treat?

No, not in our area because though they leveled the whole area, believe it or not, none of us were hurt. When we were underground we were safe, unless it was a direct hit. Most of those shells landed on the airfield. We had three medical companies—A Company, 1st Marines; B Company, 5th Marines; and C Company, 7th Marines. And there were line company corpsmen. We saw casualties with our company in action.

What was the situation with malaria?

When you got malaria, you might have it five times. Everybody was getting it over and over again. I had it five times—twice on the island and three times in Australia. Those were recurrent attacks. If they evacuated people who had it five times there would have been no one left in the field. By the first of December, we had more casualties—four- or five-thousand casualties from malaria, dengue fever—than we did from actual battle.

What did they do with you when you got it?

When the survey replacement units came out in December, the 1st and the 5th Marines were evacuated. They sent them to Brisbane and stuck them out in a swamp loaded with mosquitoes. So they were always in the hospital. All day long in Brisbane you could hear the ambulances taking men to the hospital. Since we came in last, we stayed last. We didn't leave there until January 9. On New Year's Day we moved to the beach.

Anyway, we were sent to the beach by Lunga Point and were there seven days when we got the word that the army was coming in, and we were to be relieved. We were all exhausted. We had no clothes. All I had was my shoes, no socks, no underclothes. All I had was a pair of torn dungarees and a khaki shirt. They came ashore with Higgins boats. We climbed over the sides into the boats. When we got to the ship we couldn't make it. We started up the cargo net and fell back into the boats. Sailors were tying ropes around us and pulling us up. I had gone to Guadalcanal weighing about 150; I left weighing about 110.

What did you do with the malaria cases? How did you treat them?

Atabrine and plenty of fluids. And whenever they could, they would put them back on the line. They had no choice. If you had malaria ten times, they would finally evacuate you. There were no replacements. If you were to send everyone back with two, three, four cases of malaria, you'd have nobody left. . . .

So you weren't getting medical supplies in either?

Just what we had brought in with us. That was it.

Did you guys feel abandoned?

The first couple of months, yes. Until we came in on September 15, the first guys who had come hadn't seen anybody since August 7. When they had that big sea battle of Savo Island, and they lost those five cruisers, the U.S. ships hauled ass and never came back. They went ashore with a thirty-day supply of food and ammunition. So they had to replace that with captured Japanese rice.

Did you actually eat any of that captured rice?

No, because the other two regiments had exhausted supplies. When we came in, we shared what we had with them, because we were able to bring stuff in, even though we were only there a couple of days before they took off. We didn't see them again till October, when the army came in. Once the army came, they came with sea bags, brand new uniforms, food, medical supplies, M1s, new helmets, everything. We said, "Look at these candy asses!" At night, we'd sneak into their camp and help ourselves because they had so much stuff! They couldn't get it off the beach fast enough.

So, the whole time you were on Guadalcanal you were patrolling.

We were in garrison and on patrol. We had sections we moved around in. Sometimes the 5th got hit pretty bad, and they would be pulled back toward the airfield, and the 7th would take their place.

If the 7th got hit, then the 1st would take their place. There was the Raider Battalion. When the 2nd Marines were in Tulagi the first week, there was the heaviest fighting over there when they ran into a garrison of over two-thousand Japs, and they were dug in. So that was a hard battle. Finally, they had to bring them over by Higgins boats to the island to replace some of the units. They never fought in Tulagi anymore. Everything was on the Canal after that first week.

Did you go out on patrol with these people?

Oh yes. We crossed the Matanikou River, we crossed in the northern part of the Tenaru River. We went about forty miles, as far as the patrols could go. We'd find the Japs on the road dead, on the trails, but we would never catch up to them. And then we'd pull back.

How did they die? Who shot them?

Disease and hunger. They were in worse shape than us because they would be dropped off and then our planes would come and bomb their food supply and sink their ships. But they could go sixteen miles a day with a little ball of rice. But they found out they were not supermen, that they could be defeated. And their diet caused them to explode when they died. Within a couple of hours they were bloated. And the next day, boom, they exploded. The maggots were all over them. An American boy would take two days before he'd turn purple and start bloating. We'd pick them up and wrap them in a poncho and bury them.

When did you leave Guadalcanal?

When January 1943 came, we left on the transport USS *Hays* (AP-39). The word got out that we were not going to Brisbane. . . . We were being assigned to General Douglas MacArthur's 6th Army and were going straight to Melbourne.

CAPTAIN BEN L. SALOMON'S
MEDAL OF HONOR CITATION
Saipan, 1944

The President of the United States of America, authorized by Act of Congress, March 3, 1863, has awarded in the name of The Congress the Medal of Honor to CAPTAIN BEN L. SALOMON, UNITED STATES ARMY for conspicuous gallantry and intrepidity at the risk of his life above and beyond the call of duty.

Captain Ben L. Salomon was serving at Saipan, in the Marianas Islands on July 7, 1944, as the Surgeon for the 2d Battalion, 105th Infantry Regiment, 27th Infantry Division. The Regiment's 1st and 2d Battalions were attacked by an overwhelming force estimated between 3,000 and 5,000 Japanese soldiers. It was one of the largest attacks attempted in the Pacific Theater during World War II. Although both units fought furiously, the enemy soon penetrated the Battalions' combined perimeter and inflicted overwhelming casualties. In the first minutes of the attack, approximately 30 wounded soldiers walked, crawled, or were carried into Captain Salomon's aid station, and the small tent soon filled with wounded men. As the perimeter began to be overrun, it became increasingly difficult for Captain Salomon to work on the wounded. He then saw a Japanese soldier bayoneting one of the wounded soldiers lying near the tent. Firing from a squatting position, Captain Salomon quickly killed the enemy soldier. Then, as he turned his attention back to the wounded, two more Japanese soldiers appeared in the front entrance of the tent. As these enemy soldiers were killed, four more crawled under the tent walls. Rushing them, Captain Salomon kicked the knife out of the hand of one, shot another, and bayoneted a third. Captain Salomon butted the fourth enemy soldier in the stomach and a wounded comrade then shot and killed the enemy soldier. Realizing the gravity of the situation, Captain Salomon ordered the wounded to make their way as best they could back to the regimental aid station, while he attempted to hold off the enemy until they were clear. Captain Salomon then grabbed a rifle from one of the wounded and rushed out of the tent. After four men were killed while manning a machine gun, Captain Salomon took control of it. When his body was later found, 98 dead enemy soldiers were piled in front of his position. Captain Salomon's extraordinary heroism and devotion to duty are in keeping with the highest traditions of military service and reflect great credit upon himself, his unit, and the United States Army.

KAMIKAZE ATTACK
LIEUTENANT WALTER B. BURWELL
Battle of Leyte Gulf, October 23–25, 1944

Lieutenant Walter B. Burwell was a medical officer aboard the USS Suwannee *(CVE-27) when it was struck by two Japanese suicide (kamikaze) aircraft on October 25, 1944.*

The escort aircraft carrier *Suwannee*'s sick bay had one standard hospital bed and four tiers of three bunks. We also had an operating room, and adjacent to that, a pharmacy and a sick call area, and a dental office. For the ship's company, we had a senior medical officer; I was the junior medical officer. Each squadron usually brought a surgeon with them. We also had about twelve corpsmen and a chief pharmacist's mate. We had a dentist aboard as part of our Ship's Company Medical Division. Of course, he would help out with first aid, health and sanitation inspections, and things like that, but he was kept pretty busy with his dental duties, because in those days the general public had pretty poor dental hygiene. And a lot of these boys coming aboard had probably never seen or heard of a dentist before.

Earlier Operations
The *Suwannee*'s first deployment was to support Operation Torch, the invasion of North Africa, in November 1942. In addition

to providing air cover and helping to destroy the Vichy French navy, we also ferried over a bunch of army P-40s Curtiss Warhawk single-seat, fighter-bomber aircraft. On the way back, we ran into a terrific storm with a fifty-nine-knot gale. Tremendous waves peeled back the forward part of our flight deck. After repairs at the Portsmouth Navy Yard, the *Suwannee* went to the Pacific. We arrived at Noumea, New Caledonia, in January 1943 and amazed the South Pacific veterans by steaming into the harbor with officers and crew at quarters in whites. We spent the next seven months or so based at Efate Island. From time to time we'd sortie out and run up the "slot" to Guadalcanal to support various operations. We made a quick trip back to San Diego in September 1943 for resupplying, refurbishing, things of that kind. But we made it back in time for the assault on Tarawa. We took part in the shore bombardment for that operation, and then, in succession, supporting landings at Apemama, Kwajalein, Eniwetok, Aitape, Hollandia, Saipan, Tinian, Guam, and Moratai.

I recall one very narrow squeak off Saipan one night. Our radar had picked up a bogey some miles out. You could hear reports of the action on our PA public address system. "He's fifteen miles out, ten miles," and so on. As the plane approached, our spotters actually saw him release a torpedo, which came straight for us. I was at my battle station in the forward battle dressing station, which was at the waterline, and I heard the torpedo strike the side of the ship and then glance off. You could hear it bouncing off throughout the length of the ship—glunk, glunk, glunk, glunk. It never exploded. The explanation was that the pilot released the torpedo so close to us that it didn't have time to arm before it struck. I remember when we got back into dry dock, seeing the scars along the starboard side of the ship where the torpedo had scraped from front to back.

Leyte Gulf
On October 12, 1944, we left Seeadler Harbor in Manus, Admiralty Islands, to participate in the Philippines invasion, supporting

the landings at Leyte. As I remember, our fleet was divided into three groups—Taffy 1, 2, and 3 off the east coast of the Philippines. Our group, Taffy 1, was the southernmost and was to support the landings on Leyte. The army seemed to have no great trouble with the initial landings on October 20, and we were able to successfully repulse Japanese aerial attacks on our group.

But of course, the Japanese navy came down to try to knock us out of our positions. By October 18, we had received reports from our search planes that the Southern Japanese Fleet had put out from Singapore and was heading for the Philippines. By October 22, our submarines had spotted the Japanese Center Force heading for San Bernardino Strait. The Southern Force was destroyed at Surigao Strait during the night of October 24. At the same time, Admiral Kurita's force came through the San Bernardino Strait to the north, expecting to catch us in a pincer maneuver. Even those of us doing mundane jobs were aware that something was going on from all the radio activity and reports.

On October 25, we had gone to general quarters at dawn. After being released from general quarters, I had had breakfast and gone back to my stateroom to take a shower. Our captain announced on the PA system that the whole Japanese fleet was attacking Taffy 3 to the north of us. I looked out on the forecastle, and sure enough it looked like there were a hundred ships on the horizon. At that point, general quarters sounded, and I had to go below to my battle dressing station in the forward part of the ship. It was one deck below the main deck—two or three below the flight deck. We were just about at the waterline. There was nothing unique about the battle dressing station; it contained twenty-five to thirty bunks and medical supplies stored in lockers, and was just below and aft of the catapult engine room. There was an open deck one deck above so you could look out on either side. This was ordinarily used as a barbershop and had a couple of barber chairs there. Many times during general quarters, I would sit in one of those barber chairs because it was the most comfortable thing I could find.

The Kamikazes

Shortly thereafter, we were hit by the first kamikaze. Our sister ship, the escort aircraft carrier *Santee* (CVE-29), was actually hit first, but nineteen minutes later, another kamikaze managed to get through all the antiaircraft fire and crash into our flight deck about amidships and penetrate to the main deck. This attack did not do nearly as much damage as the second attack the next day.

On the morning of the twenty-sixth we had maybe twenty-five wounded in the forward battle dressing station from the action of the day before. And we had things pretty much under control by that evening. In fact, we were not even at general quarters. My stateroom was only two decks above our battle dressing station, and I told my corpsman that I was going up there to get a change of clothes and maybe lie down a minute, and that if he needed me to come and get me. For some reason, exhaustion just got the better of me before I even got up there, and I crawled into a bunk in an adjoining sleeping compartment just forward of our battle dressing station and fell asleep.

I was asleep when the second attack occurred. The thing that woke me up was the sound of our antiaircraft guns going off. When I heard the guns, I jumped up and started for the dressing station. Just as I got to the doorway there was a terrific explosion and we lost our lights. I went into the dressing station and helped our corpsmen pull some of the wounded out from under wreckage when there was a second explosion. That one shattered all the bulkheads and broke water mains.

After the first explosion, my corpsman lit out for my stateroom to get me, thinking that's where I was. But when he got up there he found that my stateroom had been demolished and thought I was gone. I will never forget how after we got working again, he looked up and saw me and said, "My God, you can't be here." Indeed, he thought I was dead. "I'm so glad I'm not here by myself," he said.

The second explosion forced us to evacuate the battle dressing station. After the first explosion, there was smoke and fire fed by aviation gasoline pouring onto the deck above us. The wreckage in the passageway and ladder to the deck above by bomb and ammunition explosions, prevented entrance or exit to or from our dressing station. But up to that point we could have remained where we were, at least temporarily. However, the second explosion further wrecked our compartment, buckled our bulkheads, and ruptured water mains above and in our compartment, so that we began to flood. As the water level rose to knee height in our compartment, the ship was listing uncomfortably and lying dead in the water without steerage because of destruction of the bridge and wheelhouse. Isolated from the rest of the ship with only the reflection from the gasoline fires above and a few flickering battle lamps for light, I saw my wounded partially covered with wreckage and already awash and knew that we had to evacuate.

I think there were about thirty of us in the compartment, including two corpsmen, two stretcher bearers, and perhaps twenty-five wounded resulting from the action of the day before, mostly consisting of extensive burns, blast and fragmentation injuries, traumatic amputations, compound fractures, and multiple severe lacerations. About half the wounded were able to help themselves to some extent in dragging themselves about, but the remainder required stretchers to be moved.

Though I did not know the extent of damage to the compartments aft of us, I knew that they were unoccupied and sealed off during battle conditions. I informed my corpsmen that I would try to find an escape by this route, as it seemed to offer our only hope of evacuation. We opened the hatch to the adjacent compartment, and I was able to get through it and lock it behind me without flooding from our compartment. Feeling my way with the help of a pocket flashlight, I found the compartment to be intact and dry, though without light or ventilation. Then I worked my way aft through several adjacent unoccupied compartments in the same way until at last I reached an open space on the main deck. Now, feeling certain that we could make our way out by this route, I returned to my group in the forward battle dressing station. There, with my corpsmen and stretcher bearers, and with the valiant help of some of the mobile wounded, we were able to move our stretcher-bound wounded through the hatches from one compartment to the next without leaving or losing a single member of our party, to finally emerge on the open deck. From there, we entered the chief petty officers' mess, to find two corpsmen tending to about twenty more wounded. So we joined forces to organize an amidships dressing station and began to gather additional wounded in that area.

On the deck above, we found about fifteen or twenty more wounded, mostly burns and blast injuries, who had made their way into bunks in the chief petty officers' quarters. There was no immediate possibility of moving them to our already overflowing and understaffed amidships station. One of my corpsmen and I gathered up what medical supplies we could carry and made our way up to the chiefs' quarters to treat the wounded there. Just as we arrived at the entrance to the compartment, a sailor, apparently in panic, came running along the passageway screaming, "Everybody's going over the side! The captain's dead! Everyone on the bridge has been killed! Everybody's abandoning ship!" Now, havoc! Now, contagious panic and cold fear! The wounded who had crawled into the compartment began struggling to get out, screaming hysterically, "Where's my life jacket? Who took my life jacket? Turn that loose! Gimme that! No, it's mine!" Some were shoving toward the entrance, fighting and scrambling over one another. My heart sank as I stepped into the threshold to block the entrance and shout over and over, "Get back into your bunks! There's no order to abandon ship! You don't need your life jackets!"

I could see this was only having limited effect; so, with much inward trepidation but outwardly extravagant bravado, I made myself step into the compartment from the threshold, remove my own life jacket and helmet, and hang them in clear view on a coat hook near the entrance. Then, I had to consciously force myself to move away from the entrance and the comfort and security of my life jacket and go into the compartment to tend the wounded, fearing that at any moment some panicky sailor might snatch my life jacket and bolt, setting off a wild melee. It seemed to me that time hung in the balance for an eternity, but finally one after another of the men quieted down and crawled back into their bunks, so that gradually things began at last to calm down and sort themselves out.

In the meantime, one of our corpsmen tending the wounded on the flight deck saw the plight of those isolated by fire on the forecastle. He came below to report that medical help was critically needed there. It seemed to me that we would have to try to get through to them. So he and I restocked our first aid bags with morphine syrettes, tourniquets, sulfa, Vaseline, and bandages, commandeered a fire extinguisher, and made our way forward, dodging flames along the main deck. Along part of the way, we were joined by a sailor manning a seawater fire hose with fairly good pressure. Although the seawater would only scatter the gasoline fires away from us, by using the water and foam alternatively as we advanced, we managed to work our way up several decks, through passageways along the wrecked and burning combat information center and decoding area, through officers' country, and finally out on the forecastle. Many of the crew on the forecastle and the catwalks above it had been blown over the side by the explosions. But others trapped below and aft of the forecastle area found themselves under a curtain of fire from aviation gasoline pouring down from burning planes on the flight deck above. Their only escape was to leap aflame into the sea, but some were trapped so that they were incinerated before they could leap. By the time we arrived on the forecastle, the flow of gasoline had mostly consumed itself, and flames were only erupting and flickering from combustible areas of water and oil. Nonetheless, the decks and bulkheads were still blistering hot and ammunition in the small arms locker on the deck below was popping from the heat like strings of firecrackers. With each salvo of popping, two or three more panicky crewmen would leap over the side, and we found that our most urgent task was to persuade those poised on the rail not to jump by a combination of physical restraint and reassurance that fires were being controlled and that more help was on the way. Most of the remaining wounded in the forecastle area were severely burned beyond recognition and hope. All that could be done for the obviously dying was to give the most rudimentary first aid consisting of morphine, a few swallows of water, and some words of companionship, leaving them where we found them and moving on to others.

Nonetheless, within an hour or so after being struck in the last attack, power and steerage had been restored, fires were out, ammunition and gasoline explosions had ceased, pumps were working, and ruptured water mains had been shut off. But it was miraculous that we escaped destruction during this period, because we were vulnerable to further air or submarine attack.

By this time we had done what we could for the wounded on the forecastle, and I moved back to the amidships dressing station. From there my corpsmen and stretcher bearers were searching out and gathering wounded. By nightfall, we began to run short of medical supplies, and I realized that we needed to salvage the supplies left behind in the forward battle dressing station. I was able to recruit a small group of stretcher bearers to help me, and we successfully made our way back to the forward battle dressing station. We found the compartment was still flooded with knee-deep water, but most of our supplies were salvageable in wreckage above this level. We were able to load up our stretchers with plasma, dressings, sulfa, Vaseline, and morphine and haul them out. After two or three trips we had all our supplies safely out and distributed elsewhere.

Coming Home

For the ensuing three days we still had our hands full continuing to search for, find, and care for our many wounded scattered throughout the ship and burying the dead at sea. Then we proceeded to Kossol Roads, in the Palaus, where we transferred our most seriously wounded to two hospital ships, the *Mercy* AH-8 and the *Bountiful* AH-9. From there we went to Seeadler Harbor, Manus Island, to further "lick our wounds" for five days. There we cared for our less seriously wounded and made temporary repairs so we would be seaworthy enough to proceed to Hawaii.

We arrived at Pearl Harbor on November 19. As we limped up the channel to the naval base, every navy ship at anchor or in dock there "manned the rail" in a salute to the *Suwannee*, and our radio received this message: "Welcome to Pearl! Your successful fight against great odds will live as one of the most striking tales of naval history. The people of our country and those of us in the naval service are gratified and proud of your outstanding performance of duty against the best the enemy could offer. As long as our country has men with your heart, courage, skill, and strength she need not fear for her future. To each and every one, a 'Well Done'— signed, Admiral Nimitz."

We stayed in Pearl Harbor only overnight, just long enough to transfer our remaining wounded to the naval hospital and to take on supplies, and then we headed for major repairs at the Puget Sound Navy Yard in Bremerton, Washington, where we docked on November 26, 1944. The repairs took about a month. Because I was junior medical officer, I had to stay aboard for a week or so while it was being repaired, and when the first section came back from leave, I was able to go on leave. While I was on leave, orders came through for me to report to the Naval Dispensary, U.S. Training Center, Gulfport, Mississippi. I went to Bremerton to be released and to pick up what was left of my belongings. While there, I walked through the ship once more. I realized I must have led a charmed life. The bunk I had been lying in at the time of the first explosion had been destroyed by the second explosion. It was absolutely unbelievable.

I departed with great pride in my ship and shipmates and their accomplishments, for I had witnessed innumerable instances of cool courage, bold bravery, and unselfish heroism blended with faith, friend-ship, and self-sacrifice. But I will say that I had gained no fondness for naval warfare, and I was thankful to go on to other endeavors.

Note: For his heroic work on Suwannee, *Lieutenant Burwell received the Silver Star.*

PRIDE IN HER SERVICE
Kristin Rothwell
Battle of the Bulge, December 16, 1944, to January 28, 1945

In the dead of winter with snow and subzero temperatures at times, U.S. soldiers, with the help of allied forces, fought brutally during World War II against Hitler's army at the Battle of the Bulge between December 16, 1944, and January 28, 1945.

Not far from the front lines, Dorothy Steinbis-Davis, RN, served the wounded—many of whom suffered from frostbite and other cold-related injuries—and saw many more casualties as they were brought to her small detachment, part of the 57th Field Hospital.

Working in the mobile unit, made up of four physicians, a dentist, a medical administrative officer, five nurses, several enlistees, and a small surgical team, proved to be a demanding and exhausting task for Davis.

"Our patients were those who were critically wounded and needed extensive nursing care," said Davis, a second lieutenant with the U.S. Army Medical Corps. "The mortality rate was high—at times, over 20 percent. This was emotionally difficult. A patient you had over the past twelve to fifteen hours, and who you thought would survive, may have died when you returned to work after a few hours of sleep."

With gunfire ringing out just a short distance away, there were many times when she and her crew didn't know if they were going to be able to evacuate before the area was overrun by Germans.

"Transportation in these situations was always a grave problem," she said.

She added, "You are afraid, but on the other hand, you really had to stay focused on what you were doing."

Though Davis' detachment wasn't officially assigned to the Battle of the Bulge, they were on the "French rim," just close enough to treat any wounded in the area. At one point, the small detachment supported twenty-four battalions of troops, including a number of civilians who required emergency medical care before they could be transported to civilian hospitals.

"I can distinctly remember crawling into my bedroll after one exhausting day and thinking, 'My God, what if we should lose the war?'"

During the Battle of the Bulge, Davis recalled how the hospitals often suffered from mass confusion, particularly with the continuous need for blood and not knowing the state of the combat situation. Between October 1944, when Davis' detachment first joined the theater of operations, and April 1945, the hospital moved forty times.

Davis explained that many of the moves took place at night in blackout conditions so that the roads would be available during the day for use by the tanks, infantry, and the Red Ball Express, a fleet of over six thousand trucks and trailers that delivered over four-hundred thousand tons of ammunition, food, and fuel to the Allied armies.

When possible, a schoolhouse or large building was selected for a makeshift hospital. On several occasions, Davis said that her crew would move into a building still occupied by a German hospital.

Because most of the buildings were so war-ravaged, Davis said that oftentimes patients on litters would be waiting for medical service to arrive. Nurses and doctors would immediately have to begin preparing the patients for surgery while the enlistees set to work cleaning the area, setting up a generator for electricity, and assembling an X-ray unit, operating room, and post-op ward.

By mid-March, as the war was nearing the end, the entire 57th Field Hospital was assigned to Toul, France, to care for 355 Allied national patients, most of whom were Russian, as well as Yugoslavian, Serbian, and Polish nationals, who had been liberated from the Germans.

The prisoners, who had been forced by the Germans to work in the lime mines near Metz, France, suffered from tuberculosis, osteomyelitis (infection of the bone caused by the seeding of the bacteria within the bone from a remote source), mine injuries, and various nutritional diseases.

"The prisoners' state had been reduced to one of animals in their struggle for existence," said Davis, who helped improve their health status so they could withstand their return trip to Russia.

Davis said the devastation and destruction around her could scarcely be imagined—roads littered for miles with debris and cities destroyed to almost nonexistence. But her job in Europe was not over yet.

When her unit reached Germany, they worked at several airstrips to serve as air-holding hospitals before the wounded were air-evacuated back to the United States once physically able. Some days, Davis and her crew saw up to a thousand patients come through.

For three or four hours before a flight, the medical staff would feed and medicate the patients and change their bandages. "Many of them had never been on an airplane before, so we really tried to make them feel comfortable and tried to control their worries," said Davis. She learned many years later that the planes, used to bring food, gasoline, and equipment to Europe, were soaked in gasoline—not a good mix when there were several oxygen tanks set up for patients to withstand the long flight home.

After the war, Davis married a member of the 57th Field Hospital, Colonel William V. Davis, an adjutant from Illinois who had served in the U.S. Army since 1938 and who survived the bombing at Pearl Harbor.

Though Davis retired from the U.S. Army after serving two years, she continued to use her nursing skills volunteering with the American Red Cross, an organization she still dedicates her time to—as a registered nurse—sixty years later. Over the years, she helped run school health programs, provided immunizations and eye checks, and has volunteered for numerous other activities.

Davis, who originally wanted to be an "airline stewardess"—a profession that required a nursing background—soon realized that nursing was her love. Several years before graduating from nursing school at the University of Minnesota, she not only signed up for the American Red Cross when representatives came to her hospital to recruit nurses, but she also enlisted in the U.S. Army, which would recruit her as soon as she graduated, passed her boards, and turned age twenty-one.

"I fell in love with nursing, and then when the war came along there was no thought of becoming an airline stewardess," said Davis. "The Nurse Corps changed my whole life."

ATTACKS ON JAPAN
LIEUTENANT COMMANDER SAMUEL ROBERT SHERMAN
March 19, 1945

*Lieutenant Commander Samuel Robert Sherman was a flight
surgeon aboard the USS* Franklin *(CV-13) on March 19, 1945,
when it was heavily damaged by a Japanese bomber near the
Japanese mainland.*

I joined the navy the day after Pearl Harbor. Actually, I had been
turned down twice before because I had never been in a ROTC
[Reserve Officer Training Corps], located at many colleges to train
students for officer commissions reserve unit. Since I had to work
my way through college and medical school, I wasn't able to go to
ROTC summer camp or the monthly weekend drills. Instead, I
needed to work in order to earn the money to pay my tuition.

When most of my classmates were called up prior to Pearl Harbor, I felt quite guilty, and I went to see if I could get into an army
unit. They flunked me. Then I went to the navy recruiting office, and
they flunked me for two minor reasons. One was because I had my
nose broken a half dozen times while I was boxing. The inside of my
nose was so obstructed and the septum was so crooked that the navy
didn't think I could breathe well enough. I also had a partial denture
because I had lost some front teeth, also while boxing.

But the day after Pearl Harbor, I went back to the navy and they welcomed me with open arms. They told me I had ten days to close my office and get commissioned. At that time, I went to Treasure Island, California, a naval station in San Francisco Bay, for indoctrination. After that, I was sent to Alameda Naval Air Station east of San Francisco, near Oakland, California, where I was put in charge of surgery and clinical services. One day the team medical officer burst into the operating room and said, "When are you going to get through with this operation?" I answered, "In about a half hour." He said, "Well, you better hurry up, because I just got orders for you to go to Pensacola to get flight surgeon's training."

Nothing could have been better, because airplanes were the love of my life. In fact, both my wife and I were private pilots, and I had my own little airfield and two planes. Since I wasn't allowed to be near the planes at Alameda, I had been after the senior medical officer day and night to get me transferred to flight surgeon's training.

I went to Naval Air Station Pensacola Florida in April 1943 for my flight surgeon training and finished up in August. Initially, I was told that I was going to be shipped out from the East Coast. But the navy changed its mind and sent me back to the West Coast in late 1943 to wait for Air Group 5 at Alameda Naval Air Station.

Air Group 5

Air Group 5 soon arrived, but it took about a year or so of training to get up to snuff. Most of the people in it were veterans from other carriers that went down. Three squadrons formed the nucleus of this air group—a fighter, a bomber, and a torpedo bomber squadron. Later, we were given two marine squadrons, the remnants of Pappy Boyington's group.

Since the marine pilots had been land-based, the toughest part of the training was to get them carrier certified. We used the old USS *Ranger* (CV-4) for takeoff and landing training. We took the *Ranger* up and down the coast from San Francisco to San Diego and tried like hell to get these marines to learn how to make a landing. They had no problem taking off, but they had problems with landings. Luckily, we were close enough to airports so that if they couldn't get on the ship they'd have a place to land. That way, they wouldn't have to go in the drink. Anyhow, we eventually got them all certified. Some of our other pilots trained at Fallon Air Station in Nevada and other West Coast bases. By the time the USS *Franklin* (CV-13) came in, we had a very well trained group of people.

I had two marine squadrons and three navy squadrons to take care of. The marines claimed I was a marine. The navy guys claimed I was a navy man. I used to wear two uniforms. When I would go to the marine ready rooms, I'd put on a marine uniform and then I'd change quickly and put on my navy uniform and go to the other one. We had a lot of fun with that. As their physician, I was everything. I had to be a general practitioner with them, but I also was their father, their mother, their spiritual guide, their social director, their psychiatrist, the whole thing. Of course, I was well trained in surgery, so I could take care of the various surgical problems. Every once in a while I had to do an appendectomy. I also removed some pilonidal cysts and fixed a few strangulated hernias. Of course, they occasionally got fractures during their training exercises. I took care of everything for them, and they considered me their personal physician, every one of them. I was called Dr. Sam, and Dr. Sam was their private doctor. No matter what was wrong, I took care of it.

Eventually, the *Franklin* arrived in early 1945. It had been in Bremerton, Washington, being repaired after it was damaged by a kamikaze off Leyte in the Philippine Islands in October 1944. In mid-February 1945 we left the West Coast and went to Naval Base Pearl Harbor first and then to Ulithi in the Caroline Islands, west Pacific Ocean. By the first week in March, the fleet was ready to sail. It took us about five or six days to reach the coast of Japan, where we began launching aerial attacks on the airbases, ports, and other such targets.

The Attack

Just before dawn on March 19, 1945, our bombers took off, escorted by about nine of our fighter planes. The crew of the *Franklin* was getting ready for another strike, so more planes were on the flight deck. All of a sudden, out of nowhere, a Japanese plane slipped through the fighter screen and popped up just in front of the ship. My battle station was right in the middle of the flight deck, because I was the flight surgeon and was supposed to take care of anything that might happen during flight operations. I saw the Japanese plane coming in, but there was nothing I could do but stay there and take it. The plane just flew right in and dropped two bombs on our flight deck.

I was blown about fifteen feet into the air and tossed against the steel bulkhead of the island. I got up groggily and saw an enormous fire. All those planes that were lined up to take off were fully armed and fueled. The dive bombers were equipped with this new "Tiny Tim" heavy rocket and they immediately began to explode. Some of the rockets' motors ignited and took off across the flight deck on their own. A lot of us were just ducking those things. It was pandemonium and chaos for hours and hours. We had 126 separate explosions on that ship; and each explosion would pick the ship up and rock it and then turn it around a little bit. Of course, the ship suffered horrendous casualties from the first moment. I lost my glasses and my shoes. I was wearing a kind of moccasin shoes. I didn't have time that morning to put on my flight deck shoes, and they just went right off immediately. Regardless of that, there were hundreds and hundreds of crewmen who needed my attention.

Medical Equipment

Fortunately, I was well prepared from a medical equipment standpoint. From the time we left San Francisco and then stopped at Pearl and then to Ulithi and so forth, I had done what we call disaster planning. Because I had worked in emergency hospital service and trauma centers, I knew what was needed. Therefore, I had a number of big metal containers, approximately the size of garbage cans, bolted down on the flight deck and the hangar deck. These were full of everything that I needed—splints, burn dressings, sterile dressings of all sorts, sterile surgical instruments, medications, plasma, and intravenous solutions other than plasma. The most important supplies were those used for the treatment of burns and fractures, lacerations, and bleeding. In those days the navy had a special burn dressing which was very effective. It was gauze impregnated with Vaseline and some chemicals that were almost like local anesthetics. In addition to treating burns, I also had to deal with numerous casualties suffering from severe bleeding; I even performed some amputations.

Furthermore, I had a specially equipped coat that was similar to those used by duck hunters, with all the little pouches. In addition to the coat, I had a couple of extra-sized money belts which could hold things. In these I carried my morphine syrettes and other small medical items. Due to careful planning, I had no problem whatsoever with supplies.

I immediately looked around to see if I had any corpsmen left. Most of them were already wounded, dead, or had been blown overboard. Some, I was later told, got panicky and jumped overboard. Therefore, I couldn't find any corpsmen, but fortunately I found some of the members of the musical band whom I had trained in first aid. I had also given first-aid training to my air group pilots and some of the crew. The first guy I latched onto was Lieutenant Commander MacGregor Kilpatrick, the skipper of the fighter squadron. He was an Annapolis graduate and a veteran of the USS *Lexington* (CV-2) and the USS *Yorktown* (CV-5) with three Navy Crosses. He stayed with me, helping me take care of the wounded.

I couldn't find any doctors. There were three ship's doctors assigned to the *Franklin*, Commander Francis (Kurt) Smith, Lieutenant Commander James Fuelling, and Lieutenant Commander George Fox. I found out later that Fox was killed in the sick bay by the fires and suffocating smoke. Smith and Fuelling were trapped below in the warrant officers' wardroom, and it took twelve or thirteen hours to get them out. That's where Lieutenant Donald Gary got his Medal of Honor for finding an escape route for them and three-hundred men trapped below. Meanwhile, I had very little medical help.

Finally, a couple of corpsmen who were down below in the hangar deck came up, once they recovered from their concussions and shock. Little by little, a few of them came up. Originally, the band was my medical help and what pilots I had around.

Evacuation Efforts

I had hundreds and hundreds of patients, obviously more than I could possibly treat. Therefore, the most important thing for me to do was triage—separate the seriously wounded from the not so seriously wounded. We'd arranged for evacuation of the serious ones to the cruiser USS *Santa Fe* (CL-60), which had a very well equipped sick bay and was standing by alongside.

Lieutenant Commander Kilpatrick was instrumental in the evacuations. He helped me organize all of this, and we got people to carry the really badly wounded. Some of them had their hips blown off and arms blown off and other sorts of tremendous damage. All together, I think we evacuated some eight hundred people to the *Santa Fe*. Most of them were wounded, and the rest were the air group personnel who were on board.

The orders came that all air group personnel had to go on the *Santa Fe* because they were considered nonexpendable. They had to live to fight again in their airplanes. The ship's company air officer of the *Franklin* came up to Lieutenant Commander Kilpatrick and myself as we were supervising the evacuation between fighting fires, taking care of the wounded, and so forth.

He said, "You two people get your asses over to the *Santa Fe* as fast as you can." Lieutenant Commander Kilpatrick, being an Annapolis graduate, knew he had to obey the order, but he argued and argued and argued. But this guy wouldn't take his arguments.

He said, "Get over there. You know better." Then he said to me, "You get over there too."

I said, "Who's going to take care of these people?"

He replied, "We'll manage."

I said, "Nope. All my life I've been trained never to abandon a sick or wounded person. I can't find any doctors and I don't know where they are, and I only have a few corpsmen, and I can't leave these people."

He said, "You better go, because a military order is a military order."

I said, "Well, what could happen to me if I don't go?"

He answered, "I could shoot you or I could bring court-martial charges against you."

I said, "Well, take your choice." And I went back to work.

As MacGregor Kilpatrick left he told me, "Sam, you're crazy!"

Getting the Franklin Under Way

After the air group evacuated, I looked at the ship, I looked at the fires, and I felt the explosions. I thought, well, I better say good-bye right now to my family because I never believed that the ship was going to survive. We were just fifty miles off the coast of Japan (about fifteen minutes flying time) and dead in the water. The cruiser USS *Pittsburgh* (CA-72) was trying to get a towline to us, but it was a difficult job and took hours to accomplish.

Meanwhile, our engineering officers were trying to get the boilers lit off in the engine room. The smoke was so bad that we had to get the *Santa Fe* to give us a whole batch of gas masks. But the masks didn't cover the engineers' eyes. Their eyes became so inflamed from the smoke that they couldn't see to do their work. So, the executive officer, the ship's second-in-command, came down and said to me, "Do you know where there are any anesthetic eye drops to put in their eyes so they can tolerate the smoke?"

I said, "Yes, I know where they are." I knew there was a whole stash of them down in the sick bay, because I used to have to take foreign bodies out of the eyes of my pilots and some of the crew.

He asked, "Could you go down there (that's about four or five decks below), get it, and give it to the engineering officer?"

I replied, "Sure, give me a flashlight and a guide, because I may not be able to see my way down there, although I used to go down three or four times a day."

I went down and got a whole batch of them. They were in eye-dropper bottles, and we gave them to these guys. They put them in their eyes, and immediately they could tolerate the smoke. That enabled them to get the boilers going.

Aftermath

It was almost twelve or thirteen hours before the doctors who were trapped below were rescued. By that time, I had the majority of the wounded taken care of. However, there still were trapped and injured people in various parts of the ship, like the hangar deck, that hadn't been discovered. We spent the next seven days trying to find them all.

I also helped the chaplains take care of the dead. The burial of the dead was terrible. They were all over the ship. The ships' medical officers put the burial functions on my shoulders. I had to declare them dead, take off their identification, remove, along with the chaplains' help, whatever possessions that hadn't been destroyed on them, and then slide them overboard because we had no way of keeping them. A lot of them were my own air group people, pilots and aircrew, and I recognized them even though the bodies were busted up and charred. I think we buried about 832 people in the next seven days. That was terrible, really terrible, to bury that many people.

Going Home

It took us six days to reach Ulithi. Actually, by the time we got to Ulithi, we were making fourteen knots and had cast off the towline from the *Pittsburgh*. We had five destroyers assigned to us that kept circling us all the time from the time we left the coast of Japan until we got to Ulithi, because we were under constant attack by Japanese bombers. We also had support from two of the new battle cruisers.

At Ulithi, I got word that a lot of my people in the air group who were taken off or picked up in the water were on a hospital ship that was also in Ulithi. I visited them there and was told that many of the dead in the air group were killed in their ready rooms, waiting to take off, when the bombs exploded. The marine squadrons were particularly hard hit, having few survivors. I have a list of dead marines that makes your heart sink.

The survivors of the air group then regrouped on Guam. They requested that I be sent back to them. I also wanted to go with them, so I pleaded my case with the chaplain, the XO [executive officer], and the skipper ship's commanding officer. Although the skipper felt I had earned the right to be part of the ship's company, he was willing to send me where I wanted to go. Luckily, I rejoined my air group just in time to keep the poor derelicts from getting assigned to another carrier.

The air group commander wanted to make captain so bad that he volunteered these boys for another carrier. Most of them were veterans of the USS *Yorktown* and USS *Lexington* and had seen quite a lot of action. A fair number of them had been blown into the water, and many were suffering from the shock of the devastating ordeal. The skipper of the bombing squadron did not think his men were psychologically or physically qualified to go back into combat at that particular time. A hearing was held to determine their combat availability, and a flight surgeon was needed to check them over. I assembled the pilots and checked them out and I agreed with the bombing squadron skipper. These men were just not ready to fight yet. Some of them even looked like death warmed over.

The hearing was conducted by Fleet Admiral Chester W. Nimitz, commander-in-chief, Pacific Fleet and Pacific Ocean Areas.

He remembered me from Alameda, because I had pulled him out of the wreckage of his plane when it crashed during a landing approach in 1942. He simply said, "Unless I hear a medical opinion to the contrary to Commander Sherman's, I have to agree with Commander Sherman." He decided that the air group should be sent back to the States and rehabilitated as much as possible.

In late April 1945, the air group went to Pearl, where we briefly reunited with the *Franklin*. They had to make repairs to the ship so it could make the journey to Brooklyn. After a short stay, we continued on to Alameda. Then the navy decided to break up the Air Group, so everyone was sent on their individual way. I was given what I wanted: an assignment as senior medical officer of a carrier—the USS *Rendova* (CVE-114), which was still outfitting in Portland, Oregon. But the war ended shortly after we had completed outfitting.

I stayed in the navy until about Christmastime 1945. I was mustered out in San Francisco at the same place I was commissioned. As far as the air group officer who had said he would either shoot me or court-martial me if I didn't evacuate with the air group personnel from the *Franklin* to the *Santa Fe*, well, he didn't shoot me. He talked about the court-martial a lot, but everybody in higher rank on the ship thought it was a really bad idea and made him sound like a damned fool. He stopped making the threats.

HOW A GOLDBRICK SAVED MY LIFE
Dr. Thomas M. Brown
Iwo Jima, 1945

When we reported in for duty at the 5th Marine Division about March 1, 1944, Dr. Charles Hely and I were assigned to the 27th Regiment, where we quickly took over the command and operation of its sick bay. We were [jointly] endowed with the title of regimental surgeon. At last someone had recognized how talented we were and positioned us where our abilities would be properly used! Two weeks later superior rank moved in: Charley became the doctor for the 3rd Battalion and I for the 2nd. Yet for one short moment we were in our glory as regimental surgeons.

Early on in that two weeks it became obvious to us that the regiment was strongly victimized by a plague of sore feet and bad backs. Most of those bad feet and backs belonged to "goldbricks," our terminology for fakers. So Charley and I rose to the occasion with the original practice of "Second Opinion." When I had seen a man from our own respective battalion two or three times for the same minor complaint and reached the conclusion that there was no real physical basis for the complaint, I would tell my patient that I wished for him to be examined by Dr. Hely for a second opinion. Likewise, my fellow doctor would send his goldbricks over to me. From our standpoint, it was a good system.

One big, strapping marine was referred to Dr. Hely by me. After a few minutes of a good examination I heard Charley say in his best gruff voice, "Mac, there's not a confounded thing wrong with you. You are an excellent physical specimen and in good health. You're nothing but a goldbrick. Now, get your butt out of here and don't ever come back again unless you're really sick or need an immunization."

The young private's jaw dropped as he hurriedly slunk out of that 27th sick bay. Until that day we were seeing over ninety men at each of those two-a-day sick calls. To my amazement, after this incident, attendance at sick call dropped off sharply.

D-Day [for the invasion of Iwo Jima] arrived, and as soon as our tractor hit the beach, I looked for wounded needing medical help. Since all the wounded I saw upon landing were dead, I hastily plodded across that beach of deep, black sand . . . and started up the escarpment. A barrage of artillery shells screamed in, so I hit the deck and started eating sand. After a couple minutes the barrage ceased. While I was lying there, a piece of shrapnel dropped out of space, its momentum spent, and hit my left thumb. This produced a little bleeding, but the wound was insignificant.

With the cessation of shelling, I backed down to the bottom of the escarpment and looked about. About fifty yards to the right was a battered blockhouse perched at the top of a gully. Recognizing this blockhouse as a good [location to establish an] aid station, I crawled up and sat a few feet below it. As I turned to beckon to the two corpsmen standing below, I noticed small bits of dirt spitting out of the right side of the gully near me. Why would anyone want to kill me? I had never hurt anyone.

That thought expired in about ten seconds, as it became obvious to me that the enemy was trying to eliminate me. The corpsmen saw the firing and wisely concluded it might be best to stay where they were. As I sat there in the gully, I tried to determine if [the enemy] had seen me or were just firing in my direction. So I used the age-old deceptive maneuver of raising my helmet on my rifle's muzzle.

Ping! Ping! My question was immediately answered. They hit the helmet all right but couldn't quite get down to it when it rested on my head.

A marine rifleman passing by well to my right saw that bit of action. He bravely walked to the side of the only door of the block-house and tossed in two grenades. After the dust and smoke cleared, he looked in, then grinned my way and called, "I got three of the bastards, Doc!" He got his first enemy and saved my life in the process. I looked up at him in gratitude. It was the goldbrick we had kicked out of sick bay! Being called that name had helped him to become a first-class marine. He went through the entire battle of Iwo Jima without a scratch.

TRIBUTE TO CORPSMEN
Robert De Geus
Iwo Jima, February 19–25, 1945

From 1944 to 1945, I was a navy corpsman attached to a U.S. Marine Corps rifle company (F-2-26, 5th Division, FMF) in the PTO during World War II. There is nothing unique about being a member of six or seven corpsmen assigned to a company of marines. It is unique to have had the privilege to have stood in the company of so many brave and heroic warriors in a world-renowned event, the battle for Iwo Jima, in February and March 1945.

The violence of war is well documented, and stories of personal tragedy and extraordinary achievement in war abound, but I believe individual acts of bravery in battle are just part of the teamwork engaged in by many. For instance, I have the greatest admiration for litter bearers in battle, often prime targets by the enemy, many times caught in helpless situations, defenseless and alone in No Man's Land, and nearly always in harm's way. Litter bearer tales of survival are rare, but there is little doubt that many surviving battle casualties owe their survival to the heroics of warriors handling stretchers of canvas, wood, and metal in a violent, chaotic environment. Other than individual marines "enlisted" on the spot for litter duty, many of the 5th Division litter bearers came from musician ranks.

These were composed of members of regimental bands and musical groups who in their element of music were great morale boosters but had little combat training with rifle units. This was an obvious handicap for most of them.

As a navy corpsman attached to the marines in battle, I realized well the value of the months of preparation and training received in the navy and Marine Corps. It seems amazing to me that these military organizations could take a scrawny 115-pound eighteen-year-old and invest time and energy in the process of converting such an undisciplined individual into one capable of enduring a job performing physical tasks that often look impossible.

My wounds [suffered on Iwo Jima] were not serious, but shrapnel damaged my right shoulder. Being right-handed, this significantly handicapped me, because I couldn't use my right arm. I saw that I would become a burden instead of the help I thought I could be. As a result, my greatest regret about being wounded and evacuated after only a few days in battle is that I didn't finish my job to those men. Many wounded soldiers feel this way. Somehow we have let down our comrades by being wounded and taken out of the action and out of harm's way. This has troubled me for many years. I didn't want to leave my outfit, because I felt deeply that I had [not] finished what I was sent to do. Obviously, I did not have a choice.

I don't want this to sound trite, but emotionally I believed I had not done enough to fulfill the expectations of the preparations and training I was given, even though during my time in the battle I tended to many wounded men and undoubtedly helped some survive whom I will never know about. After being wounded, I realized that for the good of the team, I had to leave for treatment for my wounds.

For a long time, I battled with guilt and also anguish that I did not know what happened to the marines I treated on the battlefield. It was even worse to not know what happened to those I left behind. In the end, I was evacuated to Guam, then Oakland, California, and eventually to Great Lakes Naval Hospital, near Chicago.

After a brief stay at Great Lakes, I returned to Oakland for re-assignment with the navy until March 1946. Looking back, I believe there are many factors that contribute to one's survival in battle. One is pure luck. Two is training. Three is timely medical teamwork and treatment. Four is national support and caring. And five is faith.

Many battle casualty survivors know about individual acts of bravery and sacrifice by corpsmen, doctors, buddies, and even unknown angels on the battlefield who by chance became life-saving factors. I don't feel I ever did anything especially heroic, other than just doing my job as a corpsman, but I am proud to have seen and to have worked among those who by chance came to be part of a special history. When the time comes, if it hasn't already, may their souls rest in peace with the knowledge of a job well done.

IWO JIMA MEMOIRS
Tony Moreno
Iwo Jima, 1945

Moreno was a corpsman with the 5th Marine Division, 27th Regiment, 2nd Battalion, Easy Company, 2nd Platoon. The following was written in September 2002.

After intensive but brief training to become a corpsman in San Diego, we received orders to depart. On February 19, 1945, I landed on Iwo Jima with the 5th Marine Division, 27th Regiment, 2nd Battalion, Easy Company, 2nd Platoon. Puffs of smoke from the distant beach could be seen as we approached in the early morning hours. It was almost like a nightmare that in a matter of minutes we were to land on the enemy-held island of Iwo Jima.

I awoke from this trance as the amtrack to our right caught a direct hit, exploding and rapidly sinking, as the ammo of the hand grenades and bazookas was ignited. We watched helplessly as most of the marines with the exception of those few lucky ones that dove into the sea were killed immediately. We had our orders to move forward and deposit the marines on the beach. Already on land were marines from the first and second waves.

The equipment I had to carry onto the island included a carbine, a seventy-pound medical supply backpack, and my first aid kit. My orders were to quickly get to my destination with the medical supplies. With the bombing going on, this was made more difficult due to the volcanic ash on the island that made me slide with each footstep. On my way I saw a marine without a head and two others with phosphorous explosive burns/fires on their backs from a direct hit.

This incident caused my adrenaline to kick in, making my movements light as a feather as I went to help the two marines. Their calls for help made my load feel lighter, and even though I was scared, I felt better because I was able to help my buddies. After leaving the medical supplies at the medical station, I moved forward to find my company and platoon.

On two different occasions during our occupation and as I was treating casualties, I reached for my backpack of medical supplies and found it missing. The only surprising and logical explanation was that in the confusion and noise of the bombing it had apparently been torn off by flying shrapnel. I later met my need for supplies when I picked up a pack from a dead marine buddy.

On or about the sixteenth day of the operation, at midday, a sixteenth-inch shell landed about sixty feet away from us. We instinctively went down for cover in our foxholes. We waited for the inevitable password "Rags" letting us know of injuries or dead marines. There was an enormous cloud of dust and volcanic ash. The cloud of dust settled. Guess what—we discovered it was a dud, as we saw the rear end of it sticking out. We all gave a sigh of relief and an Amen, especially the corpsmen and the men who did not become casualties.

About the eighteenth day of the battle at dusk, a "Rags" call was passed through the foxholes, and I took off calling out the password "Rags" to find and help the injured men. A platoon had a direct hit in their foxholes and three very young marines were seriously injured. I gave medical aid to one with a torn and bloody twisted leg. Shrapnel had seriously ripped and torn another marine's chest. The other young man's head and throat were bleeding badly from torn, cut, and ripped flesh wounds. After rendering aid, my problem was getting back to my foxhole—it was a dark night. God was with me.

Toward the end of the campaign, all our leaders were killed or injured badly. Lieutenant Jack Lummus was selected to lead our last charge that morning. We could see the ocean at the other end of the island. He encouraged us without concern for his own safety to charge forward and we did. Little did we know that he would step on an antipersonnel mine.

Lummus' right foot was blown away. His left foot hung from the ankle and was bleeding, with the flesh of the thigh blown off. His lower body was bloody and ripped to pieces; it was a horrible, bloody, and sordid scene. Bill Wallace, corpsman from Chicago, and I from Texas were there to render the best first aid we could offer. We tried to make him as comfortable as possible, trying to give him water which he spewed out. We leaned him against a rock and waited for litter bearers to take him to the aid station for further treatment. Lieutenant Lummus (who played for the New York Giants before the war, and might have been a significant player after, had he not been killed) died as he uttered in a weak voice to Dr. Brown, "Well, Doc, the New York Giants lost a mighty good end today."

I would like to acknowledge the devotion and dedication of Dr. Tom Brown, for his medical attention to the injured. Also, I wish to thank for their support my fellow corpsmen, Roy Brown, Emil Graff, Raymond Hansen, Glen Lougee, Lester Murrah, and Bill Wallace.

A CASE OF PORK AND BEANS
Dr. Thomas M. Brown
Iwo Jima, 1945

Jim Huddleston of Muncie, Indiana, and formerly of 2-28, [of the U.S. Marines], related the following bit of history as the absolute, sworn truth. His wife, who was not with him at the time of this revelation of history, independently verified his statements at a later date and alleged that he had related the story to her as absolutely true after he returned home from overseas. This is his story:

Following the capture of Mount Suribachi [on Iwo Jima], our regiment reorganized and headed north to join other elements of the 5th Division in the savage struggle to capture the rest of the island. This was a few days after we had raised our Red, White, and Blue above the hill. Our squad was sitting in foxholes waiting for the order to move out to destroy a bunker a short distance ahead of our platoon. It was a formidable installation and had been a difficult obstacle for our company the past few hours. We sat and sat in those foxholes leaning back against the hot, volcanic soil for the longest time. An hour must have passed before the order to move out finally arrived.

We were so bored with sitting there leaning back against the hot earth, we were ready to go the second the order arrived. Our helmets were strapped, carbines loaded with safeties off and lying across our laps, and packs on our backs. We all jumped out and started running forward in squad formation. Some were firing away as they ran, and some were throwing grenades as others covered with protective fire. We anticipated crossfire, but none like what we received. They were waiting for us and gave us a warm welcome.

As I ran, the enemy fire seemed to be coming from all directions. I went forward about twenty-five yards when something hit me in the back real hard and knocked me over on the ground. I fell so hard my breath was knocked out of me. As I fell, I knew I had been hit, but didn't know how badly. As I lay there face-down on the ground, something warm began oozing over [my back] where I was hit. I yelled, "Corpsman!" as loudly as I could. "I've been hit," I screamed through all the noise and chaos.

A voice replied, "I'll be there as soon as I can, buddy." By then I felt the warm blood oozing down over the left side of my body. I reached under with my right hand to that area. Sure enough, it was thick, red blood. A feeling of increasing weakness spread through me as my vision dimmed. "Hurry, Corpsman, I'm losing blood," I pleaded.

"I hear you, Mac. I'm almost through with this man. Hang on."

By now my fatigues on the left side of my chest were saturated with blood. I could feel it oozing through them. My vision was rapidly dimming. I was sweating like crazy. "Hurry, Corpsman. I'm bleeding to death."

"I just finished this man, Jim. I'll be there in a jiffy. Hold on, I'm coming."

And he was. He knelt at my left side and lifted up my pack to check the wound in my back. There was a pause interrupted by a soft whisper, "Oh, my God, Jim!" There was another pause, and the corpsman broke out in loud, hilarious laughter. He just kept on laughing and laughing, while I was lying there, dying and dying. What's this guy's problem? I thought he was cracking up. Finally he was able to control himself and stop.

"You dumb-ass marine," he quipped, "there's nothing wrong with you. They hit you in your pork and beans."

Much can be said about the state of mind when one is dying. Jim did receive the Purple Heart Medal for bona fide wounds incurred later in battle.

WOUNDED ON OKINAWA
Frances M. Doss
Okinawa, 1945

This is a small piece of a great story about Desmond Doss, a conscientious objector (C.O.) for religious reasons during World War II. He became a medic, and the story that follows shows how a man who wouldn't wield a weapon still managed to save seventy-five men in the midst of battle. Frances M. Doss is the wife of Desmond Doss.

"Is that Okinawa? Doesn't look very big," remarked a soldier.

"No, I think that is just a small island near Okinawa. It is called 'Ie Shima.' 'Shima' means 'island.' There is another island named 'Zamami Shima,' I think," volunteered another soldier.

Yet another soldier volunteered more information. "You know, I just heard that Ernie Pyle—that war correspondent—was killed on Ie Shima just a day or two ago. It's too bad. He always stayed right with the men and told exactly what was happening to the soldiers on the battlefield."

For a few days the 77th Army Division stayed on board ship in the area. But by April 20 they were on the island of Okinawa itself.

The 77th had many new recruits, because so many had been wounded and killed on Guam and Leyte.

One thing made the soldiers sad when they landed on Okinawa. The Japanese had told the native Okinawans that Americans would treat them cruelly, rape their women, kill their children, etc. So to get away from these "terrible" Americans, they told the people to hide or maybe kill themselves. The mothers believed the Japanese, and when Americans landed on the island, they saw evidence that many mothers had slit their children's throats and then killed themselves. Another method they used was to throw the children into the ocean from the high cliffs and then jump in themselves. Hundreds lost their lives this way. The ones who didn't soon learned that the Americans were not as cruel as the Japanese said they were.

Stretching across the island was what was called the Maeda (Mie?-da) Escarpment. It was a four-hundred-foot cliff, going almost straight up on the front side. The top of it was about seventy-five to one hundred yards wide, then it sloped off down the back side.

Although the Americans didn't realize it until later, the Japanese were dug into the very center of that big hill. There were two and three stories of dugouts inside, connected by ladders from one story to another.

The 77th Division bivouacked in the front of the four-hundred-foot cliff. Their job was to kill the Japanese on the top and back side of the escarpment. They began to realize what a job it was going to be.

Desmond wasn't required, as a medic, to pull guard duty. But the soldiers had been fighting hard and losing a lot of sleep, so he volunteered for guard duty at times. One time, down near the bottom of the escarpment, he and another soldier were pulling guard. He took the first watch. After a couple of hours, he woke the other soldier—who immediately went back to sleep.

Then Desmond heard something. There was a big hole beside them, and he could hear voices down the hole—and they weren't speaking English! There were grenades right beside him, and he knew that if he dropped a grenade down the hole, he would have some dead Japanese. Desmond felt this was the greatest temptation he ever had to destroy life. He believed that if a Jap threw a grenade that landed in his lap, he would be justified in throwing it back before it exploded, but he felt it would cause confusion if he, a CO, would drop a grenade and kill someone. He poked the other soldier—he was snoring, and Desmond wondered if the Japanese could hear him. But again he went off to sleep immediately. So Desmond settled down as far away from the hole as he could get and prayed for the rest of the night for the Lord's protection. His prayers were answered, and again they weren't hurt.

From the bivouac area below the cliff, the soldiers could climb up about 360 to 365 feet, even though it was very hard because of the steepness and the roughness of the terrain, caused by the bombing of the island by the navy and air force. But the last 30 to 35 feet went almost straight up, even leaning about 5 feet out at the top from what it was 30 to 35 feet below.

Later, Lieutenant Gornto asked Desmond to help out. "Doss, could you and a couple of fellows get those navy cargo nets over there, and rig a ladder up that last 30 to 35 feet. I think you can do it by splicing the nets together with 2x4s."

"Yes, sir. We'll try," said Desmond.

They spliced the cargo nets together with the 2x4s and tied them into the coral rock at the top edge of the escarpment. Other soldiers used the rocks they found in the area to make a rock wall near the edge of the escarpment for the little protection it might give them.

"That's a good job, fellows," said the lieutenant. "It will sure help us to get up and down a lot easier and safer, I hope."

It was April 29, 1945, when the real battle for the Maeda Escarpment began. The fighting was on top of the escarpment after the soldiers got to the top. One big problem they found was that the Japanese had been there for so long and had dug trenches and foxholes that the Americans couldn't even tell were trenches or foxholes. The area would look like natural terrain, but unseen guns were sticking out to shoot the unsuspecting Americans.

Henry D. Lopez, in his book *From Jackson to Japan* (used by permission), says, "Japanese defenses on Okinawa were the most rugged and impregnable ever assaulted. . . . The terrain of Okinawa with its countless knolls, ridges, and promontories of coral-limestone rock . . . lent itself most favorably to the conduct of a determined defense."

"Okay, fellows, we're going up on top again today. Those cargo nets are up, so we can get on top more easily. You have plenty of ammunition. Do your best, men." Lieutenant Gornto was giving them last minute instructions.

Desmond went over to where Gornto was. "Lieutenant," he said, "I believe prayer is the best life saver there is. The men should really pray before they go up."

"Fellows," called Gornto, "Come over here, and gather around. Doss wants to pray for us."

That wasn't what Desmond had in mind. What he had in mind was that none of them knew whether they would survive this battle, and he felt they should be reminded to pray for themselves before they went up the cargo net. But when Lieutenant Gornto put it that way, Desmond did pray. "Dear Lord, bless us today. Be with the lieutenant and help him to give the right orders, for our lives are in his hands. Help each one of us to use safety precautions so that we all might come back alive. And, Lord, help all of us to make our peace with Thee before we go up the net. Thank you. Amen."

With that, they all started up the cliff and the cargo net. They reached the top and almost immediately got pinned down so they couldn't move on. Company A was fighting to their left, and was hitting fierce opposition. The first five men who reached the top were killed.

The message came up by radio from headquarters asking how many of the Company B men had been killed or wounded.

Desmond reported none so far. So they gave the orders that Company B should take the whole hilltop by themselves since Company A was pretty well shot up. Uncle Sam has to sacrifice lives at times to gain important objectives, and this Maeda Escarpment was an important objective.

So Company B started across the top of the escarpment. They knocked out eight or nine Japanese pillboxes. The miracle of the story was that not one man was killed and only one man was injured—by a rock that hit his hand.

It was such an outstanding happening that headquarters soon heard about it and the message went back even to the States.

"How did you ever do it?" was the question asked.

The men of Company B answered, "It was because of Doss' prayer."

The next day a member of the Signal Corps arrived at the Company B area. "We've heard about the good job you guys did yesterday. Can I get a picture?"

"Yes," said Lieutenant Gornto. "Doss, go up on the escarpment and let him take your picture."

Desmond said to the signal corpsman, "Come on up with me."

"Don't believe I will. I haven't lost anything up there and don't intend to." However, in the end the signal corpsman accompanied Doss to the escarpment and photographed him.

Medal of Honor Day

It was time to go up on the escarpment again. Desmond was reading his Bible when Captain Vernon approached him and said, "Doss, would you mind going up on the escarpment today? You know, you are the only medic we have left, and we really need you."

"Yes, Captain. I'll go up. But do you suppose I could take time to finish my private devotions?" asked Desmond.

"Okay, we'll wait for you," the captain replied.

Desmond bowed his head in prayer. He figured he was ready to join the group in about ten minutes. Some told him it was half an hour. But none of them were anxious to go up and fight so they were glad for the delay.

The soldiers actually thought the hardest battle was already fought, and that this day was just a mop-up job. Desmond did mention prayer to Captain Vernon, but he said, "Sorry, Doss, we've already started to push off." So nothing more was said.

The 155 men left in Company B went up the escarpment. Right away they faced the hell of war. Everything seemed to go wrong. One Japanese position the group could not seem to rout. The Americans heaved satchel charges (bags of TNT) and other high explosives into the Japanese position, but they pulled the fuses out before they exploded. Finally several of the men grabbed five-gallon cans of gasoline and heaved them over into the enemy foxhole. Then Lieutenant Phillips threw a white phosphorus grenade. The resulting explosion was more than they anticipated. There was a terrific explosion in the foxhole itself, but even more further down in the hill. Evidently all of the high explosives the men had thrown into the foxhole went off, but also an ammunition dump down below.

Then what happened was unexpected. Japanese came from all directions from other foxholes and trenches—probably figuring it was now or never. There were so many Japanese and they fought so hard, it would have been suicide to stay up on top. The soldiers were told to retreat. It was supposed to be an orderly retreat, but it ended in panic.

Desmond was up on top with his men until they all left. But what about the wounded men who were scattered around on the top of the escarpment? He couldn't go off and leave them. He knew many of them had families at home.

He started for the nearest soldier. He was badly hurt. Desmond dragged him over to the edge of the escarpment and looked around to see what he had to use. There was a litter and the one rope they had used for hauling up supplies. He rolled the wounded soldier onto the litter and tied him on as well as he could. Then he dropped him over the edge as he hung onto the rope. Part way down he thought he was going to lose the man, but the rope held and the litter landed safely thirty-five feet below at the bottom of the cargo net.

Some of the fellows had dropped to the ground at the bottom of the cargo net to rest for a minute before proceeding on down the cliff. "What on earth is going on?" they wondered as they noticed the litter coming down.

"Take him to the aid station pronto," yelled Desmond from up on top. "He's hurt bad."

As a couple of fellows started on down the cliff with the wounded man, Desmond pulled the rope back up. It took a long time to lower that man. He tied a bowline knot with two loops, brought another man over to the edge, slid the two loops onto his legs, doubled the rope again, and tied it around the man's chest. Then he let him gently over the edge. The Lord had provided a tree stump on top of the hill. Desmond wound the rope around the stump and let up on the rope gradually. That took the load off him as he let the man down.

Desmond kept praying, "Lord, help me get one more."

Why the Japanese didn't come over to the part of the escarpment where they were and finish them all off, Desmond didn't know. His only explanation was that God took care of him and his men, and later he had time to thank God.

It took him about five hours, but he rescued all of the wounded soldiers. It was a tired, thankful, blood-soaked medic who came down the Maeda Escarpment that day. And, unbelievably, he was not wounded.

The members of Company B who had witnessed this conscientious objector soldier medic doing what he did were astonished, and it wasn't long before the rest of the company heard about it too. Then others.

When he arrived back at the bivouac area, he heard welcome words. "Doss, those fatigues are blood-soaked. Besides you are covered with flies, and we don't have any fly spray. We're going to have to find you some different fatigues."

It wasn't long before he was dressed in a clean uniform. He decided to go off in a quiet place somewhere and read his Bible. He certainly had something special to thank his God for this time.

While he was gone, General A. D. Bruce from the 77th Division headquarters arrived at the camp. He had heard of Desmond's feat, and wanted to shake his hand. He also suggested that he should receive the Medal of Honor, and asked those who could start the process to get it going. Desmond was told this later, because he was not there to shake the general's hand. He wished he had been.

How many men had Desmond let down from the escarpment? The top brass said, "Let's see. We had 155 men go up and only 55 men got down the hill on their own. So you must have saved 100 men."

"Couldn't be," said Desmond, modestly. "It couldn't have been more than 50. I wouldn't have had time to save 100 men."

So they compromised at 75, and that is the number on Desmond's Medal of Honor Citation.

Two weeks later there were still places where the Japanese were fighting hard. It was decided to try Japanese tactics: They came out of hiding early in the morning to find sleeping Americans and kill them. Why shouldn't the Americans do the same?

They decided to try it. One very dark night the soldiers marched out of the bivouac area. Desmond plastered a piece of adhesive tape on the back of each man's pack so they could follow each other from the faint glow it made. But it was so dark even that didn't help. They finally got near the area where they were to be next morning. Desmond and three others found a hole and crawled in.

Then they saw it coming—a grenade! The other three managed to crawl out, but Desmond was too far back in the hole. The grenade landed at his feet. Almost without thinking, he put his heavy army boot on top of the grenade. BOOM! He felt himself flying into the air, and he saw stars that weren't there. When he was on the ground again, he felt his leg area. The leg was still there! But it was bleeding badly. He bandaged the leg as best he could.

He must get out of the area because it was Japanese territory, so he and another soldier started crawling over the hill into American territory. They found a hole there. Since the other soldier was wounded in his shoulder, Desmond borrowed his shovel to dig the hole a little wider. Then they crawled in to spend the rest of the night. Desmond knew he was losing a lot of blood. He would feel woozy and then lie with his head down the hill. When it began to get light they looked around a little. They saw that when Desmond was shoveling the hole out the night before, he came within inches of hitting an artillery dud. If he had hit that, there wouldn't have been a greasy spot left, as the saying goes.

Again God had cared for Desmond Doss.

Soon after daybreak, the litter bearers came to pick up the wounded. They loaded Desmond on the litter and started for the aid station. On the way, they found a soldier who had been wounded on his head when the Japanese opened fire. But they only had one litter and not enough men to carry two soldiers. Desmond rolled off the litter and told them to take the other man who had the head wound.

"We don't want to do that, Doss," they said. But Desmond insisted. "I've been out here for five hours and I will be okay for a while yet. Take him."

"Well, okay, Doss, but we'll be back shortly."

While they were gone, Brooks, a friend who had been slightly wounded, came by.

"Doss, what happened to you? Oh, I see. If you lean on me, do you suppose we could manage to get to the aid station on our own? Come on, let's try it," suggested Brooks.

They started out, but hadn't gone far when a Japanese sniper shot a bullet that hit Desmond's arm. It went into his wrist, came out below his elbow went in above his elbow and lodged in his upper arm, shattering his bones and nerves. If the bullet hadn't hit Desmond's arm, it probably would have gone through Brooks' neck, possibly killing him.

"Brooks, give me your gun," Desmond said. Brooks wondered why this man who had never carried a gun, wanted one all of a sudden. But Desmond knew. He put it against his useless arm and asked Brooks to wrap his field jacket around his arm and body. It made a splint for the arm. They went on toward the aid station, but Desmond had lost so much blood he passed out. Brooks ran to the aid station, and got the litter bearers there to go out and pick Desmond up. The aid station they arrived at was not the First Battalion aid station. That caused an interesting happening in Lynchburg, Virginia. When the litter bearers came back to get Desmond, he was gone. So they reported him killed in action, and that report went back to Lynchburg and was printed in the paper there. But when Desmond was in the hospital after surgery on his leg and arm, he asked a nurse to help him finish a letter to his folks, which he sent home.

The day after it came out in the paper that Desmond Doss was killed in action, Mother Doss went to work as usual at the shoe factory. Her fellow workers were shocked. "Mrs. Doss, how can you come to work when your boy was killed?"

"But he wasn't killed! He got wounded, and is in the hospital, but he will be okay eventually. You see, we got a letter from him just yesterday." The next day the paper printed a retraction.

When Desmond arrived at the field hospital, the doctor looked at his wounded arm and leg, and said, "Doss, we are marking you for stateside as soon as we get you fixed up a little." Desmond decided that was one nice thing about being wounded. Surgery for Desmond meant taking out seventeen pieces of shrapnel from his wounded leg and setting his wounded arm, putting it in a heavy cast. After surgery, he was put on a hospital ship heading east this time. It was about that time that he noticed his little Bible was missing! He must have dropped it out on the battlefield. He sent a message back to his fellow soldiers, asking them to keep an eye open for it. His friends fanned out across the area, and it was found and returned to Desmond. He treasured that Bible.

The hospital ship took him to Guam, and a plane flew him on to Hawaii.

"My arm really hurts, and besides, it smells terrible," Desmond told the corpsman who was helping him.

"We'll have the doctor take a look," the soldier replied.

The doctor had to cut out a piece of the cast to get to the arm. He found the gauze bandage wrapped around and through to the bones, and the arm was infected. When he saw the condition of Desmond's arm, he had a few well-chosen swear words to say about a certain doctor on Okinawa.

"If that man were a veterinarian, I wouldn't even take my dog to him!" he exploded.

"Doctor, is there anything you can do to make this cast more comfortable? It's awfully heavy, and it doesn't let me stand up straight," said Desmond as the doctor worked on his arm.

"Well-l-l, it is getting in kind of bad shape. If it gets in a little worse shape, we might need to change it."

So Desmond saw to it that the cast did get in worse shape in a very short time. As a result, the old heavy cast was removed and a new type made of metal strips and covered with muslin, and called an airplane splint, was put on his arm.

When the doctor finished with Desmond's arm, it felt much better—and it didn't stink.

Then it was across the Pacific—toward home.

DAY BY DAY ON OKINAWA
Ed Strohmeier
Okinawa, 1945

Strohmeier was a marine platoon corpsman. His story is taken from notes collected by him and put into book form by a friend, Harry Murray, whose story is also presented in this book. At this point in his narrative, Strohmeier is with his company, attempting to hold Half Moon Hill on Okinawa.

It became apparent, about this time, that the companies to our right and left had not advanced as they were expected to. As a result, we were a good distance in front of the lines, and the Nips were concentrating everything they had upon us. At the rate we were losing men, I didn't see how we could be expected to hold the hill until morning. There were no replacements, and it was very unlikely we would be relieved, because we had just come to the front.

A few minutes later we received word to make a "strategic withdrawal." We were to return to the company CP.

I assure you that it wasn't long before we were off of Half Moon. Some of the men didn't have time to pick up their packs or other equipment. I was more fortunate. Mine was in the general direction in which I was going, so I stopped long enough to grab my carbine and pack and started down the hill as quickly as possible. The Nips were expected to pull a banzai attack immediately. As we hurried up the tracks, we were continually looking to our rear in the expectation of seeing them coming over the hill.

As we came to the concrete bridge crossing over the tracks, there was a group of men from our company working with some of the wounded men who had been sent back earlier. It seems that just before we had left Half Moon, one of the young fellows by the name of Jerry Reilly had stepped on one of the mines on the railroad tracks. It had shattered his legs, and he was losing blood rapidly. There was nothing we could do for him, due to circumstances being as they were. He was screaming for Hymen, his buddy, to give him more morphine. Hymen said he had given him a whole syrette, and he couldn't give him more. I felt very sorry for both Reilly and Hymen. Reilly, because of his condition, and Hymen because he realized that Reilly didn't have a chance. We'd be lucky if we could even get him back to the CP.

One of the marines was working with a man whose face was very bloody and covered with mud. The mine had gotten him too. He seemed to be unconscious. Two of us looked at him, but we couldn't recognize him. Someone said he believed he was a replacement by the name of Kelly. I don't see how his face could ever be the same again.

I saw Hymen about thirty feet down the railroad tracks with an M1 rifle. I was wondering what he was going to do. As he came up the track toward me, he took out the clip and the shells and slammed the rifle across one of the tracks, breaking it in two. I felt very sorry for him. His face expressed the hopelessness of it all. I could see he was just about exhausted. He said something about being too tired to go any farther. He was so exhausted he began crying.

I didn't see how the few of us who were able were going to get these wounded men back over the hill to the CP. I don't know how we did it, but all the wounded were brought back. Due to the position we were in at the time, it was impossible for us to bring down the hill those four men who had been killed. We hated to leave them, but there was no alternative. We wondered if the Nips would mistreat their bodies in any way.

Although the time seemed like hours and the distance like miles, it was probably a very short time from our withdrawal from Half Moon to our arrival at the CP, which was probably only a half-mile away. However, in this short time, I experienced the thrill of terror that I will never forget. I realized that it might be necessary for us to leave some of our wounded behind. That is really a terrible feeling, especially after hearing of some of the atrocities that the Nips were capable of committing.

I took the rear right end of the stretcher and helped two of the men who were carrying a wounded man. The man on the stretcher was very heavy. This along with the deep mud made it very hard for us to carry him.

As we came around the hill into the CP, I saw Lieutenant Andrews standing near where we were passing. I said to him, "Take this," meaning the stretcher. At the same time, my carbine fell from my shoulder, and he took that instead. I was too tired to repeat it, so I went on with the men to where Brady and Swick were giving plasma to some of the wounded. Reese was helping them. It sure was good to see them again. I helped for awhile, and then went up the hill to the ridge where we were to dig in for the night. The crest of the hill was very irregular and stony. Some of the stones were very large and made good protection against rifle fire.

The Nips were still firing knee mortars that were hitting about a hundred yards to our rear. A few, however, landed quite close to our line.

I saw Oldfield and asked if I was to sleep with him again. He said he imagined so. We began digging after debating on the location of the foxhole. Neither of us wanted the responsibility of saying where it was to be dug, just in case a shell or mortar landed on that spot.

We had been digging for several minutes when we heard a very loud explosion to the right of us with immediate cries for the corpsman. I grabbed my helmet and medical kit and ran over to where a shell had hit one of the amtracks being used to bring up supplies and to take out the wounded. The shell had hit right in front of the ramp. One of the boys . . . had been standing a few yards from the amtrack and had received much of the impact. As I got to him, one of the corpsmen from the 3rd Battalion came with a splint—just what we needed. His leg was very badly shattered. Most of the flesh was blown from the bone, and the bone was broken into many small pieces. He kept wanting to rise up and look at it. I told him, if he didn't stay down, I would have to have someone hold him down. He didn't know how badly his leg had been mangled, and I didn't want him to see it, because he was suffering from shock already. We used about six large battle dressings on his leg after sprinkling it with sulfanialamide powder and giving him a shot of morphine. We tied his leg to the splint, and he was put on an amtrack and taken back to battalion headquarters. I heard later that it was necessary for them amputate. Although I was sorry for him, I was not surprised to hear this. Some of us used to kid him about having such large feet. I've forgotten what size shoes he wore, but they were quite large.

I went over to where Brady and Swick were working on their foxhole and told them about the man's being wounded and that he had been taken out by the 3rd Battalion. Brady said he had told Hymen to go back to battalion headquarters for the night to get some rest. In his condition, he would have been unable to do anything if we had needed him.

Previously, I had thought that giving the Purple Heart for "combat fatigue" cheapened the meaning of the medal, but now I had changed my mind. A "nice" wound was far less severe than complete exhaustion.

I got a few supplies from Brady and told him who had been killed or wounded. We had to keep these records straight. He told me that many of the men had said I had done a very good job on Half Moon. It made me feel very good to hear this. It was just what I needed.

It was beginning to rain, so I said good-bye and started up the hill that was becoming slicker and muddier with the beginning of more rain. Oldfield and I finished the shallow foxhole and put up the shelter-halves. We wondered how long it would be before we would have running water in our new home. It wasn't long.

We ate a can of rations and went to sleep after deciding that we should have made the foxhole both longer and wider. The rain was beginning to drip through the shelter-halves too. During the night I was awakened by several explosions that sounded very close. I didn't hear anyone calling for a corpsman, so after shivering in my wet clothes for a while, I eventually went back to sleep.

It was good to see the sky getting lighter. Oldfield and I decided that we might as well get up and try to get a little warmer by moving around. If we lay still in the foxhole, we got cramps and became stiff. If we moved, the cold rain water in the foxhole would come running into our clothes, and we would shiver even more. It wasn't too bad if you could get in a comfortable position and warm the water around you. The trouble was finding that "comfortable" position. As we literally slipped out of our shelter, we noticed the sky was still very cloudy, and we would probably have more rain. Some of the men had already gotten up and were warming some cans of chow over a "hot box." We got our chow and did the same. When everyone had gotten up, I held sick call, which consisted of fixing blisters, scratches, etc., and passing out aspirin and sympathy. Savage came over and said he had been hit in the ass on Half Moon and he wanted me to take a look at it. He didn't believe it would amount to anything, though. I could see that infection had already begun. I could feel a piece of metal, but it was too far in for me to do anything about it. I told him he had better check with Brady and then go on back to see the doctor at battalion headquarters.

Carmody came over and showed me his hand. The fungus infection was so bad that he couldn't completely close his hand. I told him he might as well go with Savage and let Dr. Clark take a look at it. They reported to Lieutenant Goheen that they were leaving and started out for battalion headquarters.

I went down the hill to talk with Brady and Swick for a while. The mud had become even worse than it was the night before. When I got to their foxhole, I saw Swick, and he told me that one of the shells had hit right at the side of their hole, throwing debris and mud on them, shaking them up quite a bit, especially Brady. He said that Brady was so nervous and shaken up that Swick suggested he go back to the battalion headquarters until he was better. So now Swick, with Reese's help, was in charge of the Company CP. I was sorry to hear about Brady, but I was glad he was farther behind the lines.

I talked with Swick for a while about the night before and suggested that he ask Chief Culbertson, the naval chief pharmacist's mate in charge of the corpsmen for the 2nd Battalion, for a replacement for Brady. We may have use for him if we have another day like the one before. He said he would do that.

Someone in my company called for me, so I began the difficult task of climbing back up the hill. I thought of the stories I had heard of the mud in Europe during the last war—"the war to end all wars." I wondered who the political big shot was who dreamed that one up. It made me burn.

When I got to the top of the hill, one of the men came over to me and handed me three letters. He said they had gotten some of the mail and that there would be more later. It sure was good to see familiar handwriting again. I read the two letters and opened the third, which was a birthday card saying, "I hope you have a happy birthday," or words to that effect. I appreciated the card, but I was wondering how "happy" it would be—I had a rather good idea.

During the last five or six days, dates hadn't seemed very important, and I had lost track of what the date was. I asked several men, and according to our calculations, we decided the date was about May 19 or May 20—about two or three days before my twenty-first birthday. I had wondered where I would be on that occasion. I hadn't suspected, until recently, that I would be so far from home. I was beginning to wonder if I would ever see twenty-one.

As I was thinking over the prospects of a "happy" birthday, I noticed a line of men coming toward our area. I wondered if they were going to relieve us or if they were replacements for our company? When they got closer, I realized it was George Company. They were moving up to try to take Half Moon. I saw Strickland, one of the Corpsmen in G Company. I wondered how things were going to turn out for him. We used to have a lot of fun swimming together when we were in the medical replacement battalion on Guadalcanal.

By noon, it seemed as though we might not have rain after all. The sky was beginning to clear. We hoped it would stay that way at least long enough for everything to dry out. Word was passed that we were moving again and should be ready at a moment's notice. The word was passed to "fall in" and again we were on our way. We went through several water-soaked fields and started up a hill. We could hear firing on our right side. Word was passed to halt at a five-yard interval. There was a stone wall on my right, so I took off my pack and rested against it. In about five minutes there were six or seven of us within our five-yard interval. One of the men told us to scatter out more.

I heard someone calling for a corpsman. I ran over and helped one of the men fix up one of the marines from another company who had been wounded. The wounded man's corpsman came, and I left to go back to my platoon.

About twenty yards up the hill, along the path from where I was, the Nips had dug into the hill, making an ideal location from which they fired automatic weapons. We found several machine guns and rifles. Chalkley and several other marines took the machine guns apart and destroyed the parts and threw them in all directions. I hated to see them breaking up the rifles. I would have liked to have had one to send home.

We were told that we would spend the night on this hill. After a while we moved farther up and were given our positions for the night.

Across the top of the hill, the Nips had dug a trench so they could move from one side to the other without being seen and with more safety. It was about three feet deep and two feet wide. There was a dead Nip lying along the side of it. He was beginning to bloat, and the flies had already laid their yellow eggs in his mouth, nose, and eyes. It didn't take long for them to begin their work on the dead.

Along the side of the hill which we had come up, the trench was wider at one point. Lieutenant Goheen, a friend of his (a lieutenant), and Daley were going to dig this section out wider and deeper and sleep there. Oldfield and I were to sleep just below them. We began digging, but the dirt was so loose and the side so steep that I suggested that Oldfield sleep there and I could sleep in the trench.

As we were discussing the sleeping situation for the night, one of the men called for me. He said that Dellagena had been hit by a Jap sniper. I grabbed my helmet and medical kits and ran over to where Dellagena was lying. He looked as though he were dead. I felt his pulse and his heart, but there was no indication of life. His eyes were open and rolled back. I tried to shut them. I looked for his wound and found it to be a small hole in his side. There was no blood, just a small hole. And yet it had taken his life. I hated to see it happen to him. The marine who had come for me said that Dellagena had just dug his foxhole and had risen up to rest. He heard a shot, and Dellagena fell into the foxhole.

I was sure we wouldn't be able to get him out that night, so I checked through his pockets and pack because I wasn't sure when he would be gotten or by whom. He had a little money and some Jap navy stamps. I decided I would keep these things for him and send them to his sister. (One of the men said he believed Dellagena had a sister.) I spread his poncho over him and went back to tell Lieutenant

Goheen of Dellagena's death. I got permission to sleep in the trench and got ready for darkness. Two of us had rolled the dead Nip into the trench and had thrown just enough dirt over him to keep the flies away and to keep down the stench.

We had moved over to the left that day and were now tied in with the 5th Marines on our left and George Company on our right flank. We received word that there was a possibility the Nips would pull a banzai attack and that our flares would be sent up at intervals. We also received other bad news. Fennelly, who was from Boston and had been our company mail man while we were on Guadalcanal, had been killed while carrying out George Company's wounded who had been trying to take Half Moon. Another of the "old men" gone.

We figured out how long the watches would be and who would stand them. I followed Oldfield, and Goheen's friend, the lieutenant, followed me. I had one of the late watches, so I went to sleep as soon as it was dark. Oldfield woke me when it was time for me to go on guard. He said nothing special had happened, but to be sure to watch the flat ground at the bottom of the hill. He thought he had seen someone moving down there when one of the flares lit up. He handed me Goheen's watch, a GI model with luminous dial and face, and went back to his foxhole.

I heard one of the flares going over, and it lit up out over the flat strip Oldfield said I should watch. I tried to scan the whole area at the same instant. I was looking so hard that my eyes began to hurt. The only thing I could see moving were the shadows of small bushes and grass as the small parachute let the flare down slowly, causing the shadows to lengthen and to seem to move about. I couldn't decide whether I appreciated the flare or not. I could hear them going over. Then there was a sudden flare of very bright light swinging from a small parachute, making weird whistling sounds as it came down. I can't describe it—you'd have to experience it. It's an awful sound. I figured if it shows us where they are, surely it also shows them where we are. But we would or would not have them according to what some of the big wheels thought, whether I liked them or not.

I wondered how Mathias was making out. He was one of the younger guys. He had come to me just as it had begun to get dark and said that his leg (I believe) was hurting him badly. I couldn't see anything wrong with it. He asked if he could let the doctor look at it. I told him that Dr. Clark was probably a mile away at battalion headquarters. He wanted someone to go with him, but I told him he would be risking another man's life as well as his own by going a distance like that at dusk. I told him to ask Lieutenant Goheen for permission, I wouldn't give it. Goheen told him the same thing I had told him. He said he could go back in the morning if it weren't better and if Novina, who was in charge of the machine gun squad that Mathias was in, thought he would be able to spare him.

Another flare went off, giving me the creeps again. My eyes were beginning to ache from the strain. I couldn't see anything that looked like a man moving around. After awhile my watch was over, and I gladly awakened the lieutenant to relieve me. I told him that everything had been quiet, but to watch the level strip of ground. I got down into the trench, and after putting on my mosquito net and trying to get comfortable under the shelter-half, it was only a matter of minutes until I was asleep.

When I awakened the next morning, the night had gone and the sky was becoming light. I wondered what this new day would bring and if it were May 22 yet. Maybe I was twenty-one years old already. I felt much older than that. I got up and ate a can of C rations. It tasted awful.

I went over and talked with the men in one of the machine gun squads for a few minutes. They had found several oil cans with the Nip guns they had destroyed. I needed one, so I took one. After a few minutes, I went back over to the trench and cleaned my carbine. One of the men had given it to me when he heard that I had lost mine when Lieutenant Andrews had relieved me of it after our withdrawal from Half-Moon with the wounded. It wasn't as good a weapon as the one I had before, but it would fire, and that was about all you could expect from any carbine.

Lieutenant Andrews had been wounded by a fragment from a grenade as we were coming up the hill the day before. I saw him come down hill and say something about having to go back. He had been hit. That's how we lost our "Hollywood" marine. I wondered how badly he had been hit. I hadn't seen his wound.

A short while later, we received word that we were to move out right away. This generally meant within the next hour or two. I wondered how long it would be this time. I thought that, so long as I was waiting, I might as well make myself comfortable for a while. We didn't know what we were going to encounter that day. I laid my webbed belt with the canteens and medical kits on one side of the trench and my pack on the other side. I put my carbine down in the trench and leaned it against the dirt wall and lay down in the trench with my helmet on.

I had just lain down when all of a sudden, without warning, there was a shattering blast about ten yards up the trench from where I was lying. It stunned me for a minute, and my eardrums felt as though they were broken. The ringing sound was terrific. I didn't see any blood, so I supposed that I hadn't been hit. I heard someone moaning, and I realized that the shell had exploded about where three new replacements had been talking just before the explosion. They had slept there the night before.

I grabbed my medical kit and got over to them. One was lying on the ground with his brains about five feet away from his head. I didn't stop to see if anything could be done for him. The second man was badly wounded and suffering severely from shock. He didn't know what was happening. His wounds were very bad and bleeding freely. I was almost certain he would die, either from shock concussion, loss of blood, or from the wounds.

The third man was standing and moaning. His jugular vein had been cut, and the blood was spurting from his throat. I had always feared a wound like that because there is so little that can be done for the person. He was suffering from shock and was still dazed.

I don't believe I have ever felt so helpless as I did then—one man with a cut jugular vein and the other bleeding to death from other wounds. At the same time, we were given orders to move out immediately because the Nips had gotten our range with their artillery.

Another company was moving up to our position, and the corpsman with them came over to see if he could help me. My platoon was already at the bottom of the hill and going around the side. I had to leave with them. I asked if he (the corpsman) would please do whatever he could for them, that I had to stay with my platoon. It seemed an awful thing to do, but that was the way it had to be.

He said he would do his best. I hurried down the hill after picking up my pack and carbine and reached the last man in the platoon as he was going around the hill.

We crossed a small grassy meadow and headed for a hill to the right of us. It was a rather large L-shaped hill, and as we got closer, we could see that we were not the first outfit to get there. There were several helmets and packs and other pieces of gear lying around. I saw two medical kits and wondered if someone that I knew had been hit.

The men were being given their positions and were digging in. It was almost certain that we would spend the night here. I was standing at the foot of the hill, looking for a good location for my foxhole, when there was a loud explosion to my right. I looked up and saw Lieutenant Goheen and a combat photographer sliding and stumbling down the hill. The photographer said he didn't believe he had been hit. I went to Lieutenant Goheen, and he had gotten two wounds from a grenade that a Nip had thrown from a foxhole just on the other side of the hill. The wounds didn't seem to be too serious. I had a very hard time getting the bandage to stay on his head wound. I was rather nervous, I suppose. I told him he would have to go back to see Dr. Clark. He didn't want to, but I finally got him on his way. I sure did hate to see him go. I knew no one would be able to take his place. We all thought a lot of him. He and the photographer left together. That was the last time I was to see Goheen until we went to Guam. We were told that it was necessary to put him on a hospital ship in order to keep him from returning to the company before his wounds were healed.

About this time, Carmody and Savage came back to the platoon. They had gone back several days earlier to the battalion sick bay because of infected wounds. It sure was good to see them again.

Daley, Clark, and several of the other men decided to go over the top of the hill to get the Nip, or Nips, who had been giving us so much trouble. As they started across, I wondered how many of them would come back alive. I heard several shots, and a grenade exploded. In about three minutes they all came running back.

Daley and Clark had been hit by fragments from the grenade that a Nip had thrown. Clark had spotted the Nip in a foxhole as he went over the hill and had killed him with his rifle butt. Although their wounds were not very serious, it was necessary for them to leave the outfit for further medical treatment.

Two more of the best men gone. I appreciated Savage's and Carmody's return even more now. For a while they were in charge of the platoon.

Someone on my left called for me to come over—Carr had been hit in the head by a sniper. He had tried to crawl to a better position along the ridge of the hill. One of the men crawled over the top and pulled him back over. He had been killed instantly. We covered him with a poncho, and I went back to the place where I expected to sleep.

In just a few minutes I heard the call for corpsman again, so I ran back up the hill, and Johnson said that Whitman had been hit badly. I ran over to his foxhole, and as soon as I saw him, I was afraid there wasn't going to be much I could do for him. A sniper had gotten him in the jaw. It was broken, and some of his teeth were just lying in his mouth. The bullet had passed through the jaw and entered his shoulder. He was bleeding rather freely. I gave him a shot of morphine and dressed his wounds as best I could. He was trying to talk to me, but I couldn't understand what he was trying to say. I opened a container of serum of albumin and gave that to him. I had a hard time getting the needle into the vein.

I thought of the times we had gone swimming off Guadalcanal and the talks we had had together. I felt very sorry for him, but I also was aware of the fact that it didn't affect me at all—it was just too bad—that's all. He was making the sign of the cross and repeating a prayer.

Johnson asked me how he was, and I told him I didn't think he had a chance. Three stretcher bearers came to take Carr's body out, so I called them over and Whitman was taken out instead. I was quite sure that was going to be the last time I would see him. It was. He died either that night or the next morning.

I went over to talk with Johnson for a minute. He had me worried, and I wouldn't have been at all surprised if he would have "cracked up." Most of the men in his group had been killed, and it was beginning to work on him.

Lieberman, the demolitions man with our company, decided to go over the hill and blow up several tombs where we thought some Nips were hiding. I was glad I didn't have his job. We occasionally had been receiving fire from that direction. He went over the hill, and in a few minutes we heard several explosions. He had "blown" several of the tombs with nitro-packs. When he got back over the hill, he was bleeding, so I fixed him up and sent him back to the doctor. I believe a sniper had wounded him too.

We were sure now that this would be the place where we would spend the night. Some of the men already had their foxholes dug, but, as usual, I hadn't had time. So when I began to look for a good spot, I found that they had all been taken. Carmody and Savage asked me to stay with them, but it would have been too crowded, so I dug my hole a few feet down the hill to the right of them. I knew it wouldn't be a very good spot if it began to rain. I just hoped that it wouldn't rain. It was beginning to get dark, and I could see that it was also beginning to get cloudy. I decided that, if it did rain, I would get wet anyway, so why worry?

Narcho, a Papago Indian, and another man had been given a rather high, open spot of ground to my right to dig in. It was a very bad place. They had just about finished their foxhole and had the machine gun set up. There was a shot from the other side of the hill, and Narcho fell over in his foxhole—dead. The other man flattened out and called for me. I got there as soon as possible, and between the two of us, we managed to drag him out of the hole without exposing ourselves too much. The hillside was very steep, so I let him slide down the loose dirt to the bottom. I opened his shirt, or rather his jacket, and saw that he had been hit in the chest. He, too, had been killed instantly. I wondered who was going to be next.

Narcho was liked by everyone in the company. We sure did hate to lose him. I covered him with a shelter-half and went back to digging my foxhole.

The darker it got, the more it looked like rain—all we needed for a perfectly miserable day.

Lieutenant Dale came up to the platoon to take charge. I liked him all right, but it seemed that some of the men would rather not have had him. He didn't seem like a frontline officer. He was different from Goheen.

Our supplies, ammo, grenades, and food had been brought up to the line earlier and had been passed out. We had used up almost all our grenades earlier that afternoon, so we were very glad to get more. I opened one of the cases and threw them up the hill to the guys. It amused me when I remembered how careful I had always handled grenades before, and now we were pitching them around like baseballs.

It was getting dark, so I ate a can of rations and tried to make myself comfortable in a foxhole that was too short for me. The watches had been arranged, and they said I wouldn't have to stand one. I was very glad, because I was tired.

I was awakened late that night or early the next morning by rain hitting me in the face. I pulled my helmet down over my face and tried to get more sleep. I was feeling rather sorry for myself when I heard two very loud explosions to my right. I waited for a minute for someone to call for me. It seemed I was waiting a long time, but it must have been two minutes when someone said a mortar had landed in the foxhole with Burlingham and Lieutenant Fussel. I already had my medical kit, and as I started over to their hole, someone at the top of the hill said that the other mortar had hit in one of the other holes too. It seems that it was occupied by Marton and Martinez, but I'm not sure.

I got to Burlingham and Fussel first. The shell had either hit right at the side of the hole or in it. Fussel, I know, was dead. He had received the full impact of the explosion. I took a look at Burlingham. He was groaning and semiconscious. His head was bleeding very badly, and his pants and jacket were ripped to pieces. I saw the blood flowing from his legs. It was so dark that I wasn't sure just what condition he was in. Actually, I suppose I more or less felt his wounds rather than saw them. I remember feeling the warm, rather sticky blood all over his legs and head and on my hands.

All this time there was one man yelling for me to hurry and get up to the other two who had been wounded. I told him I was doing my best. When I got there, I saw that the one boy was dead already. The mortar had hit him squarely on the back. He was in a kneeling position. I could see his ribs broken away from the back bone, and his intestines were lying under him on the ground. He had almost been blown in half. It was a terrible sight. The other man's wounds weren't so bad. I fixed him up and went down to see if Burlingham was still alive.

I cut the legs out of his pants and dressed his wounds as best I could. He had lost very much blood, and I was almost certain he would die at any moment. I didn't see how he could possibly live. I opened another can of serum of albumin and, fortunately, I found his vein without any trouble.

Two or three of the men volunteered to take Burlingham back to the company CP. I knew that if he weren't taken, he would surely die. It was raining hard, now, and the hill was very slick. We put him on the stretcher, and the men left with him. The other man who had been wounded went along with them.

(I saw Burlingham about a year later in the hospital at Great Lakes while I was waiting to be discharged. He had recovered from his head wound, but his legs were still giving him trouble. It looked as though large pieces of flesh had been blown from his leg. I had heard that he had lived, and it sure was wonderful to see him again. Burlingham told me he was wounded on May 22, my twenty-first birthday. At the time, we hadn't known the date.)

I went back to my foxhole, and Carmody asked me how Burlingham was. I told him I didn't see how he could possibly live. By this time, quite a bit of water had drained into my foxhole, so I put a hand grenade box in it to sit on and kept my feet out of the water by placing them on my shovel. It seemed that the whole hillside was draining into my foxhole, so I got my canteen cup and bailed the hole out as best I could. I don't believe I slept at all that night.

When Schnetzler was wounded on Half Moon, he gave his pistol—a Smith and Wesson .38 Special—to Daley. Clark and Daley decided that I should have it, since I was without a weapon. I kept it.

When it became light enough for us to get up and move about with safety, everyone came out of their muddy, water-filled foxholes and tried to get warm. A poncho will keep a person dry if it doesn't rain too hard or too long. It had rained all night, so everyone was soaking wet and miserable.

Word was sent back for stretcher bearers to take out the bodies of Narcho and the other boy. I went up to see the other boy. He looked bad enough at night, but now, with the light of day, it was even more terrible than I had thought. His back was simply blown away. I covered him again with his poncho and went down the hill to my mud hole and ate a can of C rations, which I didn't enjoy at all. It seemed even harder than usual to get the stuff to go down, and I knew why.

The stretcher bearers finally came, and we managed to get the body on the stretcher. Rigor mortis had set in, and since he was in a kneeling position, it was hard to keep him from falling off the stretcher. We had to tie him on it.

Narcho's body was taken out then, too. We didn't have as much trouble with him, but I felt sorry for the men who had to carry him back across the muddy hills. He certainly was heavy.

We were told later that day that we were to be replaced. We would move over to the next hill on our left flank. When our replacements came, we moved out. It was only a short distance, and we were glad to find that someone else had been there already. I believe the outfit had two 75mms there. They were a welcome sight.

We were to cover the left flank of the hill. Lieutenant Dale assigned the men to their positions, and they began to dig in on the crest of the hill.

I began looking for a good place to sleep for the night, and I thought I had found it—either a tomb or foxhole that had been cut into the base of the hill. I put my pack and other gear in the entrance and took a look around to see what kind of a position we would be in for the night.

There seemed to be about ten men on our right flank, so I went over to see if they had a corpsman with them. Fortunately, they did—a guy by the name of Glass from Wisconsin. We talked for a few minutes, and I came back to my platoon.

As might be expected, this area was just as muddy and full of water as the one we had just left. But it was a change, and that was welcomed too.

I held sick call, but there wasn't anything serious, for which I was very thankful. The evening passed very quietly until we received word that a high-ranking Japanese official had been captured and said that there was to be a major banzai attack tonight along all the lines. Everyone started digging his foxhole much deeper, and more ammunition was brought up. It was quite obvious that Lieutenant Dale was very worried about the whole affair.

There was a stone tomb that had been cut into the hill about halfway up, and I decided that was probably the best place for me to bring the wounded if we should be attacked. I moved out the earthen jars of bones and straightened things up as much as possible to make more room. I decided I had enough supplies, so that didn't worry me.

I had gotten quite squared away when I heard an explosion that sounded as though it might have been a grenade blast on top of the hill. I grabbed my medical kit and started for the top of the hill just as someone called for me. I couldn't imagine what it could have been, because some of the men had gone along the other side of the hill earlier in the day and had thrown grenades into all the tombs. I didn't see how it could have been a Nip.

When I got to the top, one of the men said that a grenade had gone off in the foxhole with Starks—a boy who had very little to say to anyone. I believe he was from the country. He had gotten heat stroke one time on a firing problem on Guadalcanal, and I had quite a time with him. Just as soon as I got there I could see that Starks was dead. I surely did hate to see it happen to him.

One of the new replacements, who was sharing a foxhole with Starks, was so shaken over it that he was unable to tell us what had happened. He simply went to pieces. Finally, we quieted him, and he told us he wasn't sure what had happened. They were going after more grenades, and when they got back to the hole, Starks yelled, "Watch out. It's a grenade," just as it exploded. From that we concluded that the pin came out of one of them and he didn't have time, or was unable to throw it out before it exploded. We certainly hated to lose Starks, especially in that way.

We had a stretcher, so I sent one of the guys after it. We put Starks on it, covered him with his poncho and took him down to the foot of the hill.

Lieutenant Dale and several other men came over to look at Starks. I went back up the hill to see how the other guy was getting along. He was still quite bad off, so I told him to go down the hill to the company CP.

I went down to the tomb and decided that I might as well stay there until something else happened. It was quite dark now with the exception of an occasional flare that was sent up. I hated those flares.

There were about three tombs in a row at different elevations. The one I was in was the highest one on the left. It was facing away from the front line, and I had no idea of what was going on.

After about an hour of sitting alone in the dark in the tomb, it dawned on me that I hadn't told any of the men on the line that this was where I would be staying all night. I was about to go out to tell one of the men who was closest to me to pass the word along. I realized that just as soon as I stuck my head out or called to them someone might take a shot at me. The closest man was about thirty yards away, so I decided that, rather than take a chance at being shot, I would just sit still and wait to see what would happen.

Once there was a lot of firing from a machine gun, and several grenades went off. But that was all that I heard through the whole night. I would have felt much better if there had been a little more noise of some kind, because I kept thinking all kinds of weird things that might have happened to my comrades, and yet I didn't dare take a look for myself.

Postscript: Strohmeier survived the war without harm and self-published book of his story called A World War II Trilogy.

A CORPSMAN ON OKINAWA
HENRY G. LEWIS
May 1945

Taking Okinawa at the end of World War II involved some of the greatest battles and casualties of all the war. Private Henry G. Lewis, a member of the medical branch of Easy Company, 29th Marines, gives this eyewitness report of the taking of Sugar Loaf Hill and his role as a corpsman in the midst of it and in subsequent fighting.

As we rested after the northern [Okinawa] campaign, the rumor circulated that maybe we would be home for Christmas. This was what we all wanted to hear, and we tended to ignore those rumors of the army having trouble in southern Okinawa.

From our vantage point on the coast, we could see what a terrible pounding the navy was taking from the kamikazes (suicide planes). Our ships were putting up such a heavy barrage of antiaircraft fire, you could almost walk from one burst to another across the sky. However, even though most of those planes were being shot down, the few that did get through were causing very heavy losses. In fact, the navy lost more men off the coast of Okinawa than it did all the rest of the war. We should have realized that as long as anyone was having it tough, things were far from over on the island.

Our short rest was interrupted by the word that we would be replacing the 27th, because the marines had to help them out once before during the Saipan campaign. It was bad enough that we were going back into combat, but to have to replace the 27th made us pretty bitter.

As we were loading our trucks to leave, we could see the first of the 27th Division trucks moving into our area. They began hollering "you'll be sorry," and we returned by barking like a dog for the "doggies." In the few instances where the army and the marines came in contact with each other, there was little love lost.

When we reached the front, the 22nd Regiment took the lead and we were held in reserve. All signs pointed to the 27th Division leaving in a hurry. They had not even bothered to pack up their personal gear. That was another thing that irritated us, the fact that the army had so many comforts. As an example, I found a toothbrush and toothpaste somebody had left. I had not brushed my teeth since we left the ship, about six weeks before. I boiled that toothbrush in my canteen cup over a fire of C-2 plastic explosives and really enjoyed cleaning my teeth.

For supper that night, we were back to K rations again, which we usually had on the front lines. As we ate, we could see about three hills further east where an army unit was dug in. Lo and behold, a truck pulled up to that army unit, and they had hot chow that night. There certainly was a difference between the army and the marines.

Just before sundown, the Japs opened up with an artillery barrage. One shell hit so close the concussion knocked me to the ground. As I lay there, I looked around to where Beacon, the company runner, was standing a minute before. All that was left now was one shoe. Heretofore, it was always someone I just knew slightly who got it, but now, I began to really feel a personal loss.

That night, as I looked for a foxhole, I realized I was without my foxhole buddy. I really didn't want to get close to anyone again for fear I would lose another of my friends, so I decided to spend the night alone. That was a real error in judgment, because that was one of the worst nights I have ever spent. My first mistake was looking for soft ground that I could dig my foxhole in. When I had almost finished digging, I realized why the dirt was soft. Just where I was making my bed was the shallow grave of some poor guy that had got it just hours before. Graves were unusual out there, mainly because no one had the time to dig one, but I found one and it was sickening. Unfortunately, it was too late to start a new hole, and I had to stay put all night.

To add to that gruesome night, I had heard that the 22nd Marines had made eleven attempts to capture a little hill called Sugar Loaf, and had been repulsed every time with horrendous losses. Actually, the 22nd Marines had received about 60 percent casualties in a matter of minutes on that hill. Tomorrow would be our (29th Marines) chance to take that hill.

(I later found out that the Japs had picked this area to make their stand, because it had been their practice artillery range. They knew how to cover every square inch with artillery fire because they had practiced just that for years.)

To say I was scared is an understatement. To make it worse, I didn't even have a foxhole buddy to whom I would have to prove my bravery. I really thought, at that time, it was me against the world. As all these things started piling up, I tried something I was not proud of. I knew the only way I could get out of going the next day was if I was wounded or killed. When the next artillery barrage started up, I held my leg out of the foxhole in hopes that I would get some sort of slight wound that would get me off the front lines. As luck would have it, I ended up with a shrapnel burn to my leg that was painful, but not disabling. After that incident, I didn't care much what was going to happen the next day; I just wanted that night to be over.

Early next morning, May 16, my group, Easy Company, took on Sugar Loaf Hill. It wasn't a big hill, measuring only three hundred yards long and one hundred yards high. They say we made three charges up that hill; I really can't say. All I can remember is running across that open field just north of the hill at a dead run and artillery and mortar shells exploding all around. The Japs let our lead units reach the foot of the hill, and when the rest of us were strung out across the field, they opened up. They had caught the greatest number of us without any cover. Their artillery was hidden on the surrounding hill where they could see every move we made. From the caves in Sugar Loaf itself, they fired their mortars at close range. To make the situation worse, you never saw the enemy. They would come out of their caves, fire a few rounds, and dive back into their cave. You never knew what direction the fire was coming from and therefore, it was impossible to know where to take cover.

I found that the casualties from the artillery fire were usually beyond help, while those hit by mortars had a better chance, but required a lot of attention. The guys hit by small arms fire, more often than not, had to take care of themselves that day.

I climbed about one third of the [way up the] hill before I was so busy with the wounded that I had to stop. I don't know how far the rest of my machine gunners got. I do know that after a few minutes, the number of wounded straggling down from the top was more than I could count. I had wounded guys lying in every shell hole there was at the base of that hill. Even as this was taking place, more and more of Easy Company was racing past me heading for the top.

One time, when things had slowed for a second, we got the word that there was heavy fighting at the top. I started up again, but before I got thirty yards, I met a guy coming down saying there was no one left alive at the top. A little later, when I heard some sergeant trying to get a group together to make another try for the top, I joined in. This was just another futile attempt, however, because before we really got started, the sergeant was killed and three of the others were wounded. As usual in combat situations like this, you never knew what the big picture was. You seemed to be always looking for someone who knew what was really going on.

Actually, I had more than I could take care of where I was, so after that last try, I did not make any more attempts to get to the top of Sugar Loaf. As the number of wounded piled up, we decided we had to call for some amtracks to help evacuate the wounded.

Almost every amtrack that tried to cross the field to get to us would be knocked out by mortar fire. The first one to make it to us was hit and disabled before we could even load the wounded. When the second one came, I had it about half loaded when a mortar [round] landed not more than a foot from me. I had one end of a stretcher and was climbing the slanted ramp to enter the bay of the amtrack. The [round] hit the slant on the ramp on such an angle that it failed to explode and bounced off to the side. There was so much going on at the time, that I did not realize how lucky I was until later. I cannot seem to remember anything else that happened that day. Easy Company's struggle for that darn hill lasted only a few hours, but seemed like a lifetime. How I returned across that field, and back to where we started our ill-fated adventure, I still do not know.

That night, the few of us that were left of Easy Company were told to join up with Dog Company to make the assault the next day. I looked around for familiar faces, but there were none. For a moment, I felt very guilty that I had made it through without a scratch.

What did remain of Easy Company looked more like the living dead than a proud fighting machine. By this time, we had no emotions or feelings. What kept us going when we were so exhausted is hard to say. We probably should not have been sent back into the assault on Sugar Loaf, but there were so few officers left, no one could or would make that decision. For our part, by now life had no meaning, and our goal was just to survive.

Captain Mabie of Dog Company decided the next day to forego a deadly frontal attack and try to outflank the hill. We were split into two groups, each to attack from a different side at the same time. I went with the group that circled the left side. Since I had been with the machine gunners in Easy Company, I was assigned to them again, in Dog Company, which put me midway along the line of advance.

The Japs let the head of our column make their way almost to the reverse side of Sugar Loaf before opening up. We all dived for cover and I found a small creek bed that afforded some cover from the fire. This time it was a little better than yesterday when we were out in that open field. As I lay there wondering what was happening at the head of our column, I heard a shot very near me. I looked around to find one of the guys that came with me from Easy Company pointing his rifle at his own hand. He had shot himself rather than go through that hell again. Some might have thought him a coward, but it was not hard to understand that everyone had his breaking point, and this guy had reached his.

The word from the head of the column was not good. We heard from the few survivors that not one of our guys in that first unit was still alive. We all froze, waiting for someone to give the word for us to join the battle at the head of the column.

The records indicate that very few officers or staff noncommissioned officers of either Easy or Dog Company survived Sugar Loaf Hill. I do not know all of the particulars, but I do know that the next time I was assigned to what they called a platoon, which should have had a lieutenant and several sergeants, the highest-ranking individual was a corporal.

Some of Dog Company that attacked the hill straight on after the diversionary attacks stayed the night on top. I do not know who they were or how they got there, but the hill was now ours. I spent most of the night trying to help the wounded that crawled out from behind Sugar Loaf under the cover of darkness.

The next day, all of what was left of both Easy and Dog Companies was pulled out on the line to regroup and prepare for our next adventure. I understand that there were more killed on or about Sugar Loaf Hill per square foot than anywhere else in World War II. A few days later, we had a visit from the battalion medical officer.

He told us how proud he was of our work during the battle and how he would like to see us all get a citation or medal. However, since he was not able to swing that, he settled for giving each one of us a battlefield promotion in rank.

Sugar Loaf Hill changed all of us. A good example of how little we resembled human beings at this time [occurred] when we finally got some hot chow. We had thrown our mess gear away, so we all improvised. Everything I got went into my canteen cup. By the time I reached the end of the chow line you could not tell what it was. Also, since I had no fork or spoon, I ate with my seven-inch K-Bar knife. What a sight, all these dirty unshaven characters wolfing down that chow like it was their last. To top it all off, there was a dead Jap only partially buried lying in front of where they set up the chow line. You had to step over him to get to the line. No one had the energy or inclination to finish burying him. If you can ignore the sight and smell of something like that and eat like there's no tomorrow, you are really not ready for polite society. Mentally, you were better off if you never thought of what was happening, or where you were. Just do what you were told, and don't question anything. The past and its connection to family and friends brought pleasant thoughts, but these were often followed by sadness. Mother wrote three or four times a week, but the mail must have been piling up at Guam. I only got two letters all the time I was in Okinawa. I read them over and over.

By this time, I had taken on the appearance of a true combat veteran. I had eliminated the unnecessary items in my medical kit (this happened to be at least half of what was issued) because on the front lines, you never had time to do anything other than the most basic treatment. I had found a map case that used to belong to some officer, which was smaller and more convenient to carry my medical gear in. I also made the decision to carry a .45 pistol rather than the rifle I was issued. I had found it difficult to do my work with a rifle slung over my shoulder. Many times I had to lay the rifle down while working, and then I had to go looking for it when I was through. This was a bad situation and could be fatal if I needed protection in a hurry. One of the officers that I attended had a .45 pistol in a shoulder holster when he died. Since it was government issue, I appropriated it. At that point, I'm sure I looked like a Chicago gangster.

Replacements from outside the division had not begun to arrive, and when they tried to reorganize us for the next offensive, it was quite a problem. It's been said that any unit that experienced over 30 percent casualties cannot sustain its fighting spirit, but the 29th had sustained about 82 percent. I was assigned to a rifle platoon where there were no [commissioned officers left]. They put a corporal named Griffith in charge of the platoon and, for a time, he did a good job. He had been a demolition man blowing up caves since we landed, but he took charge like a pro.

The guys making up the headquarters group of that platoon were a motley crew. The special weapons man was called Gladys, because he was so dainty. He didn't look like much, but I later found out he knew all there was to know about his job. The radioman was Joe Autoby, a Navajo Indian. He talked on the radio in his native tongue to other Navajos in the division so the Japs could never understand what was going on, even if they cut into our telephone lines. He was a big friendly man, but very quiet when he was not on the radio or phone. I never got to know the runner for this new platoon, because he seemed to be on the go all of the time. I rounded out that little group and probably was the strangest of all. Actually, as I look back, that was a pretty damn good outfit.

The 4th Regiment, which had taken over for us on the line, was having difficulty entering the capital city of Naha. We were hurriedly formed into new units so we could leapfrog around Naha by landing on the Oroku Peninsula just south of Naha. This time, the preparations were quite simple, because we were only going a few miles. We boarded the amtracks, went out to sea about a thousand yards, and then headed for the landing site with no attempt to disguise our mission. When we neared the beach, the navy bombarded that section until not one leaf was left on a bush. Since we had experienced the original landing, and got through it, we were a little less concerned about this landing. In fact, it came off very much like our original landing.

When we hit the beach, there were a few snipers to slow us down and there were a few anxious minutes hiding behind the seawall before we were all safely on the beach. Our regiment came in on the left flank and we moved a good mile down the northern side of the peninsula by nightfall. My platoon dug in on top of the first range of mountains. Regimental headquarters was somewhere down near the beach. Just before dark, as was the Japanese custom, they opened up with an artillery barrage. We had two killed and three wounded.

Corporal Griffith told me we could get maybe one of the wounded down the mountain to regimental headquarters, but it would be too dark for the stretcher bearers to make a second trip that night. I had to choose the one that needed care the most, and the other two would have to stay on the mountain with us until daylight. That was one of the most difficult decisions I had to make, and everyone was second-guessing me. I finally decided on the one I felt needed help the quickest, even though one of the others was complaining more. All through the night I had to listen to that guy moan, and wonder if I had made the right decision. Fortunately, the two left on top were still alive in the morning and I sent them down to get care. That decision worried me for several days, until I had a chance to talk to the stretcher bearers. They told me it probably had saved the first guy's life, and the other two were doing fine.

Replacements from the States finally started to arrive. We got a new lieutenant, named Pantana. He had been on the legal staff working at marine headquarters in Washington when they grabbed him as a replacement. You really had to feel sorry for him, because he knew the Japs would pass up many a private for a shot at an officer. The life expectancy of an officer on the front lines was very short. He kept telling us not to call him sir and not to recognize him as an officer in any way. As it turned out, we hardly knew we had an officer, and [Corporal] Griffith continued to run the platoon. Five or six days later, the lieutenant got a "lucky" wound to the shoulder and was evacuated.

We also got some replacements for the medical personnel we lost. One guy, named Windom, [had been] just eighteen hours away from liberty in San Diego. They had flown him in nonstop. As I mentioned before, they were pretty desperate for replacements at that stage of the war. Griffith brought him to me so I could help him get through his first days in combat. He kept saying that he couldn't believe he was on the front lines. He stuck to me like glue and questioned everything I did those first few days. I really didn't like the responsibility and I didn't like making friends that I might later lose. After a while, he learned how to take care of himself, and was sent to one of the other platoons. I was pleased to hear he did pretty [well].

Unfortunately, many replacements were not that lucky when they were thrust into combat situations. I understand that there were over a thousand first-day deaths among the replacements.

With the replacements we were receiving, they started making some changes in the officers of our battalion and filling in some of the vacant positions. They moved Captain Fowler of Fox Company to battalion commander. He probably was the [best] liked of all the officers, and all the men were pleased. He could have stayed at battalion headquarters in relative safety, but he liked to come up to the front every night to see how "his boys" were doing.

One particular day, my group (I can't remember what unit I was with at that time) took a particularly well fortified hill on the Oroku Peninsula by a frontal attack. Casualties were pretty light considering the hill was one of the strong points in that campaign. We had made our initial charge to take the hill and some of our guys were going back over each hole or cave they found in the hill to flush out any Japs we might have overlooked. I was working on a wounded man about twenty feet from the mouth of a small cave. You could see by the burned area around the mouth of the cave that it had already been hit by a flamethrower. The guys checking out the cave had just thrown a phosphorous grenade into the cave as an additional precautionary measure, when Captain Fowler came up. He stopped to say something to one of the wounded, when we heard a shot. Everyone hit the deck and we all tried to determine where the shot came from. The only thing we could figure out was that shot came from the little cave that should have been neutralized by now. We called in a flamethrower and hit the cave for a third time. As they were taking care of that problem, one of the wounded called out that Captain Fowler was hit.

When I got to him, he was already dead. Usually with small arms fire, death does not come that quickly, but that shot had hit him in the spleen. That Jap had waited for his one chance to make an important kill. Somehow, he had survived the original flamethrower attack and the phosphorous grenade to make his one shot count. This was typical of the fanatical Japanese. It was also very scary to realize I had probably walked past the cave and [been] in his sights several times.

(On my first leave to the States, I met Captain Fowler's father. Mom, Pop, and Aunt Binnie met my train when I got to New York, and we went to a restaurant in Grand Central Station. A man saw my 6th Marine [Division] shoulder patch and came to our table. He worked at the station and had asked every Marine with a 6th Division patch if they knew his son. He was quite pleased I could tell him how well his son was liked by his men and how he had died.)

After taking the hill, it became our responsibility to hold it. We dug in along the ridge line and tried to prepare for what we knew would be a long night. That particular night, I teamed up with Joe Autoby. We flipped, he lost, and I got the first watch. At about 1 a.m., I heard what appeared to be someone trying to climb the hill just below our post. We were close enough to the coast that the navy was keeping our area pretty lit up with parachute flares. When the next one went up, I tried to see what was making the noise. I could just make out what I thought was several figures pressed up against the side of the hill. I tried to wake Joe, but he kept falling back to sleep. I knew that my pistol was not much help at that range, so I reached for Joe's M1. Joe may have been asleep, but he held onto that rifle for dear life. Fortunately, each foxhole had been issued about two dozen grenades that night. These grenades had a ten-second delay after you pulled the pin. I had seen incidents where the Japs had enough time to throw a grenade back before it blew. I decided I wouldn't let that happen, so I pulled the pin on one, held it for three or four seconds, and then threw it down the hill. It fell far beyond the spot I was aiming for before it blew. The next time, I pulled the pin, threw it halfway and let it roll the rest of the way. After I threw five or six, it seemed like all movement in that area stopped. Several other guys on our side of the hill must have seen something similar, because it was a pretty noisy night. Even after all that, Joe was still asleep. By this time, however, I couldn't sleep, so I let him keep sleeping until morning. Every hour or so, throughout the night, I would throw another grenade. I didn't know how much good it did, but I felt better about it.

The nights had always belonged to the Japs. We would always be hunkered down in our foxholes while the Japs were on the prowl. Then the situation changed. When Captain Fowler was killed, his runner took it very hard. The runner got hold of a shotgun somewhere, and would make nighttime excursions behind the enemy lines. He was beating them at their own game. All us guys knew what he was doing, but the brass would have never allowed it if they had known. Throughout the night, we could keep up with his exploits by listening to his shotgun go off in the distance. For a while, he must have terrorized the Japs, but then one morning, he did not return.

Two days later, when we took another Japanese stronghold, we found his body. It seemed they wanted to make an example out of that guy doing what he had been doing. They had taken the can opener from a K ration and tortured him.

AN UNAWARDED BIT OF BRAVERY
Bill Lemen
Okinawa, 1945

*William L. "Bill" Lemen served as a rifleman in Major An-
thony Walker's 6th Reconnaissance Company in the fighting
in Okinawa in May 1945. This excerpt from his self-published
book,* A Special Loyalty *(2000), picks up as Lemen's unit is
fighting its way into Naha, the heavily defended capital of Okinawa. During that attack, he came across a heroic corpsman
who ended up getting a "million-dollar wound" in the action.*

We crossed the Asato under fire and entered the outskirts of
Naha. Snipers fired at us from the ruins of red tiled houses
that irrelevantly reminded me of Spanish style architecture at
home. In this suburban area, we moved up a little rise to the sound
of firing at an intersecting street above us.

Peeking around the corner of a wrecked building we heard, more
than saw, rifle, machine gun, and mortar fire directed toward us. We
could advance more effectively if [marines] fought on both sides of
the street. Bryce Hardiman volunteered to go first. He took two
steps into the street and was brought down by a wound to his chest.
Two men quickly ran across the street. From both sides we provided

123

as much covering fire as possible to those men and to two other marines who dragged Hardiman to safety and on down to the forward battalion aid station, located right behind the line.

On that day, 29 May 1945, navy corpsman Paul Smith was working in the main battalion aid station of the 1st Battalion, 22nd Marines. A radio call came in for the immediate need of two cases of blood plasma for the forward aid station. It came to Paul in a dream the night before that he would this day be wounded. A devout Mormon, he wondered if this was a message from God. But now, without thinking and without helmet, rifle or field pack, but armed with his .45 Colt pistol in his shoulder holster, Smith threw the two cases of plasma into a jeep ambulance and drove up close to the line. He could have sent another corpsman, but he appointed himself for the job.

Smith gives this account of the action:

"About 1700 [hours] I found the forward aid station, where Dr. Becker and three or four corpsmen worked hard on many casualties. Becker set up his forward aid station just beneath a hill, right in Naha. The troops fought on top of the hill; we received the casualties at the bottom of the hill. I began working on the marine wounded.

"One of the worst cases was Bryce Hardiman. He had dark, wavy hair. I didn't personally know him but had seen him around. Severely wounded with a shrapnel fragment in his chest right through his sternum, he was of course in deep shock. The hole in his chest had apparently injured his trachea or his bronchus, because bright frothy blood oozed from the wound. I plugged up the wound with a piece of two-inch roller gauze, sealed up the wound with tape and began an IV with plasma into his left arm. In a few moments his very pale color began to redden up a bit, which was a good sign. He even began to move around on his litter.

"The 22nd fought in the streets of one of the northern suburbs of Naha. With our backs to the hill and the jeep headed away from it, we placed Bryce in the jeep ambulance on the top rung to hold the stretcher. I held the plasma bottle high in the air, so it would flow into him nicely with gravity. We knew we had to get him back to more medical attention pronto, Bryce being one of the most severely wounded of the many patients in the area.

"Suddenly, a Nambu opened up with long bursts that passed right over our heads. We could hear the bullets humming very close to us. Of course, we ignored them as we always did, but in a moment another came in on us, this one right on target. Bryce let out a terrible scream as a bullet struck him through the right thigh, hitting the femur, and exiting in a nasty wound on the front of his right thigh. It was about six inches in diameter. Another bullet struck the large plasma bottle I held, with glass and plasma flying all over the place.

"The next thing I knew, I was knocked down to the ground and a corpsman named Saunders next to me said, 'Smitty, are you okay?' About then I saw smoke come up from my right pant leg, with a large black hole through my fatigues. I said to Saunders, 'Yeah, I'm okay, but look how close that round came to me,' showing him the hole in my pants. By now we were all on the ground, ducking behind a little foundation wall, about three feet in height, which saved all our lives.

"That Nambu kept firing continuously, spraying the entire area for about twenty or thirty minutes. [I hadn't felt] the round that hit me [and] knocked me to the ground, but you just don't think clearly during all the excitement of the moment. I had a million-dollar wound, through about six or seven inches of the right thigh, luckily missing the femur bone, with an exit wound of only two inches in diameter.

"Someone pulled Bryce's stretcher down from the jeep and treated his severe leg wound. We loaded the jeep ambulance down with all the cases we could, with me hanging on the back end, holding on any way I could. I knew that if the Jap opened up again, I would be the first guy hit. Fortunately, as the driver gunned out of the area, the Nambu did not fire at us.

"We got back to the main aid station close to dark. It started raining by the time they got Bryce Hardiman through the aid station, and [they] placed all of us in a large, open truck back on our way to the hospital. Being close to Bryce, I saw his condition deteriorating rapidly—that second wound really did him in. I took off my jacket and placed it over his head and chest to keep the rain off of him. He died before we arrived at the hospital. As soon as I saw his face, I knew he was dead. You get to recognize that very quickly.

"As calm as a summer morning when the bullet hit me, I don't know how I would have reacted had I not been warned in my dream. A simple wound, it never gave me a bit of trouble."

ONE DAY AT A TIME AT C MED
Lieutenant David Slossberg
Okinawa, 1945

*Lieutenant David Slossberg was company commander of C
Med on Okinawa during the last days of World War II. During
that period, James W. Fackler was assigned to this company.
He says, "We received and processed the wounded and sick
from the 7th Marines. Some needed emergency surgery in
our field hospital and when they were stabilized would be
transferred to a hospital ship. Some would be hospitalized
with minor complaints and sent back to their unit upon recovery. C Med was also a pool of replacement corpsmen for
duty in the line companies when the assigned corpsmen there
might be wounded or killed."*

*After the war, Fackler became the C Med company clerk.
He explains how he came across an invaluable log sheet.*

"The 1st Marine Division was sent to Tientsin (now Tianjin),
China, to effect the repatriation of Japanese troops. In the
spring of 1946, I was C Med company clerk. In going through the company files, I found the Daily Activity Log that had been maintained on
Okinawa by the company commander, Lieutenant (Doctor) David

Slossberg. I kept it as a souvenir. About fifty years later, my conscience started to bother me and I felt that the log should be in an appropriate repository. I transcribed the information into a computer file before sending the diary to the 1st Marine Division Association."

The following excerpt—from Monday, April 2, 1945, to June 2, 1945—shows some of the work that went into setting up a medical unit in wartime.

Monday, April 2, 1945

Entire company came ashore [on Okinawa] and set up temporary quarters at old CP of the 7th [Marine] Regiment. Area included many burial vaults, which were to be used for air raid shelters. Officers and corpsmen assigned quarters. Security posts established. First aid station set up. Situation discussed with Dr. Hagen (regimental surgeon).

April 3

Storage tent, ward tent, galley tent, and first aid tents set up. Gear continued to be hauled from beach. There appeared to be some delay in unloading gear from ships. Guards established over gear at beach. Sanitation details established. Several patients seen at first aid tent and sent to beach for evacuation.

April 4

Rifle inspection held. Arrangements made to send several ambulances to make runs from regimental aid station to our aid station and to beach. Blankets, shock sheets, plasma sent up to 7th Regiment. Bulk gear continued to arrive from beach. Nearly all equipment and gear appeared to be in good condition. All vehicles are in good running condition. Hospital setup still in an uncertain state because of uncertainty of movement. Regimental surgeon has advised us that a complete hospital setup is not necessary as casualties are light and because of possibility of our moving up at any time.

April 6

All personnel inspected. Pisano, Reno (N), Pfc., of our company suffered wound of the scalp as result of falling antiaircraft shell fragments. Sent out to off-shore ship for X-Ray. No other casualties.

April 7

Pfc. Pisano returned to company from APA 99 where he underwent treatment for scalp wound. Sick bay continues to give first aid to returning front line troops. Many skin infections treated. No diarrhea reported. Several recurrent malaria patients seen. All have responded to routine antimalarial treatment.

Advised by Dr. Hagen that C Med would move to a new area on the morning of April 8. Gear prepared for movement.

April 8

Reveille at 5 a.m. Movement started to new area. First group arrived at Ishikawa town at 12 noon and were directed to our new area by Dr. Hagen. Talked to Colonel Snedeker and Lieutenant Colonel Masters. Security conditions discussed with them. Hospital site is situated in a town—main area enclosed by 5-foot stone walls with gates at both ends. Entire area dirty and a great amount of work will be needed to make area suitable. All hands turned to at once. Vehicles unloaded and sent back for more gear. Site surveyed and general plans were drawn up.

Portable surgery erected at once. Living quarters found for Ben and officers. DDT squads from 7th Regiment sprayed all areas. Temporary wards set up in buildings. First aid set up. Galley set up. Temporary urinals and heads erected. Security watch established.

April 9

Area appears to be shaping up. Office, laboratory and X-Ray areas have been chosen and are in the process of setting up. Operating room rapidly coming into first-class condition. Cleaning of cattle stalls in compound continued. Medical storage tent erected and gear brought in. Very few flies, mosquitoes and bugs in evidence. All possible sanitary precautions are being taken, both for personnel and patients. Several bad casualties have been treated here. Lack of whole blood from supposedly prearranged blood banks has proved to be a handicap. Arrangements have been made to draw blood from donors in this area. Head [latrine] dug and put under cover. Regular head seats and boxes built. Screening to be done as soon as possible. Mess gear sterilizer set up and is in full operation. Whole blood has been drawn and administered. Casualties have been coming in small numbers. Considerable delay in moving all medical and quartermaster gear to new area because of insufficient transportation and bad roads. All hands have turned to with great enthusiasm. Morale is excellent.

April 10

[Policing] of compound continued and area is now in fair condition. Generator set up and adequate wiring set up [to power the] office, X-Ray, wards, surgery and radio. Frigidaire set up and has supply of penicillin, gas-gangrene antitoxin and tetanus toxoid received from H & S [Headquarters and Service Company]. Whole blood for several wounded marines [is] being stored in freezer. [We are] to set up ward tents tomorrow and evacuate all patients to them except for seriously wounded who will remain in small building adjacent to surgery.

April 11

Area was inspected by Lieutenant Colonel F. Giuffreda. In general he was pleased with the setup. This area was cleared for us by the engineers attached to the 7th Regiment. Patients [have been] transferred. Many corpsmen have moved into compound for security reasons. Considerable quartermaster supplies arrived today. Area visited by Dr. Stoops, ass't regimental surgeon, who was pleased with our hospital.

April 12

Construction of camouflage continued. Motor pool area completed. Inspection of facilities—found satisfactory. Area clean and very few flies and insects noted. Considerable number of casualties brought in late this afternoon and an emergency was called for all hands. We were asked for 30 corpsmen to act as stretcher bearers. Fifteen were sent but were to [act] as first aid men. All returned within two hours as they were not needed at the lines. Whole blood arrived just in time to be a great aid in the emergency. A large amount was immediately used on the casualties with excellent results. The operating room crew and surgeons worked until 3 a.m. The O.R. was efficiently run. All hands are to be congratulated for their work.

Lieutenant Colonel Giuffreda arrived to aid us in the emergency and gave aid until 3 a.m. Total admissions—37.

April 13

Sixteen casualties [were] evacuated to field hospital this morning in order to leave our facilities available for new patients. Two patients died during the day—one apparently due to pulmonary embolism and one of peritonitis. All others appear to be doing well. Several new casualties admitted—none serious. Hospital grounds inspected by Captain Kimbrough. He was greatly pleased and congratulated all hands. General Jones inspected area and hospital and expressed approval. He showed great interest in the welfare of the patients. All charts brought up to date and ward routine set. Blackout facilities proved effective for both the admitting tent and operating room.

April 14

Transferred 15 patients to div. hospital this morning. Twenty-one patients admitted—several of medical nature. All new patients appear to be doing well. Twelve patients are logged for transfer in morning. Galley camouflaged today. Head completely screened. Whole blood continues to be used to great advantage.

All patients are receiving a course of penicillin and we believe this treatment is proving of great value in holding down infections. Fifteen corpsmen [were] dispatched to the lines to be used as aid men only, and a memorandum to that effect was delivered to regimental surgeon and a copy to H & S. Censorship lifted and the men are now on a writing spree; consequently the officers will now have the added work of censoring mail.

April 15

One patient with perforating fragment wound thru left eye into brain died shortly after admission. A second patient admitted today died late in the evening after an operation during which a badly torn spleen was removed. Five pints of blood was administered but to no avail. Fifteen patients evacuated to div hospital.

[We were] advised that a monsoon could be expected on April 16. Preparations made for the storm. General situation of the hospital and compound satisfactory. Problem of treating civilians who have been coming into our sick bay in small numbers discussed. Decided to let problem go unless it becomes too great.

April 16–18

Routine hospital work continued. No outstanding events have occurred. 1,500-gallon water tank and chlorinator were erected by the engineers so that showers can be used at any time. Bomb shelters are being constructed for all hands. Galley completely screened.

April 19–22

Small number of casualties coming in. Average census is 33–35, mostly medical and skin cases. All our air raid shelters now completed. Additional supply of penicillin secured from H & S today. Memorandum on snake bite and use of antivenom received and filed.

The advancing infantry was lightly engaged during D-day operations at Gloucester, and casualties were light. Here, three corpsmen working in a small front-line aid station treat a Marine who has been shot in his left arm, December 1943. *Official USMC Photo*

An American medic administers plasma to a wounded soldier, World War II. *National Archives, Washington, D.C.*

A medic evacuates a civilian girl in the Philippines, World War II. *U.S. Army Medical Department Museum*

Robert Eugene Bush, hospital apprentice first class, U.S. Naval Reserve, earned the Navy Medal of Honor while serving as Medical Corpsman with a rifle company, 2nd Batallion, 5th Marines, 1st Marine Division, Okinawa, May 2, 1945. President Harry Truman presented the medal on October 5, 1945, the day after Bush turned nineteen. *Photo courtesy of U.S. Navy*

Kurt Oberscheven (second from right) in Korea, June 1951. As a corpsman, his quick action saved the life of Corporal Jerry T. Jolly. *Courtesy Jerry T. Jolly*

Corporal Jolly following his discharge from the Marine Corps, McAlester, Oklahoma. *Courtesy Jerry T. Jolly*

Kurt Oberscheven around the time of his reunion with Jerry Jolly, more than fifty years after saving his life. *Courtesy Kurt Oberscheven*

President Richard Nixon presented the Medal of Honor to Donald "Doc" Ballard on May 14, 1970, for his heroic actions during the Vietnam War. James DeCarlo is one of many men who credit Ballard with saving his life. *Photo courtesy of U.S. Navy*

Jim Tolomay (B Company, 1st Battalion, 1st Marine Division) rests after a sweep near the South China Sea, Vietnam, 1966. *Courtesy Jim Tolomay*

"Santa Claus" talks with a group of hospital patients during the Bob Hope Christmas Show, December 1970. *Photo courtesy of U.S. Army*

Major Jeffery Blankenship from Southern European Task Force administers medicine to a local Afghan girl during a Civilian and Veterinarian Medical Assistance (CMA/VMA) mission in the village of Jaji Maidan, Afghanistan, April 13, 2005. *U.S. Army photo by Sergeant Michael Abney*

Registered nurse 1st Lieutenant Dawn Dirksen of the 911th Forward Surgical Team checks a young girl's head in the village of Loy Karezak, Afghanistan, October 15, 2003. *U.S. Army photo by Specialist Gul A. Alisan*

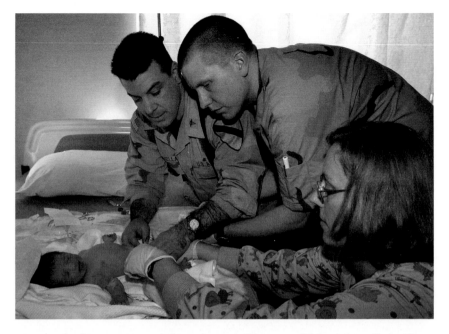

(Front to back) Lieutenant Wilson, Captain Vernon, and Major Spinella tend to Hassin, an Iraqi baby born on election day, January 30, 2005. The 86th Combat Support Hospital (CSH) deployed more than 500 soldiers from Fort Campbell, Kentucky, to Baghdad, Iraq. The 86th CSH made history recently by being the first unit in combat to collect platelets from soldiers using a technique called aphaeresis. *U.S. Air Force photo by Master Sergeant Dave Ahlschwede*

Captain Lisa Foglia, a provost OB/GYN doctor assigned to 1st Armored Division, originally from the Landstuhl Regional Medical Center, Germany, talks with Baghdad physicians on the latest equipment and technologies of emergency obstetrics during a three-day Advanced Life Support in Obstetrics course taught by 1st Armored Division doctors, October 23, 2003. *Photo Courtesy of U.S. Army*

Proceeds from this book will be going to the National Medical War Memorial to be built in Kansas City, Kansas. The statue (shown here in a scale model) will be constructed of granite, concrete, steel, marble, copper, and other materials. The memorial and adjoining Youth Education Center, history walk, convention center, and guest house will help promote peace and honor heroic service for generations of visitors. *National Medical War Memorial and Youth Education Center.*

Report on water sample received from engineers. Stanton of Malaria Control showed that the water from well on our compound (after chlorination) was safe for laundry and showers.

April 23–25

Denzil [last name deleted] was turned in as a drug addict—written up and transferred to division hospital under guard.

April 26–28

Simons, J. C., Pfc. injured in truck accident on April 27. Died April 28. Post mortem performed by Drs. Hill and Chitwood. Report of accident, course, treatment sent to division surgeon. Critical report and P.M. report also sent in.

April 29–30

Received information that C Med is to move on Wed May 2 to a new forward area. Many patients [are] being transferred to division hospital and the remainder will be transferred tomorrow. Reconnaissance made of new area today.

May 4

Area shaping up well. This hospital area being situated off the main road is somewhat of a handicap. However if the road from the hospital to Highway 1 could be fixed we would have excellent communications. All personnel have been in excellent spirits and are working with great enthusiasm.

May 5–6

[There were] four admissions on the 5th of May, while on the 6th there were 27. Many of these patients were wounded in action. Evacuation to the 31st and 82nd Army Hospitals started. Supply of blood obtained. Accurate account of blood usage and other pertinent data being recorded.

May 7–8

There has been a heavy rain for the past 24 hours causing considerable mud and making hospital work almost impossible. There is little opportunity for surgery at present as all casualties are being relieved to other hospitals after first aid and antishock treatment.

May 9–11

All casualties who can be returned to duty in several days [are] now being treated. Casualties coming in greater numbers. Major surgery being performed with satisfactory results. Blood supply is adequate and no untoward results or reactions. There is a question of injury to another corpsman, K. L. Young, PhM 2/c. So far confirmation has been impossible.

Corpsman K. L. Young, PhM 2/c, was killed in action; we were notified 5-13-45. No other casualties.

Our corpsmen are serving well with line corpsmen and in our collecting stations. Fifth ward tent erected today. Casualties are now being evacuated with more dispatch than during the past several days. Seabee organization surfaced our road into hospital area and as a result movement of traffic has been greatly facilitated.

May 15–17

Casualties continue to come into our hospital in fairly large numbers and our count is already over one thousand. Blood and plasma are proving very effective in bringing the patients out of shock and the results are a great source of satisfaction to the doctors and corpsmen. Evacuation of patients has been facilitated by the appointment of Dr. Quinn whose cooperation is greatly appreciated.

May 18–20

Jaeger, Albert E., HA 1/c, of C Med was wounded in action on May 17 and was treated at this hospital. He was evacuated to 3rd Corps Med Bn in excellent general condition. The 7th Regiment has been relieved from line duty for a well-deserved rest, and our collection section has therefore returned to this hospital. The amphibious tractor is now fully equipped and is standing by to go to the collecting section.

May 21–23

Colonel Snedeker visited the hospital on May 21 and made a thorough inspection. He visited with the patients in all wards, and once again it could be seen that the men were greatly pleased to see their commanding officer. The number of admissions have greatly fallen during the past several days, and during this lull additional police details have been used to erect a new head, repair all tents and structures.

May 24–27

Number of admissions have been low with extremely few battle casualties.

May 28–30

Blood (outdated) replaced today with new supply. Admissions still low. Transportation of patients discharged from this hospital to their regiment has been arranged. Regiment will send vehicles here as needed.

May 31–June 2

No outstanding events have occurred during the past several days. Personnel in good health and excellent morale. New ward tent to be set aside for diarrhea cases as dysentery is suspected. New head being built for the use of these cases only.

Postscript: While Slossberg's journal does not record much drama, obviously much was happening each day as these doctors, nurses, and corpsmen carried out their heroic activities. It is a mark of war that one soon becomes used to a routine and flows with it in the ever-determined struggle to win the battle and save as many lives as possible. Mr. Fackler is to be commended for his efforts to preserve the journal.

MY TIME AS A CORPSMAN
Harry L. Murray
Okinawa, 1945

Harry L. Murray was a Marine corpsman, PhM1/c, and served in the Japan theatre in 1945. This story relates activities he was involved in on Okinawa in the last days of the war.

One day we were all called topside to hear about where we were going. Just the night before, Tokyo Rose had said: "The Japanese troops on Okinawa will annihilate the famous 6th Marine Division, called the Young Tiger, the first day. They will tell you that we don't know, that it is all a secret, but you will try to hit the island of Okinawa, and we have heard about the 6th Division. We will be glad to greet you. You should hear about it any day."

Sure enough, a captain got up and told us, "Where we are going has been kept a secret and we will tell you now. It is Okinawa. We will attack the Japs by surprise." Some hardened marine, who had been on a couple of operations, yelled, "Blow it out your duffel bag." One day we saw the aircraft carrier *Franklin* pass by us with a hole in the side large enough to drive cars through. It was just creeping along, and it didn't look good.

The next day was an odd one. We stopped at the Island of Ulithi. It was supposed to be a rest stop before hitting Japanese territory. It was announced we could go ashore for sandwiches, beer and soft drinks, and a swim. I didn't care to swim or drink beer, and they put soft drinks out in water cans. Somebody had to stay in the lab, because only part of the ship's crew could go. I told the other two guys, who were swabbies, that I would stay in the lab and they could go ahead. They thanked me. Strangely, two guys were caught in an undertow and were drowned. It turned out to be the same two that I had told to go ahead. There is something deeper here, and again I asked why? Maybe what happened a week later was a warning to the ship.

We all hit the sack about midnight with plenty of anxiety. I some-how dozed off easily. One thing, I had no coffee. This, I later found, was my worst enemy. I did not realize it, nor did any of the doctors tell us, strong coffee might aggravate anxiety. Taking atabrine every day was something I have always wondered about. Some guys would turn nearly yellow, and I was one. It seemed to hit darker guys more than fair-skinned guys. One guy from Vincennes, Indiana, Bob Lasher, was dark-skinned too, and was the most yellow looking of any I ever saw. Strangely, when Mary and I got married, we moved into the apartment Bob Lasher and his wife had moved from at Mrs. Flintzer's home on North Ninth Street in Vincennes.

On that famous—or infamous—morning, our sergeant woke me up about five o'clock, saying, "Doc, it's time to get up." I believe he was more nervous than any of us. He was an old China marine, and I don't know if he thought his days were numbered, but I had trouble later that day with him on land.

Soon the firing began with all the fury the navy could muster. We looked out to sea, and there were a thousand ships firing, and planes were heading toward the island of Okinawa. It was a strange feeling. They then announced we could have orange juice, pancakes, and bacon and eggs, and all we wanted to eat. I remember it felt like they were giving us our last meal, like just before being executed. Sergeant Leedy told us to get our packs on after we had eaten. Nobody was hungry. Many had the runs and were vomiting from fear. I held well and had accepted the worst, but I was still somewhat frightened. We looked toward the shore as it got light. We were about two miles away. They were going in by waves, and we didn't know when they would call for the engineers. Contrary to what Tokyo Rose had said, we did get ashore easily.

I was about ready to climb over the side on the cargo net, when our outfit had just received the word to go in, when over the PA system they called my name to come to sick bay immediately. I told myself to forget it. I had a suspicion that it was for me to take all of the medical records ashore. I dismissed the thought and climbed down the cargo net. Just as I was halfway down to the Higgins boat, a guy cried out. It turned out to be Stocker, our cook. He weighed about 225. I caught him just enough to stop him from going to the ocean. With all of the gear, he no doubt would have drowned. He has thanked me a couple of times since the war for saving his life. The sergeant told us to keep our heads down as we were going in. The planes were flying over us, and we could hear the shells hitting the beaches, but it was fairly easy.

We went in with the 22nd Regiment and advanced the first day to the airfield, which wasn't to be taken until day three. One Jap pilot landed there, thinking it was controlled by the Japs. They drilled him with so many bullets he could have passed for a sponge. The airplane was in excellent shape.

The first night I was on the outer perimeter in a foxhole with three other guys. We had a .50-caliber machine gun and were told we would take turns of two-hour watches. I just barely remember one guy shaking me and saying it was my turn to man the machine gun. I awakened the next morning, and two guys had not been on the gun; I had never completely awakened. I believe we were all so relieved that we weren't attacked that we could have slept standing up.

As we were marching the next day, Andy Anderson, who played chess with me a lot and was a close friend about ten years older than I, suddenly turned almost white. I thought he was having a heart attack. I stopped and grabbed his rifle and pack and tried to get him along the path. Sergeant Leedy yelled at me, "Doc, you can't be that close to each other. You will become a target that a Jap couldn't refuse." I told him he could take care of the fighting, but my top job was to save the sick and wounded. We had it out for a minute or two right there. He knew I was right, and he was right as a military man, but he always wanted to be right. From then on he and I never got along. He would always go to Harvat for treatment.

The next day the kamikaze planes were tearing up our navy. We would look out to see, and it looked like hundreds of Fourths of July. The flak was so thick that you could not believe a Jap could get through it, but they did. Intelligence had underestimated the strength of the island; they had over 120,000 trained troops plus civilians. And planes from every island tried to destroy our navy so that we would pull out. I believe it was Halsey who said we may pull back and spread out, but they would never drive us out of Okinawa.

A day later I heard the ship that I had been on, the *Sumter*, was sunk by a kamikaze. Here again, I had to ask myself why?

I had several near misses during combat, but it was not like being on the front lines. Often they sent us in front of the lines to put in bridges or do some surveying. One day they asked me to go with an engineer in a small tank to survey in front of the lines. The Japanese spotted us when we rolled in with that small tank. I don't know why we even used it. It couldn't have stopped a bean shooter. Just as we got to our place to survey and got out of the tank we could hear the shells striking close to us. Nevertheless, we crawled to about where he wanted to set his tripod, and the shells were getting closer and closer. We both crawled in the same foxhole and wondered what we should do. They just about had us zeroed in. Shells were falling just about ten feet away and getting closer. We looked back at the tank and just then, a shell went right through the smoke stack of the tank.

This tank was different from any I had ever seen, and it was certainly not good for defense or offense. The engineer finally yelled that we had to get that tank out of there and get out too. I told him to get in the tank and not to wait for me to get in. I started running faster than the tank could go. We got about a hundred yards away and felt safer, but we thought it was stupid to survey that day.

Another day we went up to put in a bridge, and the Japs saw us and really came very close. One hit near me as I jumped from the truck, and my foot got caught on some of the equipment and I landed right on my head. That night, and for several days I could not sleep on my back. If I did, my neck would be pulled to the right every time. I asked the doctor about it, and he said it would go away and not worry about it. However, it never went away completely.

Another time, we went up to put in a footbridge, and our truck ran over a land mine, blowing off one of the wheels. We had a young lieutenant who was to lead us. The Japs shelled us so badly, he went back and told Captain Benger that putting in the foot bridge was too dangerous. We were about two miles back of the front lines. Captain Benger told him that we had to put in that bridge, and there could be no excuses. It ended up Captain Benger led us down that road at night and we got it in.

One particular day after I had lost my helmet up front when our truck almost got hit, they asked me to go up front, but I had no helmet. A marine loaned me his. While we were up front, they shelled our position back of the front lines. As luck would have it, a piece of shell shrapnel hit the top of the head of the man from whom I had gotten the helmet. He died instantly. This was strange to me. Every time we salute the flag I think of him, and I wonder why people don't think it was because of guys like him that we have a flag to salute.

There was one odd event that occurred while B Engineering Company was at the northern end, just before we were to go south.

They sent about five engineers to get a fresh water supply. For some reason, they had to test it for fitness for human consumption, and they had to stay through the night. During the night several Japanese soldiers attacked them while they were sleeping. The Japanese were just getting ready to kill them when one engineer cried out. One of the Japanese had his knife to the throat of an engineer who was red-headed, and I have since forgotten his name. Just then hospital corpsmen who were stationed nearby heard the call for help and came running to help them. They killed the Japanese soldiers.

The next morning the engineers came back to our camp and revealed the incident to us. The attack startled the redhead so much that it caused him to stutter. His stuttering continued for several days, and the guys began to tease him about it. I had to call the guys separately and tell them to stop teasing him because it might affect him permanently. A few days later he was back to normal.

One of the worst nights that I ever had was the night we had to put in two footbridges during the night so our troops could go into Naha. We got shelled, and I believe Lewis was hit just enough to have him put in a field hospital. Two others were hit, too, and I had the guys hold up while I had them put in the field hospital. The group that Lewis was with was up the road from where we were putting in a footbridge. Our group finished first and I knew the other guys did not have a corpsman. We started back, but I asked Captain Benger if one guy would stay with me while I tried to find the other group that was up the river from us. Captain Benger asked if anybody wanted to volunteer, but nobody did. So when they left, I started up the road by myself. I had walked about a block or so when Japs started shooting flares. When they did, I hit the deck and lay there until the flare died. It had been raining and I had on my poncho, when this flare went off close by. I jumped in a hole with two feet of water in it with two or three dead Japs. At first I thought they were alive. A minute later I said to myself, this is no place for even a hero. So I started back, because I was afraid my own men might shoot me. They would not know if I were a Jap or marine, and some guys were so quick to fire; I knew it was too much of a risk. As I went back, I was scared. I knew the 22nd Marines were on the front lines, and I approached them to stay with them until our guys came back. They had far more trouble getting their footbridge installed than we. They asked me where I was from and I stammered and paused and replied, "Vincennes, Indiana."

A lieutenant asked if anybody ever heard of Vincennes. Several replied they had. One guy, I believe, was from Lawrenceville, Illinois. He then asked me how far Lawrenceville was from Vincennes. I said, "About nine miles."

The jarhead said, "No, closer to eleven."

He then wondered why I was up front alone.

I told him and he became very nice to me, along with all the other marines there, because we had put a footbridge in under dangerous conditions. Tomorrow would be far more dangerous for them after they crossed the bridge.

Three days later, toward the end of taking the island, another strange thing happened. We were putting in a heavier bridge. Just as we finished, it was in the afternoon, when I heard a guy yell "Corpsman." About three marines had pulled a guy back and yelled for a corpsman. We were just leaving, and I ran over to see if I could help. I saw a marine with half his face shot off. I told Lilly, who was the corpsman under me, to tag him because he was dead, and Graves Registration would pick him up. Just then a blood bubble came from where his nose had been.

I said, "I think he's alive, Norm. Get some plasma."

Norm got the plasma started, and I asked for four or five engineers to help haul him to our truck. We got out of there fast, because we were now bunched up and real targets for the Japs. Fortunately they missed us. We dropped him off at an aid station nearby and went on.

Here I have to get a year or so ahead of my story. . . . I ended up in Vincennes, at one of three tuberculosis hospitals, I believe, in the state. It happened in 1947; while a patient, I went into town to the dentist. While talking to the dentist, Dr. Johnson, he told me he had a nephew who had been in the 6th Marine Division and was from Sullivan, Indiana.

He later told me his nephew's face was practically shot off, and he had been hit near Naha, but he was still alive. I remembered it as having happened the same day, as I had taken care of the marine. This was quite a coincidence. I wrote Norman Lilly, the corpsman that was with me that day. He remembered it, but Norm could not recall as clearly as I, because he had been through a lot of stress at that time; the next day had been my birthday, so I could recall it easier than he. In retrospect, if Norm had not been with me, I doubt that we would have gotten the plasma quickly enough to save the marine.

Now I am going to take you forward a number of years, in fact to 1997. The marines were having a minireunion down in Florida. One of the corpsmen under me had been Bud West. . . .

One morning, I got a call from him down in Florida. "Murray, I ran into a guy who has been to Vincennes several times and he is from Sullivan, Indiana, and wants to come to our reunion."

I replied, "The only guy I ever heard of from Sullivan was the guy Lilly and I took care of just out of Naha. What is his name?"

He told me, but it didn't sound familiar; I didn't recall his name. I asked West if the marine had a scar on his face, and he replied that he had a large one. Then I asked West to ask him if he was related to Dr. Johnson in Vincennes. He replied yes, and the rest is history. He came to the reunion in Vincennes, and we became acquainted. His name is Carl Sproatt and he lives in Florida. A month later, he and his wife visited us, . . . the *Vincennes Sun-Commercial* wrote it up, and a lot of people saw it as a classic story. . . .

While at Naha Airfield, the Engineers settled in there for the end of the war. . . . For three days they called us, Company B Engineers, to blow up a cave.

When we got to the cave, we found out there were a lot of Japanese soldiers in there and they were coming out at night and shooting at our marines. The general gave orders to blow it up if they did not surrender. The next day we went back with ten drums of diesel. We lit them and rolled them into the cave. There was a heck of an explosion. The Japanese still did not surrender. Just as we went back to get some demo, a Philippine doctor and his wife came out dressed in dirty white uniforms; they begged us not to blow the place up because there were twelve hundred civilians being held as hostage, and we had already killed and badly burned a couple hundred. He asked us for permission to try to persuade the Japanese to set the civilians free.

Our officer called the general and asked what we should do. He said give them two hours, and then load up the cave with demo and blow it to kingdom come.

Just after we stacked the entire demo at the entrance of the cave, the Japanese freed the civilians. Now it became my job. I told one of the marines to run to a field hospital nearby and bring all the corpsmen and plenty of tincture of green soap and water. Meanwhile we started bringing out hundreds of wounded and very sick civilians; some of them had tuberculosis, and one or two had leprosy. Two died as we stretched a chain of hands helping them up the steep hill. I have since thought if I ever got tuberculosis from someone, it was then.

Two hours later, we shook the whole end of the island with the demo charge, which blew up the large three-story cave with seven hundred Japanese soldiers.

(I ran into a student at the University of Evansville while going to school there who was from Okinawa. He told me there was a large plaque placed there, telling about what happened to hundreds of people dying at that spot.)

Just a week previous to this, on Okinawa, a marine had told a Jap to stop and he didn't and it turned out to be a boy. The marine came and asked me to try to save the boy's life. When I got there I found that the bullet had torn over a foot of flesh from the boy's leg. I went against the rules and gave him plasma and poured sulfa on his leg and put about thirty not-too-neat stitches in his leg. I have often wondered if he got well.

When we first hit Okinawa we were at the northern end, and we went through it like Grant taking Richmond. Three marines with the engineers came across a lady who was very sick and asked me if I would take care of her. Here again, it was against the rules, but it was the right thing to do. When I got to the lady's house, she was lying on a mat. She had an extremely high fever and pain in her belly. I was sure it was peritonitis. There were no children; just she and her husband, who was afraid she was dying, and I was afraid too. I bathed her body and explained to her husband to give her two sulfa pills every four hours night and day and push a lot of water through her. I gave him some sodium bicarb to help settle the effect of the sulfa on her stomach. I left and never thought much about it. One month later we were marching through a town, when suddenly a civilian ran up to me and pulled my arm. I didn't know who he was, but I got out of line and followed him. He showed me his wife, who was getting well, and she gave me a big smile after her husband told her who I was. When I started to leave he actually knelt down and kissed my hand. Probably one of the most unusual incidents occurred the first week we landed on the island. Three marines and I were on a routine patrol. The island itself had experienced almost a month of constant bombardment by ground, air, and naval forces. Practically everywhere we looked, there were shattered homes and farms. We came upon a house that was completely demolished. We looked at it for a couple of minutes and started to leave, when we heard a sound. It was the sobbing of a child. We tried to find where the sobbing was coming from. We lifted up panels and boards and found three small children lying across the bodies of their dead parents.

When they saw us, they became frightened and clutched the bodies of their dead parents, just hoping to squeeze one more ounce of love and protection from them. Their parents had apparently committed suicide, and the children, not knowing what to do, had pulled the panels and boards around themselves and trusted that somehow or some way their parents would revive.

The oldest was a little girl about nine, and the two younger brothers about three and five. The little girl's face had dirty circles around her eyes, and her hair lay partially in her eyes and was matted with tears. Her younger brothers were also crying, with circles around their eyes. They had dirty, torn clothing and were pot bellied from the lack of proper food.

When we got them from beneath the wreckage, the little girl clutched her two brothers as if trying to protect them from us. She began to cry loudly and said something which we could not understand. She became frustrated until she demonstrated what she wanted us to do. She had her two small brothers kneel down and she whispered something to each and kissed them tenderly. She then knelt down beside them and while the tears streamed down her cheeks she cried out loudly: "Peestol, peestol," as she pointed to the necks of her brothers and her own.

We understood immediately and we picked them up in our arms, while almost crying ourselves. We never said a word, nor did they. It was a strange experience for them. Here we were, men who were not going to hurt them, but it was so bad that they just wanted to die. We started walking down the road, and all we could hear was the crunching of our shoes through the dusty road and distant gunfire and convulsive sobs of the children.

We searched incessantly for a place to leave the children, but no people would listen to us. Evidently, their custom is that if they accept the children, they are their responsibility the rest of their lives. We finally came to a place and again the people refused, but we used our rifles and let them know we wanted the children to stay there, and we would be back the next day to check on them.

The next day we went back with K rations, C rations, and hard candy bars. When we arrived at the home, they were eating. Strangely, however, the owners and their children were sitting on one side of the room, and the three orphans were on the other side of the room.

When the children saw us they ran to us and were very glad to see us. We played games and showed them how to eat the rations, and of course the candy. They were more interested in that than anything. The chocolate bars are really hard and you have to chew them in your mouth for a few seconds before it comes together. We showed them coin tricks by taking pennies out of their ears. For several minutes the small one was looking in the ears of his brother and sister trying to decide where they came from. We also explained to the people someone would eventually pick the children up and they should be there, safe and sound. It then came time for us to leave. Our outfit was moving on the next morning, and so we knew that we would never see them again.

As we started to leave, all of the children started crying and wanted us to stay. Finally we explained to the girl that we had to leave. I will always remember the smallest boy clutching to my pants and legs and in his own way crying and begging us to stay. They, we suspected, had not been treated this nice in their whole life. Finally the girl explained to her small brother that we had to go. He somehow bravely fought back the tears. We hugged each one and then we started down the hill into the valley, and we kept looking back and waving to them as they did to us. As we descended into the valley we looked back and all we could see were three small specks on the horizon waving, waving, and waving goodbye. We never saw them again. Those thoughts still linger and I doubt they will ever go away. . . . I [also] think of all of those guys that were killed. The real heroes will never know that they were true heroes. I have often thought how hard it must have been for parents to have lost a boy and to hope most of all his death wasn't in vain.

We got aboard an LST and headed for Guam. We knew for certain that it would not be long until we hit Japan, and we were not looking forward to it. When we got to Guam, I was surprised to find it was a far more advanced island than any we had seen. There were thousands of planes parked and ships at anchor and sailors and civilians running around. We didn't have those land crabs as we had on Guadalcanal, and it seemed nice, but that issue lay in the back of our minds.

When we got there, the 3rd Marine Division was already packing up to head to a real small island off Japan. We got new replacements and everything was happening quickly. While on Guam I got aboard the *Missouri* and saw a couple of friends on it. As I was coming back by a boat from the *Missouri* and got on shore, I heard someone yell, "Hands Harry." I knew that voice and I had heard it before many times. I looked to try to find where he was calling. It was Louis Duesterberg, a very good friend of mine whom I had worked with before he went to Annapolis to become a naval officer.

When he got ashore we got to talk for quite a while, and he told me he would come to visit me on the island. It was about three weeks later we got news from some Army Air Force flyers saying the war would be over in a month, and there would be no landing on Japan, but they still continued with the invasion plans. A week or so later we heard about the atomic bomb and how our bombing was tearing Japan to pieces. We all celebrated, because we now knew that it was practically over. Guys were now looking forward to going home. Rumors were out that they had stopped sending guys from Europe, because we would not need them.

Just two days before Japan surrendered, I got a high fever and I didn't know what it was. I had over 103 degrees temperature. I was checked in at the field hospital with malaria and dengue fever. I was really hurting. Two days later, they had the big celebration; the war was over. The island went crazy and I was in the hospital. It took me a week to recover, and I got back in time to hear big plans were being made for the 6th Marine Division.

Since the 4th Marine Regiment had been among the first to be captured by Japan at Corregidor, 4th Marine Regiment was sent to

Japan to bring back the 4th Marines that had been captured at Corregidor. I might have gone but they chose four other corpsmen. One was Harvat, who was my corpsman. He liked the idea of going, and I wanted to go, but they had other plans for the rest of us in the engineers. We found out a few days later we were to go to China and make the Japanese surrender. They had not given up yet. We knew this would not be much of an operation, so it was good news, but we had been looking forward to going home, as thousands were now doing. . . .

About two weeks later, they put the engineers aboard to go to China, but four corpsmen and I were left as rear troops to be sure everything was clear on Guam before we left. The commanding officer was one of them, and I had to give him shots before he could go to China. I had to sign over supplies that we didn't want nor need.

About three days later we got aboard an LST and headed for Tsing Tao, which was one of the largest cities in China. When we got there, we pulled in the harbor the same time as the guys who had gone before. I believe this was done because some of the top brass were on our ship.

They sent in about a hundred marines heavily armed to see if the Japanese would surrender. They did in about two hours and we went ashore. When we unloaded our equipment, the Chinese had never seen large trucks and tanks such as we had. They would come up and touch it and laugh. They knew now that they were finally free from the Japanese. They were very happy. Little kids came up saying, "Joe, peanuts, fifty cents?" They had a pillowcase half filled. We all bought some. We had not eaten peanuts for two years. Some others came asking us to buy eggs—a half pillow case—for fifty cents. We bought them too. When we got to our quarters, we were placed in a Japanese School. It was nice, but their tubs were square cement, about two feet square. Their commodes lay right on the floor; we had to squat to use them. We finally built our own.

It turned out to be great duty. We could go on liberty every other night. We found out we could get a bath by a bath boy, a haircut, a shave, and a rubdown while they pressed our trousers for just one dollar. We could go out and have steak and eggs for seventy-five cents. Later they substituted tomatoes for the eggs. We could never see any nice Chinese girls—they were locked up and not permitted to associate with us. The officers had a nice hotel right on the beach. It was reported to be the best in China.

Postscript: Harry Murray later returned to the United States and spent time recovering from tuberculosis. He went on to work as a research scientist and wrote this story for a self-published book.

IMMEDIATE CARE SAVED MY LIFE
James C. Johnson
Germany, 1945

During World War II, I was fighting in Germany on December 2, 1945. Because of a quick-thinking corpsman, I am alive today. This is my story.

I had been a defense worker in the United States during the early parts of the war, exempt from the draft. But I waived my exemption and enlisted in the army on January 7, 1943. I was placed in [Company A, 771st Tank Destroyer Battalion] and landed in France shortly after D-Day. My unit joined General Patton's Third Army. However, Patton moved so fast in his penetration into Germany that he ran out of fuel, stopped in his tracks. Our battalion was immediately reordered to join General Simpson's Ninth Army to aid in the push to drive the Germans out of Holland. Although the effort saw great success, many good men died in the fighting. I remember a tank destroyer burning next to mine during the fighting. A high explosive shell had set it aflame and killed everyone inside. I was reminded over and over that that could have been me and my comrades.

During a temporary stop on December 2, I decided to leave the tank destroyer and scout ahead. I searched ahead of our group, trying to figure what course of action we should take next. A squad of German soldiers spotted me. They immediately laid down a [barrage] of mortar fire to trap me, but I found a ditch left by a tank or truck track and hid in it to escape the explosions. Once it stopped, I jumped up and hurried back to report to my group. I almost made it to the tank destroyer, but with only yards to go, a bullet knocked me to the ground. I soon discovered it had shot through my right thigh.

A fellow soldier from the tank destroyer ran to help me and wrapped my thigh. My leg had two holes in it: one where the bullet entered and another where it exited. Someone called in the Medical Corps by radio, and a jeep quickly arrived. The corpsmen bandaged my wounds to prevent further loss of blood, and they took me to the jeep. The two corpsmen who were helping me, I soon learned, worked on the front lines saving soldiers from shock, bleeding, and loss of limbs. They were risking their lives daily, as I was.

A few miles down the road an ambulance met us, and the corpsmen placed me on a stretcher for another long ride. When the doors of the ambulance opened, my heart dropped. Standing before me were four German soldiers still in their uniforms. But they had no weapons; they were prisoners of war.

They pulled me out on the stretcher and carried me into a large building, where other wounded soldiers lay on the floor in rows, many of them crying out with pain. I was now in Liège, Belgium. Soon, another American soldier knelt beside me and informed me, "I will be flying you to England tonight."

The next day, to my amazement, I lay far from the sound of shelling and tank destroyers. I now had a hospital bed in Cardiff, Wales. Over a lengthy recovery period, I learned that my ward especially served soldiers who had lost legs in combat. One young man had both legs blown off in a minefield. We all agreed that most of us were still alive for one reason: quick-acting, courageous medical corpsmen had helped us at the critical moment and kept us alive.

I believe that I would have died from loss of blood from my wounds had it not been for the brave, dedicated men of the Medical Corps. Today, I don't even know the names of the men who saved my life. But their faces are etched in my memory. I count it a privilege to be able to tell you this story today.

DOCTOR QUACK
William F. Carroll
China, 1944–1945

D r. Jim Kinder, who died recently in a tragic automobile collision, was more than an outstanding pediatrician caring for the children of Cape Girardeau, Missouri. I first met him in Hanchung, China, about Christmas of 1944. He was a young medical school graduate who had been called into service as a captain in the U.S. Army Air Corps before he had completed his internship. He never complained about this. He was a patriotic guy who believed in serving his country.

He was tall and looked half starved. He had a painfully thin face and a ragged crew cut. He was wearing a worn A-2 jacket and GI shoes. He didn't look old enough or wise enough to be a doctor.

He was part of the Chinese-American Composite Wing, a volunteer group of fliers who had been organized with the approval of FDR at the request of Chiang Kai-shek's wife to be a part of the 14th Air Force under General Claire Chennault.

Dr. Kinder had already experienced bombings and enemy action at several forward air bases as a flight surgeon and had most recently left Kweillin in Southeast China, just a step ahead of the invading Japanese army.

Being temporarily without a base, he received orders from the brass to go north to Hanchung to be a part of the 1st Bomb Squadron.

He was a veteran of a year and a half of combat service in China by the time I met him in Hanchung. He knew virtually everyone in the 14th Air Force from buck sergeants to Chennault.

Everyone liked Jim Kinder. Rank meant nothing to him. He was as at ease with the enlisted men as he was with the officers. He endured the rats and fleas and dismal living conditions with the rest of us. With irreverent respect and affection, we called him Dr. Quack.

He quickly established a small infirmary and hired a Chinese nurse to assist him. His equipment was simple and limited. His pharmacy looked like a collection of old brown bottles. But he was creative and skillful. With limited resources, he treated everything from dysentery, which everyone had, respiratory ailments, wounds, and fractures to the occasional case of venereal disease. The closest hospital was Chengtu, miles away by air.

Dr. Kinder was a flight surgeon in the true sense of the word. As often as he could, he was on the planes, getting his flight time like the rest of us. He had no regard for danger. He would go anywhere he was needed in order to give medical care. Jim Kinder, our Dr. Quack, understood us. He knew our needs, which included recreation. Hanchung was at the end of the China supply line. Mail calls were infrequent. We had no PX. Our mess hall was limited to eggs, chickens that looked like crows, rice, and water buffalo.

Doc joined us in the local native restaurants, which accounted for the dysentery. He was generous with his medical alcohol, which we cut with water, lemon powder, and a crude sugar for our parties. Doc managed to get enough stateside whiskey to serve two ounces per man after missions.

When we located a Taoist temple at Mewo Tai-dz a few kilometers north of Hanchung, he would send us there for R&R several days at a time. On a few occasions, Doc joined us on rest flights to Sian for some good food and a change of pace. He was one of the first to go whitewater rafting on the Pau River.

After two years overseas and away from his family and home in Cape Girardeau, Doc James was skin and bones, sallow, worn out and sick. He was more than ready to leave China but shared some of the regrets at leaving felt by those of us who had seen less of the war. We left Hanchung and flew over the hump from Kunming to Calcutta, where we boarded a troop ship for Uncle Sugar. We separated at Camp Kilmer on arrival, not knowing when, if ever, we would meet again.

But Dr. Quack wasn't about to forget the friends that he had made. Gradually, cards began coming from him, and then letters (pecked out with two fingers on his finicky old typewriter with lots of strikeouts and handwritten interlineations). A network of Hanchung friends was thus established.

In 1977, Jim and his wife, Mary (a great broad if there ever was one), invited their Hanchung friends to a reunion at their country home in Cape Girardeau. After more than thirty years, we were together again. Me, Nicklenose Wilson, Hairline Halla, Buck Blake, Deacon Larson, Ponza Hodge, and Dick Varney, our old commanding officers. And our wives, who had heard of our wartime exploits.

For several days we relived the past and learned about each other and our lives after the great China adventure.

We learned that Jim Kinder had completed his medical education, had taken a residency and specialized in medical education, had taken another residency and specialized in pediatrics. He and Mary had raised four boys. Our Dr. Quack was now James A. Kinder, MD, FAAP, caring for children in his hometown.

It was no surprise to any of Jim's Hanchung friends that he was an active practitioner until he was past eighty years of age, or that when he closed his office he took his skills to the county's public health center, where he continued to care for Medicaid patients who needed someone like him to help them, just as he had helped so many of us.

Young or old, Jim Kinder, our Dr. Quack, was a great and dedicated doctor. He spent his life well. He will be remembered.

A NURSE'S TALE
Captain Ann Bernatitus
The Pacific Theater

The Bureau of Medicine and Surgery recorded the following interview between its historian and Captain Bernatitus on January 25, 1994.

Captain Ann Bernatitus established her fame during the evacuation of the Philippines early in World War II. As a nurse, she tended many of the wounded men who fought and eventually were driven from Bataan and Corregidor.

Were you born in Pennsylvania?

I was born in this house. This is the old family homestead. Mother and Dad built it. I think it was built about 1905. Nobody has lived here but the Bernatitus family.

When did you decide you wanted to be a nurse?

I always wanted to be a nurse. There was nothing else for girls to do in those days but be a schoolteacher or a nurse. My parents couldn't afford to send me to college. My school friend, whose mother was a widow, told my mother, who was also a widow, to let me go for training. My mother then decided to let me go for training locally. That girl went to New York for her training.

Where did you go?

I trained at what was then the Wyoming Valley Homeopathic Hospital in Wilkes-Barre. While I was in training, someone from the army came to Mercy Hospital to talk about military nursing, and we had to go. That was where I got the idea of the navy. In those days, things were pretty bad.

That was during the Depression?

Right. There were no jobs for nurses, unless you were one of the old-timers. They had private duty nurses in those days, but only the rich could afford them. I wasn't thinking about going in the service at that time. It wasn't until after I graduated. I had no job. I then decided to take a postgraduate course in operating room technique and management at the University of Pennsylvania Graduate Hospital in Philadelphia at 19th and Lombard. I applied and was accepted for a six-month course.

Even after I finished that, there were still no jobs. First of all, I think I was too young at that time to get a job as a supervisor of an operating room. I stayed on at Penn and did general duty for forty-five dollars a month and my board.

When was that?

I went in training in 1931 and I graduated in 1934 but, as I said, I stayed on. I saw an ad in one of the nursing magazines that said they would find you a job, so I applied. One day I got a telegram saying there was an opening for a staff nurse, not a supervisor, but a staff nurse in the operating room at the New Rochelle hospital in New York for eighty dollars a month and board. I grabbed it. So I went to New Rochelle and worked in the operating room there rather than being a staff nurse. I was doing what I had trained for.

After so many months, I realized I would have to get New York registration to be able to stay on there. At that time, I got a letter from my former director of nurses at Wyoming Valley saying she would give me a job as an operating room supervisor at the Nanticoke State Hospital in the area. But they would only pay me seventy dollars a month. But I took it mainly because my mother felt better that I was close to home and not out in the big city. The superintendent who gave me the job had been an army nurse back during World War I.

I think at that time I had written for an application to join the Navy Nurse Corps. For the longest time, I didn't hear from them. So I wrote a second time and finally got an application form from the Bureau of Medicine and Surgery. I had to go to Philadelphia for a physical.

Did you have to take some kind of examination?

No. This was in 1936. What was happening after World War I, like always, was like we're doing right now: cut, cut, cut. Somewhere along the line, I had heard that there were only 325 nurses in the Nurse Corps. Some had resigned after World War I and some had been furloughed. They were slowly calling them back. And they were also accepting new applicants. It seems that I went for the physical exam on the first of September, and on the twenty-fifth I was on my way to the naval hospital in Chelsea, Massachusetts.

How did the navy brand of nursing differ from what you had experienced before?

First of all, I had been working in the operating room, which meant my job was different from a regular staff nurse that was out taking care of patients. In those days, when you joined the navy, you were on six-months' probation. That was the stipulation. For those first six months, you wore the uniform and hat you graduated with and had in civilian life. They put you on a ward with an older nurse, and you just learned the language and the routine.

Of course, that was the era before navy nurses even had ranks. You were probably addressed as Miss Bernatitus.

Right. In those days we were neither fish nor fowl. We were not officers and we were not enlisted. We were in between. We did not get the pay of an officer but we got more than the enlisted.

So there you were at Chelsea, a provisional nurse. How long were you there?

I was there the first six months. Then the navy would decide whether to keep you or throw you out. New nurses were coming into the corps roughly every two to four weeks. I found myself supervising the corpsmen and keeping the books. Every morning you went on duty and had to count all the blankets, the thermometers. I think we had to count the glasses. And then you had to scrub the floors. You had to keep the curtains at the windows just so.

They had inspections?

Only once a week, on Friday, when the captain and chief nurse would come through. When the chief nurse visited the ward every morning, you had to accompany her, as the nurse on the ward. You stopped at every bed to tell her what was wrong with the patient and how he was getting along. Maybe what medications he was getting. Not like now.

And you were responsible for so many corpsmen?

Yes, so many corpsmen who were assigned to that ward. You taught them how to do things and saw that they did them. There were times you actually did nursing—took care of a patient. If there was a critically ill patient, you took care of him yourself.

How long were you at Chelsea?

Exactly two years. If you were the youngest nurse on duty, you took turns doing morning duty and afternoon duty, and then we all took turns doing night duty. It was the older nurses that got the assignment for straight morning duty, no afternoon duty. We worked from eight to three, and the afternoon nurses worked from three to ten. The night nurse came on at eleven and stayed until seven or eight the next morning.

All of a sudden, we had nurses assigned to the linen room. You had to check it out to see if it was all there and what condition it was in. There was a seamstress to mend it if necessary. And, by golly, I got assigned to this job as straight morning duty. A lot of the older ones didn't know what that was all about.

That was considered to be a plum assignment?

Oh, sure. Then they decided to open some World War I buildings. They had no dispensary. They had a dispensary in the Navy Yard at Charlestown, but they didn't have a hospital for dependents. So they decided to open a hospital for dependents but did so before it was really set up. Then they hired some civilian nurses to come in and run it. That turned out to be a disaster. The nurses couldn't understand the navy way of doing things. Finally, one day I went down for lunch and on the bulletin board was a note from the chief nurse. It said, "Miss Bernatitus, see me in my suite." I thought, "What did I do now?" I went in and found that they had decided to put a navy nurse in charge of the other nurses in the dependent hospital and I was it. I looked at her and said, "I don't know anything about obstetrics. I'm an operating room nurse." She said, "Tomorrow morning you go over there." So I did. They put me in charge of the two floors. The lower floor was an outpatient clinic and an older nurse was assigned there. There was a death in her family and she had to go on emergency leave and never came back. So I ended up with the first floor too. And that's how I ended up with three floors.

After that I got orders to go to Annapolis.

When was that?

In 1938. The navy was a real nice place in those days. The nurses lived separately; they had their own mess. You were served; the food was always good. Life was good.

Was it as good when you got to Annapolis?

Yes. Annapolis was a smaller station. In Chelsea, the building we were quartered in was at least a hundred years old. The rooms were enormous with big, high ceilings and big windows. At Annapolis, we all had individual rooms. The place was beautiful. We could date the midshipmen. Some midshipmen would get their eye on you and then you were "dragged" to the hops at the academy. You had to walk from the nurse's quarters across the drill field to get to the dancing place. It was very nice. You learned a lot. I was exposed to things I had never been exposed to before. The older nurses would feel sorry for you and take you places. It was such a nice, close group all the time. You knew everybody in the house.

How long were you there?

I was there maybe two years. I remember at that time the Nurse Corps would send nurses to George Washington University for a course in dietetics. And they'd send nurses elsewhere for a course in physiotherapy. At that time they were looking for nurses to sign up for these courses. The announcements were on the bulletin board. At that time I was relieving in the diet kitchen. The chief nurse kept asking me whether I wanted to go to dietetic school. I had filled out the form we used to get every year asking us where we wanted to go next. I had the Philippines down. "Suppose I go to dietetic school and there was an opening in the Philippines, I wouldn't get it." So I didn't sign up and sure enough, I got the Philippines.

How did you get there?

I didn't have much of a vacation. I had to go to Norfolk, Virginia, to the hospital there to meet the other nurse who was going with me, Mary Chapman, and get the ship. We went over on the transport ship *Chaumont* (AP-5). I think I took an overnight ferry from Baltimore to Norfolk and met Mary there. We stopped at Guantanamo Bay and then through the Panama Canal.

I wasn't a sailor and didn't enjoy the trip. I was seasick all the time.

Did you stop at Pearl Harbor?

Yes. We had marines aboard they were taking to Midway, where they went ashore. Then we went on to Guam and arrived in the Philippines in July 1940.

What was your impression of the Philippines?

I had no idea what the Philippines looked like; I hadn't read up on it or anything. Of course somebody met us at the dock to take us to Canacao. All I can remember is the smell of copra, which seemed to be everywhere. The nipa huts, the kids running around naked. The houses on stilts, the carabao. But life was very good out there too. We went to work at eight o'clock. You went to lunch and then didn't have to go back on duty.

You had the afternoon off?

Yes, because only one nurse had to go back to supervise. We had golf, bicycling, swimming. You could go to the markets if you wanted to. For five dollars a month you took your shoes, put them outside the door, and the houseboys would take them downstairs, polish them up, and when we got back they would be sitting by your door. It was the same with the women who did your laundry. On your way to work you dropped it off in the washroom and when you returned there it was all pressed for you. Just before war was declared, we had one shop across from the Army and Navy Club run by a woman originally from Philadelphia named Rosie. Nothing was on display. She would say "I've got just the thing for you." You might go in to buy a pair of stockings and you would come home with an evening dress. She would serve you a drink first. Anyway, I bought this two-piece slack suit. Rosie was taken prisoner and I don't know how many years later, I got a bill from Rosie. Apparently, she had kept her records and the bill came from Philadelphia.

You probably had signed a chit for that dress.

Sure. That's all you ever did.

Did you have individual rooms there?

Yes. Did Dorothy Still Danner or Bertha Evans St. Pierre tell you
how we found out that the war had started?

Bertha said that her boyfriend at Cavite Naval Base phoned her.

Ed. Yes. He called her around six o'clock in the morning. The telephone was downstairs on the first floor. And she came running up
the steps and into my room. "Ann, war's been declared."

*Even before you got to the Philippines, had you been hearing anything
about war?*

I don't recall when we were going out. But one thing happened
that made us aware that something was cooking. Mary Chapman was
going to get married and had put in her resignation. When the *Chaumont* would come in to the Philippines, somebody already had their
orders to go back to the United States, but the ship always brought
someone out as a replacement. The chief nurse Miss Laura Cobb had
us at a meeting and said, "I would suggest that anything you have,
you pack up and ship back." Mary Chapman was going to be on that
boat, so I packed up a Hong Kong chest that someone had picked up
for me and all the other things I had bought from the Chinese man
who used to come to the nurse's quarters. He came with his valises
packed with linens and things, and he would spread them on the floor
and he'd tell us to just sign the chit. You wouldn't have to pay for
the things right then. So I packed all these things up and sent them
with Mary Chapman's things.

Did the stuff go out with the Chaumont?

Yes.

But Mary Chapman didn't.

No. I'll tell you why she didn't. When we heard about Pearl Harbor, they started sandbagging around the hospital because it wasn't

on a solid foundation, just on these corner posts that held it up. And it was a three-story building. They assigned us so many hours duty and then somebody would come and relieve us. I remember I was coming off duty some time in the early morning hours when the siren went off that the planes were coming to bomb Nichols Field. When the war was declared all the patients who could go back to duty were sent back to duty. They sent the Filipinos home. Anybody who couldn't be moved ended up under the hospital.

They put them under the hospital, protected by sandbags?

Yes. I stayed there, I don't remember how long because I had started to go over to the nurse's quarters already. The captain then decided to evacuate the patients to Sternberg Hospital in Manila. He decided that two nurses and two corpsmen had to accompany them.

Were the patients transported by ambulance?

I don't recall, but we went by car. Laura Cobb lined us up in the living room asking for volunteers to go. First thing you know, Mary Chapman volunteered. There were no other volunteers. I don't remember how many times she said, "Who's going to volunteer?" Nobody would. So, I got real bright and said, "Why don't you make us draw straws? Then no one can ever come back at you and say, 'If you hadn't made me do this, this wouldn't have happened.'" Laura thought that was a good idea. So she went out to the other room and got long applicator sticks with cotton on the end and held them in her hands like this. And she went over to Goldia O'Haver. Goldia then pulled one out. It was long so she knew she didn't have to go. She came to me and I pulled the short one. So I had to go.

That afternoon they took us to the nurse's quarters at Sternberg. You wouldn't believe it. When those nurses came off duty, they always served tea, and those nurses were having tea. War had been declared, and they were having tea.

Was that on the ninth?

Yes. It must have been. It was the day after the war began that the decision was made to evacuate the patients. [Bernatitus refers to her notes.] Those sixty-eight enlisted men and veterans who were ambulatory went back to their ships on December 8. Nichols Field was bombed on the ninth. The remaining patients were transferred to Army Sternberg Hospital, to be accompanied by two corpsmen and two nurses.

When we got to Sternberg they had us in some kind of a barracks for the navy patients. Mary Chapman, who was senior to me, took morning duty and I had to take night duty. I have it here. [Referring to her notes:] We were located in one of the barracks recently vacated by the Philippine Scouts. On December 10, the Japanese bombed the Navy Yard at Cavite on Sangley Point.

You were at Sternberg while all that was going on?

Yes. We were out in the courtyard of the nurses' quarters watching all this. There were foxholes dug there. It says here [referring to the notes] they were bombed by approximately 125 planes flying at twenty-thousand feet. The patients who were brought in were given first aid at the Navy Hospital and transferred to Sternberg immediately. On December 11, medical personnel at Canacao evacuated and reported to Sternberg in Manila. Within two or three days of reporting, Captain Davis received orders to establish a temporary hospital at Balintawok. That was just outside Manila. One half of the navy medical personnel went with the group. I think that was Laura Cobb, Margaret Nash, Eldene Paige, Bertha Evans, Edwina Todd, and Helen Gorzalanski.

You were still at Sternberg at this time?

Yes. This was where we separated [again referring to notes]. Those remaining were divided into teams and assigned to units being set up in other areas of Manila. Dorothy Still, Susie Pitcher, and Edwina Todd went to the Jai Alai Club. Mary Chapman and Mary Harrington went to Holy Ghost. Dorothy Still and I originally were to go to Santa Scholastica with Dr. Carey Smith and Dr. Claude Fraley and corpsmen Jones and Cary.

Santa Scholastica College was a girl's school located in the vicinity of the Philippine General Hospital. We two nurses and the two corpsmen were on the bus just about to leave, when someone came aboard and told Dorothy that she was being reassigned to Jai Alai.

So, the two of you were on the bus with the doctors and corpsmen.
Yes.

And someone came on the bus and told her that she should report to the Jai Alai Club?
Yes.

So, you were now the only nurse on the bus with the two doctors and two corpsmen?
Yes. When we got to Santa Scholastica, we found other medical personnel were there already setting up the hospital unit. Our job was to set up the emergency operating room facility. I don't recall our living quarters, but apparently they were adequate. Since we were the only navy personnel, we formed a kind of clique. In the evenings we got together and sat out on the lawn.

About this time, General MacArthur declared Manila an open city.
That's when all this happened. And why did I get picked to go to Bataan? Only for one reason. When he declared Manila an open city, they were sending surgeons out to Bataan. They weren't picking general medical men. Because of the fact that I had been Dr. Smith's ward nurse and I had the background in operating room, he picked me.

It all boils down to this. Since you had worked for Carey Smith as a surgical nurse, he knew you, he had worked with you. And since he was going, you were the logical choice.
Yes.

Bertha Evans told me that everyone at these remote locations in Manila were awaiting orders and there were no orders. There was so much confusion. The army marched their patients down and put them on a hospital ship. As Bertha recalled, "What about the navy patients? What's supposed to happen to them?" Nothing happened. They sat there. Is that how you remember it?

I wasn't with them. That was the whole trouble [referring to her notes]. On December 22, Dr. Smith informed me about 7 p.m. that Manila was to be declared an open city and that surgical units were selected to go to Bataan on Christmas Eve. Our unit was included.

So you and Dr. Carey Smith and Dr. Fraley, and corpsmen Jones and Carey, as part of that unit, were to go to Bataan.

Yes.

Dr. Smith told you that you had been selected. Who gave him the orders?

Whoever was in charge of Santa Scholastica. The army was there, so I don't know. It says here [referring to her notes] that on the twenty-fourth we left at 6 a.m. and were taken to Jai Alai, where the convoy was to form to go to Bataan. Being alone, I sat on the curb to get out of the way, when one of the navy nurses, Dorothy Still, assigned to Jai Alai, came out and found me. She wanted to know what I was doing there. I told her I was going to Bataan. She asked me where it was and I told her I had never heard of it until two days ago. At that time, I recall walking into the Jai Alai building to see how they had set up approximately one hundred beds on the porch. This is in Dr. Davis' diary. It was about this time that Dr. Davis at the Philippine Union College in Balintawok received orders to evacuate the patients and personnel to Santa Scholastica. According to a newspaper article on March 17, 1946, by Captain Lea Sartin, approximately 160 navy and 100 army patients were treated and facilities were prepared for 700. Captain Davis ordered the Canacao unit to stay together and serve until further orders came. New orders never came.

What about the convoy to Bataan?
    It formed up at Jai Alai.

Did you see the other nurses?
    No. Just Dorothy. I was waiting on the curb to get on the bus to go to Bataan.

So you never saw any of them until after the war?
    Yes. That's right. Anyway, the convoy took off for Bataan. There were twenty-four army nurses, twenty-five Filipino nurses, and me, the one Navy nurse. As we passed through the villages, the natives came out and cheered us, giving us the "V" for victory sign. Many times during the trip the bus would have to stop and we would dive into gutters along the roadside because the Japanese planes were overhead. Late that afternoon we arrived at Camp Limay, Hospital Number 1. There were twenty-five wooden one-story buildings, fifteen of them wards. A water pipe outside each ward provided water. The utility room for the bedpans and what have you was the back porch. The buildings were in a rectangle, with the operating room building at the upper end and a generator and water towers alongside. At the farther end was the building housing the nurses' quarters and the officers' mess hall. The remaining buildings were along each side. Behind the buildings on the left side of the beach was a warehouse in which were stored the equipment and supplies for the hospital. In the center of this area was grass and trees and foxholes dug everywhere. We were assigned two to a room. My roommate was Arlene Ellen Francis.
    The first few days I was assigned ward duty, but this was changed, and I was reassigned to the operating room. You know, they really left me alone. I only worked when Dr. Smith worked. He was the one who took care of me. The army nurses didn't bother me. I was a member of Dr. Smith's team.
    Let me go on. [Reading from notes:] Everyone was involved in setting up the hospital. All the supplies and equipment were crated and

stored in the warehouse on the beach. The crates were neither marked nor stored as units, so the navy crates had to be opened before you found the items for your particular unit. I recall a crate being opened and in it were surgical gowns wrapped in newspapers dated 1917.

The operating room was a long, narrow building with approximately seven or eight tables set up in the center. Along the window openings were the cabinets with supplies. There were shutters with a stick to keep them open. I'm a bit vague on how we sterilized the gauze and linen, but it seems to me it was done in a pressure cooker operated by kerosene. The instruments were sterilized by placing them in a foot tub filled with Lysol, then rinsed in alcohol. The period of sterilization depended on how fast they were needed. As the patients were brought in, they were assigned to a table by Dr. Weinstein of the Army Medical Corps. The team assigned to that table took care of the patient regardless of what type of surgery was indicated. Casualties were heavy, and the operating room was an extremely busy place.

We got there on December 24. On January 23, 1942, Camp Limay moved to Little Baguio farther down the peninsula. We had two meals a day: 9 a.m. and 4 p.m. The wards were just concrete slabs with corrugated roofs. They were open on the sides. The operating room was on a little knoll.

On March 3, the hospital was bombed, even though the warehouse on the beach had a big red cross.

You were there when the bombs dropped.

Are you kidding? Outside the operating room was a bench. I almost killed myself trying to get under that bench.

Did you hear the planes coming?

Yes. The alarm would sound and then you could hear the bombs coming down—a whistling sound. On April 7 the Japanese apologized. It had been a mistake. That hospital was right next door to the ammunition dump.

I imagine there were killed and wounded.

Oh, yes. Every operating table would be filled. They would come in from the field all dirty. You did what you could. There were lice; I kept my hair covered all the time. He, Dr. Smith, did a lot of leg amputations because we had a lot of gas gangrene out there. I remember one patient we were operating on. Dr. Smith didn't want to sew him back up. He had died. I remember telling him that I didn't want him to do that if anything happened to me. He said, "I'll sew him up just to shut you up." We were washing the dirty dressings that they used during an operation. We would wash them out and refold and sterilize them and use them again.

The operating theater and everything were right out there in the open? No screens or anything?

No. It was just the wards that were open. The OR was in a building. It was at Limay where we had the long row of tables. At Little Baguio it was in a building. I can't remember exactly how many operating tables we had. As you walked in, there was a setup for ear, nose, and throat.

What were you eating?

I remember Dr. Fraley would go down to Mariveles scrounging for food. One time he came back with lemon powder. After that, everything was lemon. After I got home I didn't want any lemon.

When did you write this document? It's dated November 26, 1975.

Yes. I've added on to it from time to time when I would get some other document, like Sartin's diary.

You said the Japanese apologized after the attack on Little Baguio.

That was on March 30. On April 7, the following week, they bombed us again. It was terrible. By that time, they had stopped advancing for a while. Things were kind of quiet at the front lines. But we were getting a lot of patients with malaria, dysentery, all that. We ran out of beds. You'd go to bed at night, and when you awoke the next morning, you'd get out there, and there would be all these two- or three-decker bunks made of wood and patients in them. There wasn't much surgery going on, but the nurses taking care of the sick were very busy.

When Dr. Smith was operating, Dr. Fraley got the job of being an assistant to the colonel in charge of the whole outfit, Colonel Duckworth. He would go to the navy facility down at Mariveles and scrounge instruments and whatever. The submarine tender USS *Canopus* (AS-9) was there, and the men aboard would make things we needed in the shops on the ship.

The second time we were bombed, they hit one of the wards. There were patients who were tied in traction. The nurses had to cut the ropes so they could fall to the deck. There were pajamas in the treetops. During this time we were not busy in the operating room. The army nurses were unhappy because the operating room nurses weren't working as hard as they were. We really didn't have a chief nurse there with us. Anyway, they got talking about naming somebody to be the head nurse to make all the rules or decisions. How do you do that? In the army and the navy, it's usually the senior nurse that gets the job. Well, you would die laughing. Who was the senior nurse? I was. Can you imagine what would have happened? There would have been another war. Well, they finally appointed somebody from the other hospital up at Cabcaben that was out in the open. Our hospital was intended to be the operating unit. We would then ship them up there for convalescing.

So, you didn't get on that well with the army nurses. You kept to yourself?

That's right. I always did.

You mentioned earlier, before we had the tape recorder on, that your relations with your fellow navy nurses were strained at some point. Was that after the war?

Yes. After the war. Once I left, that was it. When they came home, I wrote to some of them but never got an answer. A lot of it stemmed from the time I got promoted and made junior grade. I was a chief nurse.

When was this?

Right after I came home. I jumped over a lot of nurses that had been in for fifteen years. The ones that were jumped over were not very happy.

Let's go back to Little Baguio. At some point, there was not a lot of surgery going on. How long were you there? This was in April 1942.

We were bombed for the second time on April 7. On the eighth, we were transferred to Corregidor. That's when the front lines collapsed.

How did you get there?

I don't remember what kind of boat it was, probably one of the things that used to ply between Corregidor and Canacao. Anyway, it was after supper. We ate at four o'clock. About eight o'clock they told us to take what we had—and we didn't have much—and put us on buses. I left Dr. Smith and Dr. Fraley there. Later on, Dr. Smith showed up on Corregidor; Dr. Fraley didn't. I think I had all I owned in a pillowcase. To get to Mariveles, they had a road they called the Zig Zag trail, with a drop-off on both sides. We met the fellows coming up, going to the front lines.

You know that picture of me in the coveralls?

Wasn't that picture taken much later on when you were on the Relief?

Yes. The picture of me is on the hospital ship *Relief* (AH-1) but those coveralls were made for me at Little Baguio. The Quartermaster Corps made those for us. Anyway, we got down to the dock at Mariveles and we had to stay there for a while waiting for a boat. Some of the men that were there asked us where we were from. They were shocked to find us nurses. Finally when the boat arrived, we got on. It must have been a ferry. I remember sitting in the passageway on a wicker chair. I was carrying my camera; I never gave that up and brought it home with me. They were shooting back and forth over us. When we got to Corregidor I don't think the people there knew we were coming, because that night we had to sleep two in a bunk.

I remember the following morning, the army chief nurse came to me. She took me out to what we called the hospital exit to show me what Bataan looked like with the ammunition dumps going up. I felt real bad because I knew one of the officers that was left there to do the job.

What did you see when you looked across at Bataan?

Fireworks. You wouldn't believe. They had bombs and everything. The army nurses still over there were farther up the peninsula and they were being evacuated too, but they didn't get to Corregidor until the next day. I was less scared on Bataan than I was on Corregidor. When the Japanese bombed, the whole place just shook.

You were in the Malinta Tunnel?

Yes. We were in the hospital tunnel. The Malinta tunnel ran like this [gesturing], straight through and the laterals went off it. When you went into the hospital lateral it was like this [gesturing]. At the end of this would be another lateral. The main tunnel was where MacArthur and Wainwright had their headquarters.

Did you ever see MacArthur while you were on Corregidor?

No. I never laid eyes on the bugger. He was egotistical.

Did you work in the hospital there until you were evacuated?

I didn't do much work when I got to Corregidor because I had dysentery. Of course, the army was in charge, so Dr. Smith wasn't working either. I remember only doing one amputation with him.

Where did you live there?

Off the hospital lateral were these other laterals. One was the nurse's quarters. Another was the mess hall. Another was the operating room.

So you had laterals off laterals?

Yes. It was not a clean tunnel. It was just rock.

You were over there at least a month.

We went on April 8 and left on May 3.

And while you were there the Japanese were bombing and shelling constantly. It must have been bedlam in that tunnel. Did you ever get out of the tunnel?

You would try to get out at night. The fellow I told you was responsible for blowing up the ammunition dump, well, he finally showed up.

How did you get selected to be evacuated from Corregidor?

I don't know how I was picked. I remember the planes came in first to evacuate people. [Reading from notes:] Two navy PBYs seaplanes took several army nurses and fifteen other passengers on April 29.

You were being treated to this terrific bombardment every single day, and then one day they come to you and say "By the way, we're taking you out of here." Is that how it happened?

Two PBYs came in first, and they took some nurses on it. How they picked them, I don't know. We were called to the mess hall and told we were going to be leaving that night. They stressed that weight didn't matter as much as size. All I had was a duffel bag. I always said that I didn't want to go off there on an airplane. I would rather go by submarine. We were dreaming that that's exactly what was going to happen.

What happened then?

They told us we would meet after dark in front of Wainwright's headquarters. But then the Japanese started shelling us, so they canceled us. We were told to meet I think two or three hours later. Your name was called and you stepped out of the crowd because everybody was gathered around to see this.

Wainwright shook your hand and wished you Godspeed and he said, "Tell them how it is out here." And then I got in a car and they took us out of the tunnel down to the dock. Everything was pitch-black, just some trees standing with no leaves, no nothing, charred.

When we got down there, we got on a boat that was even smaller than the one that took us to Corregidor. Then we shoved off. We had to go through our own mine fields to get to the submarine *Spearfish*. We learned later that it was taking us so long to get out there that the submarine wasn't sure Corregidor hadn't already fallen. Finally we saw this dark shape and we came alongside of it. You could hear the slapping of the water between the two objects. Then someone said "Get your foot over the rail." And then someone just pulled me, and then the first thing I knew, I was going down the hatch. I got down there awfully fast. [Reading from notes:] On May 3 we were evacuated from Corregidor. There were six army officers, six navy officers, eleven army nurses, and one navy nurse. There was also one civilian woman, a navy wife, and two stowaways—a navy electrician's mate and one who was with the army transport.

What do you remember about your seventeen-day voyage on the Spearfish *(SS-190)?*

When they first said seventeen days, I thought I couldn't make it. But I did. When we first got aboard, I was in the control room. Everything was lighted up, and there were all these valves and what have you. They took us into the officer's mess. That's where we sat, and they gave us tea and chocolate cake. We hadn't seen chocolate cake and tea in a long time. The chefs gave up their quarters for us.

It was just a cabin with a sink in it. Four of us would go to sleep in a hot bunk. You know what a hot bunk is?

Someone gets out and someone immediately gets in.

Our luggage we brought with us was on the deck in that same room. I was one of the four picked to go to bed right away. The next morning when my eight hours were up four others went to sleep. You just had to kill time any way you could. Most of our time was spent in the crew's mess. Someone had a Victrola that was playing all the time. The crew would come with magazines they had stashed away someplace. We would sit and talk. And of course, the boys loved it. The crew was fed first. Anything they served was wonderful for us. We hadn't seen food like that. They gave us one bucket for four of us when we went to bed. And that was for bathing and washing. Of course, if you went to the john you had to have an escort. Down in that submarine, the only thing you heard was the sound of the screws turning. You know, after a while the gals were cooking for the boys.

They initiated us when we went under the equator. I had just gotten up and I had to stand in a pan of water or something.

You know, while we were on that submarine, we remained submerged during the day, and at dusk we would surface to charge our batteries. When we came up we came up at an angle like this [gesturing]. And then someone opened a hatch and we felt this gush of nice fresh air come through. We had hardly done this when whish, down we went again. Well, that was an experience. They thought they sighted something. Everything was turned off and everybody was sitting around doing nothing. You could watch the men. Those who had shirts on you could just see those shirts gradually turning from tan to brown with perspiration. We must have been submerged for several hours just barely crawling. But everything turned out okay.

What happened when they found the stowaways?

They turned them over to the authorities when we got into Fremantle, Australia.

What do you remember about Fremantle?

When we got in, everybody from the admiral down was there. The navy had a hotel where people stayed, and that's where they put us up, the navy wife and me. And the army just took their nurses. I saw some of them when we were going home.

How long were you there?

Not very long. We were going to stay.

Do you know who Dr. Wassell is?

Yes. Corydon Wassell.

He was the one who was kind of taking care of Peggy and me.

Peggy was the civilian wife.

Yes.

Dr. Wassell was a legend. Lieutenant Commander Corydon Wassell, MC, USNR, was famous for his heroic care of wounded during and after the disastrous early battles of the Java Sea.

So am I.

That's right. You're both legends.

One day we were invited out to dinner at the house of one of the admiral's staff. Oh, how they were living it up. I can't remember what I had to eat but they did offer us champagne. In Australia they have a custom. Early in the morning they bring in a cup of tea and bread and butter and put it in your room when you wake up. Well, I made the mistake of drinking the tea after the champagne we had, and I'll tell you that my head spun round and round. I never knew that that could happen to you.

You know, a bath was what we wanted the most when we got to Australia. Even before we got off that submarine, each nurse got a bucket of water to go into the john and take a shower. If you don't think that was a treat. It was wonderful.

Back to Australia. One day, I realized that I had just had it. I wanted to go home. Nobody objected.

So you didn't have any official duties while you were there?

No. I don't know how soon after I said that, that arrangements were made for me to fly to Melbourne to get the *West Point* (AP-23) troopship back to the United States. The navy really took good care of me. When we got on that ship, they gave me just about the best stateroom in the house.

Did that ship come into New York?

Yes. We went through the Panama Canal again. And we had no escort with us either. In Australia, the paymaster had me list all the things I had left behind in clothes and things. I forgot how much money they gave me. But I went out and bought a dress, a coat, and a hat. When I got off that ship in New York, I was a civilian. I wasn't in uniform. But some of the army nurses who had been on that submarine insisted on wearing those dungarees they had gotten from the men on Bataan.

But you still had those dungaree coveralls they had made for you at Little Baguio.

Yes. I guess you would call it a jumpsuit.

When did you get back to New York?

In July, just before the Fourth. I think I went to the Bureau of Medicine and Surgery on the Fourth.

What do you remember about that? Did you see the surgeon general?

No. I didn't see the surgeon general, but I did see Sue Dauser, wartime director of the Navy Nurse Corps. All I could think of was all the time they spent eating.

At the bureau?

Anywhere. My sister and I went from New York to Washington, and we got there at lunchtime. Everyone was pulling out their little brown bags. It seemed like you just had your breakfast and here they were having a coffee break and then lunch, then a coffee break.

So you saw Miss Dauser.

Yes. That's the time they were trying to arrange for me to meet Eleanor Roosevelt, but they didn't succeed. We then came home to Exeter, Pennsylvania. I had a very short vacation. The people of my town were quite proud of me. They had a parade and a dinner at the high school. And they presented me with a gift from the town, and then I had to go back on duty.

Where did you go?

To Bethesda. I was there when Franklin Roosevelt broke the champagne bottle on the place.

That would have been on the 31st of August of 1942 when they officially opened the hospital.

I was there sitting in the second or third row up front on the left. *I have a photograph of that with the president standing at the podium outside. Where did you work at the hospital?*

In the Sick Officers Quarters.

How long were you at Bethesda?

A very short time. This is where I got pushed around. There were a lot of senior nurses there, but I was a chief nurse like the rest of them, so they had to consider me. I alternated on Sick Officers Quarters with another nurse. That was when the public relations place downtown was shipping me here and there selling war bonds, going to factories.

And you made speeches.

Oh, yes.

When did you get your Legion of Merit?

I didn't get that at Bethesda. I got it when I was at the dispensary in New Orleans.

Were you on a speaking tour there?

No. I had been transferred there. I finally went to Miss Dauser and said, "Look, if you don't want me in a psychiatric ward, you had better get me off this rat race." I would go to work in the mornings, come off duty, have my bag packed, go downtown to the PR public relations place, get my ticket from them to wherever I was going, and then I would ride at night and get there the next morning and go to somebody's breakfast, be interviewed. And I'm not a speaker.

You were everywhere, all over the place.

Oh, yes. The other staff nurses thought that I was having a ball just riding around going to parades and banquets. That wasn't a ball, not to me.

When did you pose for that famous portrait that Albert Murray did?

It happened through the PR group. They were pleased with my presentations. I could never just get up and talk. They would write a speech for me. And I would practice enough so that I could present it the right way. I could get the women in the audience to cry. I used to say that if you could do that, you were all right. Did you ever hear of Miss Lally?

Grace?

Yes.

She was the chief nurse on the hospital ship Solace *(AH-5) at Pearl Harbor.*

Right. She came to relieve Mrs. Carver at Bethesda just before I left, and she used to say that that wasn't the way to do it.

Who was Mrs. Carver?
She was the chief nurse. And Grace Lally used to say that you should end a speech with a poem. She used to have to give speeches too.

So at some point, they decided they needed a portrait of you.
Albert Murray was doing portraits of some of the admirals.

Where was the portrait done?
At the Corcoran Gallery.

You know, that portrait is still hanging in the Pentagon?
Really?

How many times did you go to the Corcoran to pose for him?
I can't remember the number of times. I think it was every day. I was on afternoon duty so I'd go down in the morning. I'd take a trolley or bus from Bethesda.

You left Bethesda and went to New Orleans.
Yes. And that's where Admiral Bennett presented the Legion of Merit to me.

Was he the commanding officer (CO) of the hospital?
No. He was the CO of the district. The dispensary was in town off Charles Street.

How long were you there?
I wasn't there very long, because from there they sent me to Great Lakes. I was an assistant chief nurse there, because they always had these older nurses that were chief nurses. And I wasn't there very long before I got orders for the hospital ship *Relief* (AH-1).

Where did you get the ship?

In San Francisco.

That would have been late 1944?
I remember that on April the 1st of 1945 I arrived at Buckner Bay in Okinawa because that's when they made the landings.

What were your duties on the ship?
I was chief nurse.

Then, you were in charge of all the nurses on the ship?
Yes.

What do you remember about going to the Relief *(AH-1)?*
When I got out there I was at Treasure Island temporarily while the ship was being overhauled. They were putting bunks out on the deck and loading it with supplies.

There's that famous picture of you taken on the Relief *in the jumpsuit they made for you in Little Baguio.*
Yes.

When did you actually board the ship?
[Reading from notes:] I actually got to San Francisco on November 3, 1944. The ship was being overhauled from November to February. We left for Ulithi on February 13 and arrived there on March 5, 1945. On March 11 a suicide plane crashed on the deck of the *Randolph* (CV-15). On April 1 we invaded Okinawa. The next day the *Relief* arrived along with the hospital ship *Comfort* (AH-6). At 6:10 a single-engine Japanese plane crossed her bow at about five miles, made a ten-degree turn and approached the *Relief* and *Comfort* from bow on. The destroyer *Wickes* (DD-578), on picket duty off Okinawa, came to our rescue. As the enemy plane continued straight toward the *Relief*, the destroyer's gunners placed close bursts of antiaircraft fire so near as to rock the enemy's wings. This came just as the aircraft

released a bomb, causing it to fall a few feet wide of the *Relief*. A few hours later, another enemy plane flew over for a few minutes but made no attack. During the day the ship anchored off the invasion beach and deployed to sea at night illuminated like a Christmas tree. On April 10 we went to Saipan with 556 casualties. On April 27 we went to Tinian with 613 casualties.

On April 19 the *Comfort* (AH-6) was attacked by a kamikaze with some loss of life. We alternated with the *Comfort*, taking these patients wherever they were going.

When did you write these notes?
I don't know when I did this.

You were at Okinawa during the invasion. What do you remember about that?
When we stopped retiring out to sea at night all lit up, we would stay where we were anchored, ready to pick up casualties. Every time the kamikazes would come, we would get the alarm over the loudspeaker. They would say "Kamaretta red, make smoke." And then this boat would fill the bay with white smoke so the kamikazes couldn't see.

Did you see any of these kamikaze attacks at Okinawa?
No.

Where did you go from there?
[Reading from notes:] In July we left Saipan for San Pedro Bay, Leyte, and served as a fleet base hospital in the Philippines until the end of the war. August 15 was V-J Day, the day victory over Japan was celebrated, though Japan formally surrendered on September 2, 1945, and that was a day! We had just gone up on deck for a movie when it was announced. And that bay lit up that night like you've never seen. The sky was bright, everybody firing something or another. It was beautiful. I remember standing at the rail with somebody. The person said, "Well, maybe now we can go home." And I

said, "No, I don't think so. I think we have to go get the war prisoners first." I was still thinking about Dr. Carey Smith and Dr. Fraley. So, sure enough, that's what we got orders for.

To pick up the POWS.

[Reading from notes:] So on August 28 we were en route via Okinawa for Dairen, Manchuria, to pick up the prisoners of war. We were escorted by the destroyer escort *McNulty* (DE-581) and the *Eugene Elmore* (DE-686). We picked up a Chinese man and woman. The next day the *Relief* was guided past ten floating mines. One crewmember of the *McNulty* was injured by shrapnel and transferred to the *Relief*, but he died. At 9:18 we docked with no help from anybody. It was not till September 11 that the prisoners come aboard, 753 of them. That was really something.

First of all, music was blaring from the ship and everything was all lighted up. Well, they didn't let them come right aboard. They had to be deloused first—fumigated and then given showers. Then they came aboard at 8:50. I remember the supply officer who was in charge of food came to me and said that the senior medical officer was going to give them sandwiches and I said, "Listen, if you can't give them a steak dinner and ice cream or something, we ought to be ashamed of ourselves." They would stand in line waiting from one meal to the next, and they ate bread. God, they ate bread! The men were up on the Sick Officers Quarters. The galley was in the middle and my office was to the left of it. Because all the bread and butter were on my desk, they reached in to get bread and butter, then with their trays they would go through the galley to load up, and then go out to their bunks.

Those guys must have been in terrible condition.

No, not really, and I'll tell you why. The POWs had to come down to the docks from Mukden by train, but the Japanese had blown up the rails. And so there were food drops to the men. So, they didn't look too bad.

Dr. Fraley and Dr. Carey Smith were with that group?

Yes. In fact, we had one army doctor who came ahead of them. I packed a box for Dr. Fraley and Dr. Smith—candy bars and oranges, and I don't know what else—for the doctor to take back to them.

So it must have been quite a reunion.

Oh, yes, it was. So many of the 753 people we brought out were the ones who started as the American defenders of Bataan and Corregidor.

You brought them back all the way to San Francisco?

No. We put them ashore in Okinawa. In fact, when we came into Okinawa, we couldn't land because of a typhoon, and we had to go out to sea again. That was on September 12. We came in on the eighteenth and disembarked the prisoners. I don't know how they came home from there.

Did you make another run then?

No. [Reading from notes:] On the twenty-sixth we were under way for Taku, China, and arrived on September 30, where we provided medical facilities for the 1st Marine Division, assigned to occupation duty in north China. We continued there until October 24, and then we were ordered to evacuate patients to the west coast of the United States. We picked up our patients at Tsingtao on November 1 and 2, and more at Okinawa on November 5 and 8. We then went to Guam to pick up more on November 13 and 14, and then sailed for San Francisco with 361 passengers and 386 patients. We arrived on November 30, 1945.

That was your last run on the Relief?

Yes. I was relieved when I got back. The *Relief* made only one more trip to Japan, and then she was decommissioned at Norfolk Naval Shipyard on May 11, 1946, and sold for scrap on March 23, 1948.

Where did you go after you came back to San Francisco?

I went to Brooklyn, New York. I was there a short time when I requested occupational therapy school, and it was granted. So I went to the Philadelphia School of Occupational Therapy. It was, I think, an eighteen-month course. I was then assigned to the Naval Hospital in Houston, Texas, and was there about a year when they transferred the hospital to the Veterans Administration. From there I went to Long Beach, California. I was there for about a year, and then that hospital was transferred to the Veterans Administration. I was also at Camp Pendleton and Newport.

Did you ever run into the other Philippine nurses during that later part of your career?

I was in California after I retired, and I think I saw Helen Gorzalanski. When I was in Philadelphia, one of the doctors told me that Mary Chapman had died. The first time I saw Dorothy Still was after I retired and had gone out to San Diego for a Defenders of Bataan and Corregidor convention. One of the nurses I had worked with in Texas had a cookout and that's where I saw Dorothy. I never saw Edwina Todd or Bertha Evans, or Goldia O'Haver. I had written to Bertha when they first got back and I did get a reply. Helen Gorzalanski Hunter died in December 1971. Mary Chapman Hayes died in 1970. Nobody knows what happened to Eldene Page. And then on Guam, you had Marion Olds as chief nurse and Leona Jackson, and Doris Yetter; she's in California.

She's still around?

As far as I know.

PART II: KOREA

I WILL MAKE SURE YOU MAKE IT
Harold Heilman
1950–1951

My name is Harold Heilman. My stepfather, Richard J. Hempel, served as a marine in Korea in 1950 and 1951. I do not know what rank he was or what company or platoon he served with. However, I do know his story.

He didn't speak often of the war or his involvement in it. I was a child at the time, but I remember him talking to his friends about the war on occasion. I listened on the outside of the circle, trying to fathom all the things they talked about.

What I do remember was that Dad's platoon was one of the first to "hit the beach" in Korea that year. He said, "The noise from the gunfire and explosions was incredible."

His platoon entered a firefight that led to Dad getting wounded. A mortar round exploded nearby, and he and his best friend were seriously wounded. Shrapnel struck several parts of Dad's body. One piece severed an artery in his leg. He believed as he saw the blood gushing that he would die there with his best friend.

Then out of nowhere, a medic appeared and began working on him, all the while assuring him that he wouldn't leave him, and that he would be there to make sure Dad "made it." That medic saved my stepfather's life. I don't know what that man's name was, and I don't know if Dad ever did either. But that medic became a hero to me as I listened to Dad tell his story, because the medic saved the man that would eventually become the stepdad who raised me. I know today my life would not have been as full or as happy if I had never known my stepdad.

For that, I am truly grateful. And to that medic, I have to say, "Semper fi."

I OWE MY LIFE TO A CORPSMAN
Corporal Jerry T. Jolly
June 1951

*Corporal Jolly served in the 1st Platoon of H Company, 1st
Marines, 1st Marine Division from 1950 to 1951.*

It happened on a beautiful, sunshiny day in June 1951. Our unit
fought in the Hanchun-ni area of Korea near the 38th Parallel, the
line of demarcation between North and South Korea.

The North Koreans had begun making a big push all along
that line. We had to hold it. Everyone knew the importance of
it. A major incursion into the south would be devastating to the
war and plans.

Our company plugged a hole in the line. A small knoll separated
us from the North Koreans. On our side, we hurled grenades over
the knoll, just feet away, at the enemy, killing many. The North
Koreans threw grenades over at us and many of the marines picked
them up and whipped them back. Several [marines] were shot and
wounded, but we inflicted more casualties than we took.

Everyone worked to gain better positions on the hill. At one
point, I pulled the pin on a grenade, stood, and got ready to throw.
We had four seconds on a normal grenade, so I counted, "One, two,"

and pitched it over the hill. A North Korean officer lay there, and when we charged over the hill later, I found him with his head blown off from my grenade.

One of the tricks we used to narrow our aim at the enemy was for a marine to stand briefly and draw fire. Since the North Koreans weren't very [good] marksmen, it was usually a pretty safe thing to do. One of my squad members, Tom Johnson, stood. Everyone zeroed in on where the North Koreans were hidden, but this time someone shot true. Johnson took a bullet through the right shoulder. A corpsman ran over to take care of him, but the fight wore on, with neither side making any big gains.

The hill was steep, and with our squad leader sitting down in front of us, a couple of us stood to get a better look. Another grenade was slung over the knoll. I hollered out, "Grenade!" It fell between our squad leader's legs. He tried to pick it up, but it kept falling out of his hand. I dove for the ground. The squad leader lay back against the hill and the grenade went off, taking off both legs. It appeared to me this fight was going badly, but that was not a question for me to consider. We continued on, lobbing more grenades and trying to gain a better position.

Many about me were wounded and hurt, but we suddenly got orders to charge over the hill. I got up and began running, but no returning fire stopped us. When we reached the top, we saw that the North Koreans were gone. I spotted the North Korean officer lying on the ground without his head, the one I thought my grenade had killed. We searched him and I found a picture of his family in his pocket. Until that time, I thought of the North Koreans only as the enemy, not as real human beings. But seeing his family, I realized this was a man just like me, a family man, a person with a heart and soul, hopes and fears, just like me. It was a real moment of revelation, and I think ever after that I could never think of these people as just the enemy, as less than human, as nonentities, but as people who had loving families back home, too. It struck me hard, and I knew that thought and feeling would make it more difficult for me to fight as [hard as] I had been to date.

It was then we were told, after this long fight on this hill, to pull back. A lot of guys were very angry about it, but the command explained that we'd taken one hill too many and we needed to get back to our lines. Knowing the reason we had to pull back made it a little easier.

As we wound our way hurriedly down the hill, taking what cover we could, I heard a sharp, exploding sound and spun around. Landing on all fours, stunned, I looked up and spotted blood squirting from an artery in my neck that I would later learn was my carotid artery, the most important artery taking blood to your brain. I knew instantly I had only seconds of consciousness left, and only a few more moments to live.

I tried to yell for a corpsman, but my words came out as a whisper. The shrapnel had also damaged my vocal chords. Struggling to remain conscious, I tried to find the source of the blood. A corpsman had been sitting in a foxhole in front of me. I was hit right on the edge of the foxhole. He looked up and found me on the ground.

It was then I felt him grab my neck and pinch off the artery. He rolled me over and I saw it was the corpsman. I whispered, "Don't let go." He looked into my eyes and said words I can never forget: "I won't let go, Jolly." He told me later, that in those first seconds, the carotid artery will pop out of your neck and spurt. You have only two seconds or so to stop the flow, push it back into the neck and pinch it off. He did it all that fast.

Stretcher bearers arrived, and as they trundled me down the hill, [the corpsman] held me the whole way, pinching off the artery. He told me he was very nervous about letting go, since he'd have to somehow tie it off so I could be taken to the aid station.

At the bottom of the hill, they put me in an EVAC jeep. Several of my buddies saw me on the jeep, covered in blood, and I heard them say I was dead, but the corpsman was able to tie off the carotid. Finished with me, he hurried off up the hill to help more wounded men.

The jeep took me to an aid station. There, the navy doctors took over. They worked all night trying to stop the bleeding inside my chest, because they'd now discovered I also had a chest wound. At times, I would gain consciousness just long enough to hear a clicking sound and then feel the steaming blood burst out of my rib cage.

I lost eight pints of blood from my wounds. The navy doctor, an American of German descent with the name Dent, kept notes as he worked on me. In his notes, over and over again he wrote that he feared I would die because of the loss of so much blood and because they couldn't find where it [was leaking] from. For some time they replaced blood at two different areas on my body.

At the end of Dent's notes, one day I found the words, "The boy will live, the blood has stopped flowing." I spent six months in the Corpus Christi Naval Hospital recuperating and waiting for my voice to return.

I knew I owed my life to the young corpsman who knew exactly what to do at the moment he saw that blood squirting from my neck and stayed with me all the way to the aid station. For many years, I felt overwhelmingly grateful to the navy doctors who worked on me that night and over the next few days.

Years later, I met Chuck Wright when he gave a talk at the Navy League about the Medical Memorial. I thought Chuck might be able to help me find this corpsman and thank him. I walked up to Chuck and told him my story. He said he'd help.

Both of us began searching through the Internet and Chuck even traveled to Washington, D.C., and asked around. We had no information about the corpsman, other than when he'd served in Korea. Chuck soon found out about the H-3-1 Association. That was Howe Company, 3rd Battalion, 1st Regiment. They were having a reunion. Since I had been in that outfit, Chuck thought they might have the names of the corpsmen from the unit.

I went to the reunion and they gave me a list of the men who were in my platoon between May and June of 1951. Twelve men were still alive. When I got home, I wrote letters to each of them, asking if they remembered me and if they knew the corpsman who attended to me. Kurt Oberscheven was one of them. Many of the men wrote back, but Kurt wrote too, and said he remembered the incident. He had been the corpsman who stopped the blood from my carotid artery.

I called him on the phone and, after introductions, told him, "I really appreciate you saving my life."

He said, "I was just doing my job, Jerry."

We shed many tears about it.

I told Chuck, and he made arrangements for us to fly up to Spokane, Washington, to meet Kurt. On November 15, 2003, we were reunited. We performed a ceremony for Kurt, honoring him for saving my life, with the Navy League, Marine Corps League, our family, his friends and family, and also the mayor of Spokane in attendance. My family and I presented Kurt with a bronze statue of a corpsman working on a fallen marine. There were so many tears, it was hard for any of us to say anything, but I said to Chuck later, "This was the most satisfying achievement I've ever accomplished in my life."

Today, I talk to Kurt at least once a month.

EX-MARINE HELPS FELLOW
KOREAN WAR VET WIN MEDAL
Kathy Bush
September 1951

The following article appeared in the Grand Rapids Press, *September 28, 1998.*

Sal Naimo spent nearly a half-century searching for the man who could prove he deserved a Purple Heart for wounds he suffered in the Korean War. Last month, the Florida retiree finally found him—in Comstock Park.

Armed only with a blurry photograph of the marine he called "Doc" pinching his cheek, Naimo placed a long-distance call to Tom Ambrose, who had treated his injuries on a Korean battlefield in 1951. Ambrose didn't remember the voice, but when the photograph arrived in the mail, he didn't waste any time calling Naimo back.

"I said, 'Thank you, Lord,'" Naimo, 68, of Sarasota, Florida, recalled. "You have answered my prayer."

Naimo, a retired fire chief originally from Jamestown, N.J., was a marine corporal when he suffered a shrapnel wound while serving in Korea in 1951. After a second injury in December 1951, he was honorably discharged in June 1952. But he didn't get what he thought he deserved, a Purple Heart Medal, awarded to soldiers wounded in combat.

The Navy Department had no record of Naimo's wounds. Officials told him he needed to find the corpsman who treated his wounds or two witnesses to the injury. So the search began. Naimo placed newspaper ads, checked military records, and in recent years surfed the Internet. In the end, the vast connections of cyberspace provided the critical link.

While searching the net, Naimo got a tip from the Association of FMF [full name: Association of FMF Combat Medical Personnel]. Combat medical personnel said that the man he was looking for might be Ambrose.

Encouraged, he picked up the phone August 17 to contact Ambrose, who was a Fleet Marine hospital corpsman attached to Howe Company, 3rd Battalion, 5th Marine Regiment, serving in Korea from July 1951 to June 1952.

It was the job of the corpsmen to retrieve marines injured in the field and assess and tag their injuries, explained Ambrose, who was stationed with Naimo's marine platoon on the front lines.

"You bandaged them up as best you could, and then went on to the next one," recalled Ambrose, 67. "Then they were sent to the battalion aid station."

After the war, Ambrose, a Detroit native, studied speech, radio, and television during the 1950s at Michigan State University. He then pursued a career as a disc jockey and a freelance announcer, actor, and model, moving to Comstock Park in 1963 with his wife, Charlotte.

Naimo's call gave Ambrose one of the most poignant roles of his career—that of long-lost combat buddy.

"This guy called and said, 'I have a picture of who I think is Doc Ambrose,' that's what they called me," said Ambrose, who didn't remember Naimo at first. "You just wonder how many of them really survived, who made it back."

A few days later, Ambrose received a letter and a picture of Naimo with a soldier jokingly pinching his cheek. There was no doubt—it was Ambrose.

So he called Naimo and told him, "This is Tom Ambrose, and that's me pinching you on the cheek." Ambrose recalled that Naimo was injured in September 1951 on the front lines near what was called the Punch Bowl.

"When we were in this engagement, we got hit with machine gun crossfire, and then they hit us with mortar," Ambrose recalled. "He (Naimo) got hit by mortar fire."

Ambrose recently wrote a letter confirming Naimo's injuries.

"While on duty with Howe Company, 3rd Battalion, 5th Marine Regiment in Korea, September, 1951, I, Thomas J. Ambrose, HM3, a navy corpsman, did in fact treat Salvatore Naimo for a shrapnel wound to the front of his leg, sustained while under enemy fire during combat engagement," Ambrose wrote.

Naimo will now receive the Purple Heart he has longed for.

And, Ambrose and Naimo are planning a reunion in December, when Ambrose and his wife visit their son, Tom, during his graduation from the University of Central Florida in Orlando.

"I'm really going to celebrate when I see (Ambrose)," said Naimo. "I've been looking for him for 46 years."

IN THE PUNCH BOWL
Thomas Joseph Ambrose
1951–1952

The following anecdote is from "Doc Ambrose" himself.

While serving as a corpsman (hospitalman third class) with the Fleet Marine Force in Korea near the area called the Punch Bowl, I recall one of the lighter moments:

We were being hit by a mortar barrage, and we proceeded to duck into our bunkers. In a few moments I heard a marine scream, which normally would indicate someone was hit. As I popped out of my bunker, I saw a marine across a hole holding up what was left of a can of peaches. He seemed to be at a point of tears since he had just swapped for that premium can of fruit. It was a little tough to give first aid to the can of peaches. Thankfully, that time no individual was hit.

PATIENT AND RESCUER
John F. Fenwick Jr.
October 1951

Sergeant John F. Fenwick Jr. is lucky to be alive. It was a misty morning in October 1951 when his patrol, on a mission to capture a prisoner to interrogate, accidentally collided with a superior force of North Koreans. Most of his marine comrades perished in the savage firefight that followed. The exchange left Fenwick bleeding and near death as at least four machine gun bullets ripped through his body. As a hospital corpsman pulled him to safety, the corpsman too, was severely wounded. Despite his own injuries, he did what corpsmen are trained to do: protect their patient, administer first aid, and see the wounded marine safely to the rear. The story does not end there. It took a skilled navy surgeon and his team many hours to repair the damage and put Sergeant Fenwick on the long road to recovery. He recalls that unforgettable time nearly fifty years ago when navy medicine came to his rescue.

It was October 5, 1951. I'll never forget it. I was a machine gun squad leader in Company A, 1st Battalion, 5th Marines. The captain called us in and told us he wanted a prisoner to interrogate. He told me that I was short and would be relieved in two days, and then would probably be going home. He then said I didn't have to go on this patrol. We had a brand-new green lieutenant who had only been with us two days. I figured I had better go because he'd need some advice. A good officer will listen to his NCOs who have had some combat experience.

We were northeast of Inje, close enough to the ocean to have naval gunfire from the battleship *Missouri* supporting us. We went out before dawn. The lieutenant disobeyed orders and got us all fouled up. We ended up in the enemy lines. You could hear them talking and starting their cooking fires. It was scary as hell. We then pulled off that hill and instead of going right back to our lines and taking advantage of the heavy ground mist, the lieutenant said, "Let's try that other hill." The platoon sergeant, who outranked me, kept telling him we had to get back to our lines. "You can't make a name for yourself out here, because you're gonna get everybody killed," he said.

The mist burned off and we were exposed out there, almost as if someone had turned on a light switch. Then one shot rang out. Lyons, a friend of mine, was at the point and got one right between the eyes. We were only fifty yards from some of their bunkers, maybe even closer than that.

We ran behind a nearby knoll but they continued to fire at us from two sides and the front. We got the machine gun set up on the knoll and began to answer fire. But it was like taking a motorcycle and running up against a tractor trailer. We had literally hundreds of them shooting at us. The whole platoon got shot to pieces. The lieutenant then called in supporting artillery and when they registered in, the shells landed right on top of us on that hill. I guess he fouled that up too.

Finally they corrected, and the shells began landing on enemy lines.

By then, just about all of us were hit. Our machine gun was out of ammunition and was knocked out. I was the last guy alive on that knoll. I saw some of the enemy trying to work their way around our right and get behind the hill where all our wounded were. Our corps-man, Glen Snowden, was treating the wounded below. So I grabbed an MI off the dead kid who was lying beside me and I raised myself up to shoot at the infiltrators trying to outflank us. That's when I got it—four hits in the body—machine gun bullets. We were so close I could feel the muzzle blasts. It was a Russian light machine gun. When you were in Korea a while, you could tell every weapon firing at you.

It's indescribable the way it felt. It was like being run over by a train. I was bent backward. It turned out that two of the bullets grazed my spine. I could feel everything except for my legs. It was horrible pain.

Doc Snowden came running up and grabbed me. He checked everyone else real quick but saw that everybody else up there was dead. He said, "I've gotcha; I'll get you out of here. As he started pulling me, the machine gun got him twice in his left shoulder and knocked him right down the hill. He scrambled right back up again. One arm was hanging down and useless, but he still grabbed me and got me out of the line of fire.

He began telling the unwounded riflemen how to dress guys' wounds. I had an artery severed on my left flank, and the exit wound in my back was the size of a fist. Apparently the bullets had hit my ammo belt and tumbled. Some hit my small intestine and I eventually lost eighteen feet of my small intestine, which is nothing. If they had hit my large intestine, that would have really been bad.

Snowden dragged me out of there with one hand. When I finally got back to our lines, I told the guys to write him up for a Silver Star, at least. He saved a lot of guys besides me. He grabbed a jacket off one of the dead marines and rolled it up into a ball. He was all out of battle dressings. He then put it against that hole in my back and took another jacket and tied it around me real tight, like a compress, to stop the flow of blood. And that's what saved me. He had some morphine syrettes left, and told a BAR (Browning Automatic Rifle) man, Corporal Richard Baiocchi to give me some morphine. Baiocchi then said, "Here, I'll give you some morphine."

He stuck the morphine syrette in my shoulder. I was looking into his face and saying "Thank you, pal," or something like that, and just then a machine gun burst hit him right in the jaw and sheared it off. His whole chin was gone. He also took six rounds between his wrist and elbow.

Unfortunately, I didn't get the morphine because as he got hit, the impact snapped the needle off while it was still in my arm. The pain was unbelievable. It was like someone had opened me up with a scalpel without any anesthetic and then filled up my insides with red hot embers. I forgot to mention that when Doc Snowden grabbed me, two more bullets got me in my left upper arm. One was a graze and the other went through the flesh real quick.

After Snowden got through with me, two marines grabbed each of my feet and dragged me facedown back through the rice paddies. They were under such fire that they had to run, dragging me on my face through all that muck. It's a wonder I didn't drown.

When we got back a ways they put me on a litter. I really thought I had died because when we got halfway back, I felt warm and peaceful. All the pain left me. While I lay facedown on the stretcher, I saw a real bright orange hazy light but there was no pain. I remember thinking, "Thank God, it's all over."

Right about then there was an air strike on the enemy position and that pulled me out of it. It really made me feel good thinking that the ones who got me were getting fried with napalm.

When we got back to our own lines I was still conscious. A helicopter landing pad had been dug out on the reverse slope of a hill. They didn't think I was going to make it. Only one chopper could be brought in there at a time, and there was only room for two wounded on each. There were so many wounded, they could only take the ones who had a chance of making it. Some of them went down the hill on stretchers.

A chief corpsman told one of the surgeons to look at me. I remember he had a big walrus moustache. "Sir, you had better look at this man. It looks like his color's still good." The doctor then said,

"Take one of them out of the basket and put him in." The other guy was a rifleman from Texas. He had four bullet wounds stitched across his chest. He was in one basket and I was in the other. He didn't make it. And he had three kids at home.

They flew us back to Easy Med. I remember being very scared. They put me on a slanted wooden table and cut all my clothes off. Then they put a catheter in my penis. The surgeon's name was Lieutenant j.g. Howard Sirak. He really put me at ease. And then with his finger he drew a line on my stomach and said they were going to make a small incision. That was no small incision. They ended up cracking me open—a laparotomy! Dr. Sirak later told me they put 837 sutures in me. Rather than making a colostomy, they kept snipping perforated small intestines off and resewing the ends together.

When I woke up, it was night. I only saw one Coleman lantern at one end of the tent. I was lying on the cot and felt all warm and sticky on one side. I had dysentery once and thought I had messed myself. I called a corpsman, who came to me with the lantern. He said, "Don't worry; it's just blood." I had blood and plasma going in both feet and both arms—IVs. There was a catheter tube coming out of my nose, another tube in my penis, and another coming from the exit wound in my back.

The next morning both surgeons and Doc Snowden came in. He was all patched up with his arm in a sling. They told me they had to get me up on my feet. I said, "You've gotta be kidding me. I'm dyin' here. I can't feel my legs; I can't move."

He said, "When we got in there we found three vertebrae that were just grazed by the bullet and were fractured. But you have what they call spinal shock. The feeling will return. We can practically guarantee it."

But I was really worried I was going to be a paraplegic. But for the grace of God, another eighth of an inch, I would have been. The bullets had tumbled their way through me. Then I got peritonitis real bad. I remember by the time I got to the hospital ship I was getting

500 ccs of penicillin a day. It could have been fragments of filthy clothing going through with the bullets, or stuff from the rice paddy, and of course perforated intestines. I remember the day I got hit I hadn't had anything to eat, just a sip of water. The surgeon said that if I'd had food in my intestines that probably would have been it. I wouldn't have survived.

From there they sent us to the hospital ship—the *Consolation*. They put us in slings and hoisted us aboard. It looked great. It was snow white—unbelievable! The ward was so clean and beautiful. I think it was even air-conditioned. I didn't want to get in that bunk. It was so clean and I was so filthy. There was all the crud from the front, plus blood caked all over me. I hadn't been in a bed in over a year. When they got me all cleaned up and in a bunk, gave me all my shots, and changed my dressings, the nurse, a lieutenant commander, said, "How would you like to have some ice cream?"

I couldn't believe it. I thought, "I'll really fool her." So I said, "Yeah, I'd love to have some."

And she said, "What flavor?"

And knowing they wouldn't have it, I said, "Rocky fudge."

And then she said, "Coming right up, Sarge."

Then I completely lost it. I grabbed her hand and kissed it. Then I broke down crying. "You navy nurses are really angels of mercy."

Postscript: Sergeant Fenwick incurred six machine gun bullet wounds. Two were through-and-through wounds of the left upper arm, with no permanent bone, muscle, or nerve damage. Four were through-and-through wounds of the left flank, involving the small intestine, left pelvis, left iliac crest, and iliac joint, which was destroyed by direct trauma. There was a large exit wound in the lower left back adherent to the lumbar spine with fractures of L-3, L-4, and L-5. The left artery was severed. Two of the gunshot wounds were "keyhole" rounds, which tumbled, causing large muscle and tissue damage and loss in the lumbar spine region. After a long hospitalization, he was declared permanently disabled and was discharged from the Marine Corps in 1954. He currently resides in Delaware. When asked about his care then and since, "I told my wife that if anything happens to me, the hell with these civilian or VA hospitals. Get me over to Bethesda National Naval Medical Center. I have the highest regard in the world for navy medicine."

PART III: VIETNAM

DOC WES
COLONEL HARVEY C. "BARNEY" BARNUM, USMC (RET.)

Lieutenant Harvey C. Barnum of H-2-9, 3rd Marine Division, was awarded the Medal of Honor for gallant conduct during the December 1965 Battle of Ky Phu, South Vietnam. The following is his account of Corpsman Wesley Berrard's heroic actions during that battle.

Petty Officer First Class Wesley Berrard was the senior corpsman assigned to H-2-9 [Hotel Company, 2nd Battalion, 9th Marines], 3rd Marine Division, RVN, in December 1965. On December 18, Hotel Company acted as rear guard for a battalion movement out of the Khe Sanh Mountains. This happened during Operation Harvest Moon.

Working as the forward observer attached to H-2-9, I hiked along with the command element, reporting any indication of enemy action. About 10 a.m., we heard shooting coming from the head of the column. Seconds later, all hell broke loose.

The entire battalion, in a column of companies, had been ambushed by a well-entrenched NVA force. The initial round that triggered the ambush on our part [of the column], Hotel Company, was a B-40 rocket that hit the company commander, Captain Paul Gormley, mortally wounding him and killing his radio operator. Needless to say, I hit the deck, as intense fire shredded our up front lines, mainly focused on the command element.

When I looked up to get a bead on the enemy, and then behind me to see what our column was fighting, the first thing I noticed was Doc Wes running forward through intense small arms and machine gun fire in an attempt to reach the CO. Doc went down three times as bullets slammed into his body, but he didn't give up; he pushed himself up each time and continued to move toward the wounded captain.

Reaching the command group, he administered aid to Captain Gormley, placing himself between the captain and the enemy as he stooped over the captain's body. He was hit for a fourth and fifth time while shielding and administering aid to the CO.

As things intensified, I knew I had to move, so I jumped up and ran back to where Doc and the CO were. I quickly picked up Captain Gormley, and then carried him to a concealed position. Then I returned to help Doc get back to cover. As I helped him stagger to the rear, he was shot for a sixth time.

Over the next few hours, the firefight raging around him, Doc, with six gunshot wounds in his body and in tremendous pain, continued to give aid to the wounded while refusing morphine for his own pain. When the medevac helicopters arrived to evacuate the dead and wounded, Doc even refused to go aboard until all the wounded had been evacuated. When we finally began pushing back the enemy, I assured Doc everyone had been accounted for and [was] on board the helos. He then allowed us to place him on the last evac helo. As we loaded him aboard, he was shot for the seventh time.

I have only rarely witnessed a man as shot up as Wesley Berrard . . . taking action the way he did. His courage and professional dedication to his men under fire were an inspiration to all in Hotel Company, and we talked about him frequently. His acts of bravery and personal concern for his marines have left an indelible mark on my memory. His aid and thoughtful action despite his serious wounds were instrumental in H-2-9 defeating the enemy that surrounded us. We were able eventually to break out from the ambush site and reach safety. Doc's clearheaded help gave us the manpower and the spirit to do that. Doc Wes was a true marine and a true team player.

PROFILE IN COURAGE:
DON "DOC" RION
MAJOR GENERAL JOHN H. ADMIRE, USMC (RET.)
December 1966

The author of the following essay was an infantry platoon leader in Company M, 3rd Battalion, 3rd Marines, in Vietnam from 1966 to 1967.

The more imminent combat becomes, the more important it is for marines (or combatants) to believe in the competence and dedication of their corpsmen and medical personnel who serve with them. Countless studies from the World Wars to the present day have demonstrated that once combat begins, belief in the medical competence of military doctors and corpsmen is a significant factor in maintaining high morale.

I saw this in action in Vietnam in December 1966. I was a young infantry platoon leader at the time. Our company led a combat patrol into the mountainous jungle. As the lead platoon, my men crossed the river to secure the far side for the rest of the company.

Without warning, a tremendous explosion shattered the jungle stillness. We later learned it was a pair of bombs dropped by our own aircraft. The blast erupted at least one hundred meters to my rear, but I immediately saw when my platoon returned to the river crossing site that serious devastation had wounded and killed a number of marines and corpsmen. The bomb had instantly killed about ten marines at the river's edge. Another twenty-plus lay strewn about, badly wounded, many of them fatally.

We were in disbelief, but we'd learned to expect the unexpected. While we understood the immediate need to assist those wounded and killed, we also knew that we were vulnerable to attack. We had to remain focused as we concurrently assisted the wounded [and] continued to secure the site from an enemy attack amid the carnage and confusion.

One of the wounded, the company's senior navy medical corpsman, Don "Doc" Rion, took action. Doc Rion was a corpsman of average physical stature, but his psychological state was absolutely incredible. He'd demonstrated exceptional courage and compassion in past battles while administering medical aid to wounded marines. But now he had to demonstrate that same courage and compassion regarding his own wounds.

Both of his legs had been blown off, severed above each knee. He lay on the muddy riverbank in shock and agony, undoubtedly struggling to assess his own needs and life as well as he could while deciding how he could help others. Months of experience in combat and service, though, spun him into action. He had the presence of mind to perform some of the most selfless acts of courage I've ever witnessed. He probably knew from his medical experience that he would neither survive his wounds nor the day, but he saw his final minutes as an opportunity to do what he did best: save the lives of his marines.

In the chaos and confusion of the situation, Doc seemed organized and calm. I would never presume to believe that he'd resigned himself to his fate, but I do believe that he was resolute in his determination to help others. His pain prevented much talk, but he effectively motioned and pantomimed his intentions. The marines listened as Doc guided them in caring for and treating the severely wounded. There was nothing else that needed to be said. Doc's selfless attitude and actions spoke volumes.

Doc grabbed handfuls of mud and plastered his stumps to slow the bleeding. This gave him extra precious minutes to remain conscious and to commit himself to others. That done, he directed the marine survivors about what to do for the other casualties. He did this primarily by motions and gestures, as he was becoming too weak to actively assist. Yet, his actions were an incredible motivation to the morale of the wounded and those caring for them. When someone offered to bandage Doc's wounds, Doc replied there was no time. He instinctively knew that bandages would probably do no good. His mind was set on saving others. He undoubtedly had a desire to live, but his life was of less concern to him than the lives of others for whom he'd taken an oath to serve.

Doc Rion dragged himself from marine to marine thinking quickly and clearly about what needed to be done. He was stoic; he was solemn. His verbal comments were minimal, but his relentless actions represented the maximum. On that battlefield, marines close to death respected him and relied upon him as the lone person who could save them from that death.

Doc Rion died as he was medevaced to a hospital. I know of no last words. I sense, however, that he knew he'd done his duty, because he died rather peacefully considering the devastation that characterized his final minutes. Through his efforts, I hope he knew in death that he had lived just long enough to save many others from their wounds.

Later, a report from the hospital in the rear was given to the command. It said that four or five marines had been saved from certain death because of the immediate on-scene care they received under Doc's orders.

Doc Rion sacrificed his life so that others could live. He honored the motto of the Medical Corps as well as the marine code, "Semper fi"—"Always faithful." His actions will forever remind me of the essence of courage and compassion.

THE RAZORBACK
RODNEY "DOC" HARDIN
December 10, 1966

Rod Hardin was a hospital corpsman in Mike Company, 3rd Battalion, 3rd Marines, from 1966 to 1967. His account deals with a particularly bloody operation around the Razorback, a granite ridge just south of the Demilitarized Zone.

This is about a friendly fire bombing incident December 10, 1966, behind the Razorback. We had incurred a number of casualties the night before and had carried the dead and wounded for more than ten hours to a bomb crater where the choppers could get in for medevac the next morning. When the medevac choppers were loaded, they threw off a stretcher and a lot of medical supplies to make room and lighten their load. Some of the marines were going to trash the supplies and the stretcher and make them useless for the enemy. I nixed that idea and picked up the stretcher myself after having the nearby marines line up and each take a gauze bandage and tuck it in his shirt or cartridge belt. By this time a lot of men no longer had backpacks, having discarded and abandoned them in the firefight the night before.

We moved from the crater toward the Song Cam Lo River shortly afterward. When the column reached the river's edge,

Lieutenant Edmund Hale's third platoon formed a semicircular perimeter through which the second platoon and Captain Larry Green's command unit passed, fording the chest-deep river on a rope strung from bank to bank by a capable grunt swimmer. My recollection is that the river was about thirty yards [wide], but others have told me it was narrower. As Ken Snider and Joe McDavid were leaving the river on the far side, two Phantom F-4s passed over us heading downriver.

The column came to a stop, and since I was carrying a backpack and the heavy stretcher, I squatted down for a breather. Just as I was lowering [myself] behind a large boulder on the steep river bank, the Phantoms returned from downstream, and one unloaded two snake-eye bombs into the very center of the perimeter formed by the third platoon and the remaining members of the command unit who were waiting at the river's edge to cross on the rope. The rope was severed by the blasts. Fourteen men were badly injured, Hale and Simon Waiau being among them. Thirteen others were killed outright. Three of the wounded subsequently died on the choppers. Four of the casualties on our side of the river were corpsmen, including Docs Paul Blakely and Don Rion, our senior and assistant senior corpsmen, and Doc John Grachtrup, who was within feet of me in the column and died in my arms.

The last casualty I treated was Doc Gary Pedersen, who had only been with us about a month and lost his left arm. I found him almost in the river, covered with mud. It was the combination of my battle dressing and the mud that sealed his pneumothorax and kept his lungs from further collapse. It was purely by chance that this occurred. I was unaware of the extent of his chest wound.

The other corpsmen, Mike Brown, Sam Leathes, and Lynn Thomas, had made it to safety on the other side of the river with the second platoon, command, and the FOs [forward observers] and could not get back. That left me as the only uninjured corpsman to take care of 27 casualties. Doc Blakely dressed his own wounds.

Doc Rion attempted to get up on two stubs of legs severed at midthigh in an effort to aid the wounded around him, and realizing his limitations, proceeded to give instructions to marines, including Wayne Gardin, as to how to help the victims. Rion was the second living casualty I got to after leaving Grachtrup. Don Rion was less concerned about his amputated legs than the prospect that he might have lost his means of procreation. I assured him that he would be home making babies in no time, taking a feigned swing at his obviously bare and still intact "jewels," all the time knowing that he didn't have much of a chance. I applied tourniquets to what was left of his legs, and a chopper dropped a basket to the position right where Rion was, almost hitting me. John Breckenridge and I immediately loaded Don in the basket and sent him up on the winch.

Proper mass-casualty triage would have had me treat and medevac the more viable wounded first. Don clearly was a "Green Weenie" with little or no hope for survival. The circumstances were such that we needed to get Don out of the way so we could send up others to the hovering chopper. The chopper pilot was clipping the tree tops as it was and had little room for maneuvering. So, in fact, Don went up first. He was obviously in severe oligemic shock, but still alive and aware when I saw him last. He was the only man we sent to that chopper, and he was the first man medevaced. All of our other casualties and equipment went out on two Chinooks, which came in almost before we finished getting wounds bandaged. They hovered right at the river's edge, half over the water, and we loaded in everyone as quickly as we could. When the men in the rear at Dong Ha unloaded these casualties, they found grenades with the spoons half disengaged still attached to the remains of dead marines. It was a wonder these didn't tragically explode on the choppers, or worse yet, while the bodies were being loaded and unloaded. The futility of this accident comes back to haunt me every time I hear about friendly fire incidents in the Middle East or elsewhere today. The movie *Hamburger Hill* is as close to a depiction of this kind of tragedy as any I have seen, when the men reach the top of the hill, only to be strafed and killed by their own gunships.

I realized when I started moving among the casualties still alive that a lot of them already had battle dressings in place. It turned out that the corporal, [machine gunner] Robert Schley, had turned to and functioned as another corpsman. He had voluntarily picked up the slack and probably saved several lives in the process. I did not see him after that friendly fire incident. I was sure he carried an M60 on that operation. If I had known at the time that I could have put him in for a commendation, I certainly would have. He went above and beyond in all of his actions that day.

WHERE I BELONGED
Milton C. Cochran
October 1967

A t the time I enlisted in the navy, Vietnam had begun to claim a large percentage of newspaper space. However, I liked doing my job as a stateside corpsman, taking care of navy dependents, and would have been perfectly willing to play out my remaining time in the service right where I was, doing what I was doing.

But one chilly October morning after returning from an ambulance run, my CO told me to pack my gear and prepare to be assimilated into the Marine Corps. The Marine Corps? I didn't join the Marine Corps— I joined the navy, for crying out loud! My howls for some sort of clarification fell on deaf ears, and so, after intensive field training, I flew off to join the 2nd Battalion of the 1st Marine Division, operating somewhere near Da Nang, South Vietnam. With trepidation that bordered on terror, I joined H Company.

Sending a marine to join other marines is one thing. Marines share an intangible element that binds them together as if by high-tensile steel. But I was a navy man. I didn't belong. Would the marines accept me? Would I be ostracized during my entire tour? Would I understand anything they talked about concerning everyday operations?

Things went more smoothly than I had anticipated. I did my job, and the marines did theirs. If something happened, those marines knew I crouched just a few feet away. I realized this vigilance made my comrades feel better, because they told me so. It never dawned on me that this bonding process worked both ways.

I had been with Hotel Company of the 2nd Battalion, 1st Marine Division, [H-2-1 in Marine Corps talk] for three or four months when something occurred that made it clear to me that something more than simple duty was going on. Up until then, I had never missed a patrol, an all-night ambush, or a full-scale operation. I participated in everything a corpsman is expected to be part of. As a matter of fact, because of a chronic shortage of corpsmen, I sometimes had to turn around and go back out on a patrol after just returning from one.

On this particular day, we set out on an operation in the middle of nowhere. It was our second day in the field, and for those two days I had been sick as a dog. I threw up and fought hot-and-cold sweats. To make matters worse, I couldn't go fifty feet without ducking behind a tree to relieve myself. Yet through all this, I never missed even one patrol.

The dawn of the third day broke hot, without a whisper of moving air. I felt sicker than ever. My stomach was so tender I couldn't even strap on my cartridge belt, and my medical supply bag felt as though it weighed one hundred pounds. As my squad saddled up for the day's patrol, I informed the sergeant that I just couldn't go out with them. He wasn't surprised. He had already noticed how sick I had been over the past few days.

Even today in 1999, thirty-three years later, I can still see them leaving the relative safety of the compound. As always, Jones, our point man, led the way. His cheerful demeanor never betrayed the fact that he was the most vulnerable soldier in the squad. If his always-alert eyes ever missed even one little glint of trip wire, if he lost his concentration for a millisecond, he would be the first to pay the price—probably with his life.

And I can still see Knowles, our radioman, falling in at his usual place in the middle of the squad. You couldn't miss Knowles. Since he was the tallest man in the company, with his radio antenna projecting another three feet above his head, the enemy certainly found Knowles an easy target (a fact not entirely lost on Knowles himself). I customarily walked directly behind Knowles.

As the patrol wound its way along a narrow path, becoming smaller and smaller with every step, I felt my first twinge of guilt. The minute I lost sight of my squad, I began to pace.

I had come to the marines an untried entity, but these men had placed their faith in me from day one. From the very beginning I was "Doc." I acted as orthopedic surgeon, neurologist, podiatrist, and psychologist all rolled into one. I knew all along that their respect would be earned in one way only: by my being with them on the trail or in the midst of a firefight, ready to respond to that most dreaded of all battlefield sounds, the call "Corpsman Up!" As time passed, I became more troubled. "How in the hell could I have let them go without me?" I kept repeating to myself.

Time seemed to stand still. I listened for any ominous sound that might indicate the squad had run into trouble. I made up my mind that if I heard anything—rifle fire, an explosion of any kind—I would get to them, alone and running all the way if I had to.

Everyone in camp got heartily sick and tired of me sulking around, moaning that "my squad should be back by now." I believed that if they did not return soon, I was going to have a nervous breakdown. And if something were to happen to any of those guys, especially if I wasn't there to lend medical assistance, I would spend the rest of my life in a padded room. I promised myself right there and then that I would never miss another patrol—no matter what. As long as I could breathe, I'd be there.

Finally, after what seemed an eternity, I caught a glimpse of Jones leading the squad back home. After a quick head count to make certain everyone was there, I welcomed them back. From that day forward, I never missed another patrol—until the day a few months later when I tripped a land mine, ending my tour of duty in Vietnam. Because of my injuries, I spent years recuperating in several military and VA hospitals. I was discharged from the service totally and permanently disabled.

It's common knowledge that marines feel better having a corpsman at their side in the field. Take it from me, a corpsman would rather be out in the field with the people he cares most about than anyplace else. The men of Hotel Company will remain with me forever. I remember all of them—the men whose wounds were known only to them, and the men who, even though horribly wounded, resisted leaving when told they had to be medevaced out of the field. And I can never forget those comrades who, despite my best efforts, died in my arms.

Because of the circumstances under which I left Hotel Company—a group of men whose character and stamina I feel will never be matched—I never said goodbye, nor did I tell them of my pride in serving with them.

I am doing that now.

Above all, I want them to know: I was right where I belonged.

CORPSMAN UP!
JAMES TOLOMAY
1966–1967

Jim Tolomay, who hails from North Bend, Pennsylvania, writes that his three sons "have asked me numerous times about my military service. It was impossible for me to do this because I would become too emotional and could not continue. Therefore, I decided to write about my experience, and even this was a difficult task. I am not doing this for personal recognition. I do not consider myself a hero. I was scared as hell and was just about mentally broken when my tour was over. My purpose is to have the public understand what we all went through during this time."

When I was a senior in high school in 1964, it was a time of excitement, knowing I was going to graduate. It was also a time of great concern, since the Vietnam War and the draft were going strong.

After graduation, I went for my preinduction physical. I knew it was only a matter of time before I would have to go into the service. In December 1965 I enlisted in the navy and had my first plane ride, to Great Lakes, Illinois. The other recruits and I were loaded into a bus, and we headed for the navy base. It was late at night when we arrived, and [we were] herded into a barracks that was so crowded we had a tough time finding an empty bunk.

The next day we were assigned to a company to begin our training. Those weeks ahead were tough for me, since I had never been away from home for any amount of time before. Toward the end of my training, I was given a test to help me decide what field I should strike for. I was told by a first-class petty officer that I should try for something clerical or mechanical. He mentioned different things to me but stressed the need for corpsmen. I had never heard of a corpsman before, and I asked what they did. He said that they worked in hospitals, and that the navy had a great demand for corpsmen.

I decided that this might be good duty. I signed on the dotted line, and I was on my way to Corps School after a little leave at home. This school was also at Great Lakes, and I learned to like the training. I was surprised, since, before entering the navy, I couldn't stand to even walk through a hospital: the smell used to upset me.

When I finished the training, I was sent home for leave before going to my next duty station. While on leave, the girl I was dating—and eventually married—was going to nurses' training. We discussed the different types of training we had gone through. She was surprised as to what they had taught me, for my training was only for a few months, as compared to her three years. While in Corps School, I found out that some of us would eventually be assigned to the Fleet Marines. The first-class petty officer who originally mentioned the Corps to me failed to tell me about the marines. I wonder if this may have been an oversight on his part?

My first duty station after school was the hospital at Annapolis, Maryland. This place was great, and it wasn't that far from home. I could usually make it home for a weekend, if I didn't have the duty. The Naval Academy was close to the hospital, so I got to see some of the midshipmen and some of the academy.

I was stationed at the hospital for about four months, before I received orders that I was going with the Fleet Marines to Vietnam.

I reported to Camp Lejeune, North Carolina, for thirty days of training. We had mock battles, night patrol, a tour through a simulated Vietnamese village, complete with booby traps. We had classroom instruction on Vietnamese culture, the M14 rifle, and the .45-caliber pistol.

My training being complete, I made one final phone call home, to tell my parents that I was on my way. We flew from Cherry Point, North Carolina, to Denver, Seattle, Tokyo, Okinawa, and on to Da Nang. This was all on civilian aircraft. When flying into Da Nang, the stewardess told us to stay away from the windows, because of sniper fire.

We got on the ground in Da Nang. A jeep came roaring up to our position, and a marine captain got out and asked for volunteers for recon. At the time I wasn't sure what recon was, and I figured I'd better not volunteer for something I didn't know anything about. It really paid off for me. I found out later that recon corpsmen didn't last too long.

A short time later I was assigned to B Company, 1st Battalion, 1st Marine Division. When I arrived, B Company was security for the Da Nang airstrip. I just caught the end of this good duty, then our company was sent to an area south of Da Nang. On the way to Hoi An, I saw the marines just finishing a sweep through a rice paddy, and they had a Viet Cong with half his arm shot off. Now I knew where the action was. When I arrived at the battalion area at Hoi An, I was assigned to a hut with other corpsmen, near the air station. The first night there, I heard a noise outside. The door opened, and two corpsmen carried a dead marine in and placed him on the floor. They told me he was killed in a truck accident on the way back from Da Nang. They covered him and told me a helicopter was coming from Da Nang to pick him up in the morning. Needless to say, I didn't sleep that night.

The next day I finished getting all of my gear, such as a flak jacket, K-Bar [knife], .45-caliber pistol, and helmet. That night we were told we were going on an ambush. We left the battalion after dark, and were given a password. I don't remember how far we went out into the sand dunes, but we set up our ambush along a trail. I was with our squad leader, because I was new and he wanted to keep an eye on me. We sat in the dark for about an hour, and we never heard a sound except for some monks chanting at a nearby temple. A few minutes later there was an explosion in front of our position. I was hit in the right hand. I couldn't tell how bad it was, because it was dark. My hand was numb. The marines opened fire, and everything was quiet again. We returned to the battalion area, and I learned later that a grenade was thrown at our position. I had a minor wound with a small piece of shrapnel in my hand.

From November 1966 until October 1967, I participated in numerous routine patrols and major operations, each lasting a few weeks. Many times we were flown out in the middle of the night by helicopter, not knowing where we were going. Among the operations I was on were Operations Independence, Stone, Lafayette, Canyon, Union I, Union II, Calhoun, Pike, and Medina.

Some things stick in my mind. Once, when we were in a firefight, a marine about to fire his bazooka into the tree line turned to check the rear of the weapon and saw me, in direct line of the backblast. "Doc," he yelled, "get the hell out of there." Needless to say, I did.

Another time, we were dug in for the night. I was in a foxhole with our squad leader and radioman. On our watch, we were to call the lieutenant every half-hour to tell him of our situation. The time was approximately 2300 [hours] on my watch. I was about to call, when there was noise and movement about fifteen feet in front of our position. The next morning the lieutenant gave me hell for not reporting and accused me of sleeping. When I had a chance to explain the situation, he seemed to accept my explanation.

Another time on patrol, we were hit with enemy fire coming right down the trail at us. We hit the deck, and a couple of marines rolled into the ditch next to the trail, to try and get lower and away from the enemy rifle fire. When they did this, they tripped grenades that were wired. One marine was killed and another had a sucking chest wound. I crawled to him and placed a piece of plastic tape over the wound to seal it and placed him on his wounded side.

While this was going on, our sergeant was disarming the rest of the wired grenades. I went crazy on him, yelling at him, thinking he was going to get himself killed or injure more people. He knew what he was doing. The dead and wounded were flown out in about fifteen minutes. The marines later found an M14 rifle roped to a tree, and it was pointed down the trail at us. The marines had been issued the new M16 rifles, and they were afraid the old M14 rifles would get into the wrong hands. This one sure did.

I rarely saw the enemy my entire tour, although we engaged them quite often. Occasionally we would see a few Viet Cong on patrol or some that were captured. I wasn't impressed with them.

When our battalion moved north, it was big time with the North Vietnamese regulars. When they engaged, they meant business. These individuals seemed bigger than the farmers down south. I saw about fifteen NVA running along a tree line after they broke off a firefight [with] us, and they were running in step, with their weapons all held the same way. I pointed them out to the lieutenant, and he called in an air strike.

"Corpsman up!" At that cry, I was on the move. They hit us while we were going through a cemetery, and the marines dove behind tombstones for cover. The areas near the tombstones were mined. I ran through the minefield to my commanding officer, his radioman, and other marines [who had been hit]. A gunnery sergeant helped me. I don't know how he managed, because [back at the aid station] he would just about faint when I'd give him a standard injection.

We moved from marine to marine, taking care of them as best we could, one at a time. I started IVs, gave morphine, applied bandages and tourniquets. While we were doing this, the small arms fire was very bad. I don't know why we weren't hit. When the choppers arrived to take the wounded out, they couldn't land for a while because of the intense enemy fire.

The next event was the taking of prisoners. They were not the young kids like we had seen around Da Nang. These were men intent on wiping us off the face of the earth. After the enemy fire and minefield we had just been through, these prisoners were in for a hard time from the marines. I feel to this day that they were too easy on them.

In Vietnam we had free-fire zones, no-fire zones, and pacified areas. This is like being in a fight with one hand tied behind your back. One village that we passed through on patrol was usually a problem. When the residents would disappear, we knew we were in for a bad time—either sniper fire or mines. The last blow was a mine, and it took the life of a marine. Our lieutenant finally had all he could take. Pacified or not, the village was leveled, burned to the ground.

The monsoon seasons were cold and rainy. We spent day after day on patrol, wet and cold. During the day I would tolerate being wet, because we were usually on the move, and you could keep warm. The worst time was sitting out in the middle of the night on ambush in the wind and rain, the cold rain running in a stream down the middle of your back. I shook so bad the enemy could have heard me twenty-five yards away.

There were times during the day when we would take a break, build a fire, and dry our boots and put on dry socks.

Corpsmen were issued .45-caliber automatic pistols. A couple of corpsmen in our battalion also carried rifles and participated in firefights with the enemy. They were also decorated with Silver Stars and Bronze Stars. Both were killed in action. I stayed with carrying the pistol and attending to wounded marines and staying alive. These corpsmen reminded me of a newly arrived marine assigned to our company. He was eighteen years old and not long out of boot camp. He was gung ho and wanted to kick the enemy's ass. On his first patrol, he came upon a dead Viet Cong and kicked the body. It was booby-trapped with grenades. The young marine was killed instantly.

Whenever I went on patrol, I always thought about getting shot or hurt in some way. My biggest fear was tramping on a land mine.

One time a tank ran over a land mine, which blew a track off. A couple of the marines on board had broken eardrums from the blast. One marine with a cigarette in his mouth blew smoke out his ears.

In the field we ate C rations. Once, when we were near a Vietnamese village, I traded C rations for six eggs and two loaves of Vietnamese bread. As I was scrambling eggs, it wasn't long before marines were standing around me waiting for their share.

One time my mother sent me a jar of peanut butter. It arrived the day we were ordered to go on an operation. I had a full field pack, because we didn't know how long we would be gone. I had that jar of peanut butter for about a day. During a long sweep on a hot day, I had to lighten my load. One of the marines saw this and yelled, "Things must be getting bad. Doc threw his peanut butter away."

On another operation through an abandoned village, a marine saw a cobra and started swinging a machete at it, trying to kill it. Every time he would get close, the cobra would rise up with his hood flared, ready to strike. I told the marine if he got bit, it was instant medevac, as there was nothing I could do for him.

On the completion of a long operation, nothing looked or sounded better than choppers coming in to fly us out of the area. One time, as they tried to land, a water buffalo charged. After another attempt to land, marines had to shoot it before the choppers could take us out.

I can recall an operation in which we were digging in for the night, and our squad was to be the listening post on the outside of the perimeter. After dark our squad leader got us together, and we left the perimeter for our position for the L.P. I was with him and another marine. We lay there in the pitch dark, and we were watching for some movement. In an instant, a figure appeared approximately twenty feet in front of us, and a shot was fired. The only thing I would see was the muzzle blast.

The squad leader stood up and sprayed the area with his rifle. It was over in a minute, and then it was quiet. The marine next to me didn't move. I tried to shake him. He was dead, shot right in the head, right through the helmet. The squad leader and I dragged him through rice paddies and under fences and down trails to get him back inside our perimeter. The next morning a medevac chopper coming in to get the dead marine out started to receive single-shot gunfire. Our squad made our way through a rice paddy to the tree line where the shots were fired. The shooter disappeared. The only thing we found were empty .50-caliber casings and tunnels all over. Marine engineers moved in and blew up the tunnels.

A few times while on patrol, I had the opportunity to care for some of the Vietnamese people, usually children. But the problem was they needed medical attention on a regular basis, and many times I never got to their village again.

While on routine patrols from the battalion area, I was with B Company. On large operations, our company was involved with other companies in sweeps of large areas. On these patrols and operations, I treated things such as headaches, stomach cramps, and trench foot to more serious wounds such as [punji] stick wounds (bamboo or steel stakes run through marines' feet), gunshot wounds, and shrapnel wounds. Wounds from land mines were the worst. The results were usually traumatic amputations. Whenever I heard the call, "Corpsman up," I never knew what I was going to find.

On one operation, our unit was pinned down for more than four hours. The enemy was in trees and shooting marines in the head. We were too far away from our battalion area for artillery support, so air support was called in. It was not long before two Phantom jets arrived, blazing away at the tree line in front of our position. On the second pass the jets dropped napalm on the tree line. This suppressed the enemy and we were able to regroup. Only a handful of us were left in B Company.

I remember one marine who was shot in the leg, to my left, and he kept crawling to the rear trying to make it to the dike behind me, so he could get over it for cover. He made it just about to the dike when he was shot in the head and killed. I was the only corpsman not killed or wounded in my company. We were so torn up, the colonel of our battalion radioed our captain and said he wanted to send what was left of us to the rear, at the battalion area. Our captain said we wanted to finish the operation.

We spent the night with dead marines lying all around us, covered with ponchos. The next day we had trouble getting our dead out by helicopter because of the intense enemy fire, but they were all eventually taken out. My nerves were so shot, I went to pieces when a [twig] snapped. During the many times of very serious injuries to my fellow marines, I was very close to my breaking point. I can recall while on patrol at the lead of our column, a marine stepped on a land mine and was cut in half. The corpsman at the head of the patrol called for me and was determined to save him. The marine was dead, his eyes were fixed, and there was no pulse. I walked to the rear of the column and got sick. I thought I was going to lose my mind. I tried to think of home, friends, anything to put the immediate situation out of my mind. I regained my composure only because of the mental toughness of the marines around me and their support.

I lost some good friends on that operation. One I'll never forget. He was from Loudon, Tennessee. He and I had a lot in common. We exchanged many hunting and fishing stories.

When the operation was over, I was trained to do lab work at the battalion aid station. My patrol duty was limited now. I only had to replace one corpsman, who was wounded in the middle of an operation. This only lasted for a few days, then I was flown out by helicopter back to the battalion area again. I wasn't back at the battalion very long when we received word that the whole battalion was moving north toward the DMZ. I was down to thirty days to go before I was rotated back to the States, and now we were going to go north. I was sick.

The battalion packed, and we went to Da Nang to be flown from Da Nang to Dong Ha, south of the DMZ. Upon arriving, we were told to exit the plane in a hurry because this airstrip had been receiving artillery fire from the north. We were then trucked south near Quang Tri City. We were security for an airstrip being built.

I was out on patrol again, and I just knew I was not going to make it. We did not engage the enemy while on patrol, but they did manage one last mortar attack in the middle of the night, on November 13, 1967. It just happened to be a Friday.

I was sound asleep in my cot when I heard the first round explode. I ran from the tent and dove into a foxhole. Other marines piled in on top of me, trying to get cover from the mortar fire. We made it through the night with no injuries.

My orders were finally cut, and I was headed to Dong Ha to fly to Da Nang, then to Okinawa. While waiting in Okinawa, I started to relive some of my experiences of the battles in the middle of the night. I would wake up in a cold sweat and in a panic.

I boarded a military plane on Okinawa for Hawaii. Next I flew to California and took a commercial plane home to Pennsylvania.

Upon arrival, I called my dad and asked him to drive to Pittsburgh to pick me up. I didn't want to fly anymore. It was about a four-hour drive for him. He said, "I'm on my way." It didn't seem too long before my dad, mother, and future wife arrived at the airport. Things were happening too fast for me. One minute I was in the middle of getting shot at, and then next minute I was with my family. I was not able to eat or relax.

Over a ten-year period, I relived each firefight while trying to put the whole experience out of my mind. As each year passed, I was able to handle things a little better. I will never forget the things I went through, but I did learn how to accept the things that happened, and that life goes on.

My biggest battle was within myself. You ask yourself why you were spared, and so many of your friends with the same hopes and dreams were not spared.

In 1987, I went to see the Vietnam Memorial. I approached slowly, not wanting to really go because of fear of bringing back bad memories. I looked at the names with a sickening feeling, thinking of the terrible waste of human life. I tried to find the name of my marine friend from Loudon, Tennessee. I only knew his nickname and last name. I couldn't find the name. I went to talk to a Park Service attendant and found that I couldn't talk. I started to cry. The attendant said it was okay and that she would wait. I regained my composure and gave her what little information I could remember. She found the name for me. I looked at the name and felt a calm come over me with peace of mind I hadn't felt in years. It was finally all behind me.

A MEDIC WAS THERE
Norman L. Humes Jr.
December 1967

It happened during my second tour in Vietnam. The first one, last-ing eighteen months, had been incident free, and I received no wounds. On the second round, I was assigned to B Company, 326th Engineers, with the 101st Airborne Division. I was a staff sergeant stationed at Phu Bai, Vietnam. As squad leader, I was assigned to re-inforce bunkers on Alpha 4 and Charlie Deuce, two jumping-off points in the Demilitarized Zone (DMZ).

It was December, and I had just arrived in November after a six-month stay at Fort Campbell, Kentucky, the home of the 101st Airborne Division. My squad started at Alpha 4, moving dirt over to the command bunker and shoring up the berms. It was no different from any other day in the life of a combat engineer, or so I thought.

About four hours into the project, I heard a whistle and then an explosion. I yelled to my squad to get under cover as mortar shells began falling like rain. Sometime in the midst of the explosions, I suddenly felt a burning sensation in my right leg just above the kneecap. I looked down and saw instantly my leg was bleeding badly from a shrapnel wound.

I made sure all my men had reached safety, but when I tried to get up and run for my own life, I couldn't. It was then that "Doc" Ray Thatcher suddenly showed up as if out of nowhere. A tall, lean guy from Arkansas, he spoke with a heavy southern drawl and told me to hang in there, he knew what he was doing.

He grabbed me by my arm and almost yanked it out of its socket, trying to get it around his shoulders so he could drag me. He proceeded to half-shove and half-drag me to the bunker. Every member of my squad had made it to the bunker ahead of me, so that seemed to lessen the pain I was fighting. Doc worked on me, saying I was one lucky "mother" that I wasn't dead, but he assured me now he could take care of me right. He commented, "Looks like Purple Heart time."

I hardly paid attention, I was in so much pain. Doc pulled the shrapnel out of the wound and then stitched it up, dressing it like any professional doctor might do. He then gave me a "bee sting" of morphine, and I returned to our area to see what had happened to the command center. Fifty-three mortar rounds had made a helluva mess of the whole thing, so we returned to restore it. I fought the sensation of my leg stiffening.

I have been witness to many combat injuries, and it seemed medics appeared out of nowhere each time to stick with the wounded fellow and get him to safety. I don't know how those guys did it. But I'm grateful to Doc Thatcher, the medic who was there when I needed him.

DOC BALLARD SAVED MY LIFE
James DeCarlo
March 1, 1968

First Sergeant James L. DeCarlo (Ret.) was in the U.S. Marine Corps from 1966 to 1991. During the Vietnam War he served in Headquarters Platoon, M Company, 1st Marines, 1st Division.

After being in Vietnam for eight months, we learned that the 26th Marines were getting hit hard at Khe Sanh. Half of our company was sent to reinforce them. We climbed off the choppers and ran for the nearest foxhole. I landed on top of two other marines and a navy corpsman named Doc Ballard. As we got into firing position, I heard someone yell, "Corpsman up!" Without hesitation Doc was on his way to where he was needed.

By nightfall, the fighting had slowed down. I was receiving instructions for a night patrol at the command bunker. As I relayed the instructions to my men, Doc asked if we were the marines going out on patrol and if we brought any corpsmen with us? Since nobody knew how long we would be at Khe Sanh, our corpsmen were back at our company headquarters. Doc grabbed his medical kit and said, "I guess I'm going with you." He had been working hard all day and was badly in need of rest, so I asked for another corpsman. He said he was the only corpsman available and that he always went on patrols in case someone got wounded and needed his help.

Later that night, we were taking a break when all of a sudden the sky lit up as bright as the Fourth of July. We had walked into an ambush. Tracers and hand grenades were flying everywhere when from out of nowhere the Viet Cong were on top of us. They were firing at us and slashing us with their bayonets. I felt a sharp pain cut through my side and I fell to the ground. My radio operator saw me get hit, he yelled for the corpsman. Within seconds Doc was at my side demanding that I lie still so that he could stop the bleeding.

When all the firing stopped, Doc was scouting the men that weren't hurt, asking what their blood type was. Men began to donate their blood for me as Doc started a blood transfusion. His concern was that there would be enough blood to keep me alive until dawn so that he could call in a medevac chopper to get us all out of there. Doc continued to keep me alive on the chopper until we arrived at the hospital, where the doctors took over. At the hospital when I regained consciousness I asked the nurse if she knew where Doc was. She replied that he had returned to his unit. I will always remember the night Doc Ballard saved my life. That was March 1, 1968.

NSA STATION HOSPITAL, DA NANG:
A PERSONAL HISTORY
JAMES CHAFFEE
Da Nang, 1967–1969

In May 1999, I was in the colonial style bar of the Furama Hotel, on the beach right next to the site of the old China Beach USO. A loud and boorish former army nurse anesthetist, claiming to have served with an army hospital in the Central Highlands, was yammering in my face. I had told him about NSA Station Hospital, which had been located a few miles south of this place, near the foot of the Marble Mountains, and that in our triage we had no nurses; in fact, there were almost no nurse anesthetists at the hospital. He essentially called me a liar, told me the navy was run by nurse anesthetists, then berated the whole unit, saying we could have provided better service had we staffed with nurses. Cutting him short, I insulted him, the army, and nurses in general, and he left the bar.

I had the privilege and good fortune of serving as a hospital corpsman at the Naval Support Activity Station Hospital, NSAH for short, near Da Nang from October 1967 until June 1969. Situated on the sandy strip on the east side of the Han River across from Da Nang, between the Han River and the South China Sea, the hospital sat near the Marble Mountains just to the south. These five outcroppings dominated our landscape. Part of a cluster of bases just north of the Marble Mountains, where the Da Nang perimeter ended, the hospital was across the Main Supply Road from MAG-16, a Marine Corps helicopter base on the beach. The hospital was on the west side of the road, the river behind it. On the south perimeter was a Seabee camp, and south of that, at the foot of the northernmost inland Marble Mountain, Nui Tho Son, was a dump.

Across the road from the dump, on the beach at the foot of the big Marble Mountain, Nui Thuy Son (now generally referred to as the Marble Mountain in tourist guides), was the 5th Special Forces HQ. North of that was a POW compound, and then came MAG-16. Farther north the road to the China Beach USO exited the main road. On the hospital's north perimeter was a pagoda attached to the hamlet on the east perimeter, between the hospital and the river.

The original hospital was destroyed just before its completion in an attack in October 1965, when MAG-16 was overrun. When I arrived, the rebuilt facility was a major field hospital with air conditioned wards and operating rooms, and a large staff of specialists in areas ranging from tropical medicine and thoracic surgery to neurosurgery.

I was temporarily assigned to Receiving II, part sick bay and part outpatient clinic. Receiving I was next door, just off the chopper pad. This was the triage, where I would spend the bulk of my tour. But first I was permanently assigned to the same sort of medical ward as my previous assignment at Naval Hospital Yokosuka, Japan.

The Vietnam War would explode with the 1968 Tet Offensive, coinciding with my 21st birthday, just around the corner from my arrival. The year would be the most devastating of the war in terms of American casualties.

Hospital corpsmen at the Yokosuka Hospital received orders to Vietnam in groups. The previous groups had been sent to the Fleet Marine Force (FMF). A substantial number would not return alive. Our future seemed ominous as we received fresh combat casualties at the Yokosuka facility. The seriously wounded were evacuated as soon as possible, and Yokosuka was one of the stops. We saw some of those we had served with returned, or read their names in the *Stars and Stripes*.

Surprise was the general response to the orders for NSA Station Hospital. Some of us were unhappy, having looked forward to serving with the "grunts," but most were puzzled, with no idea of the facility's location or its mission. I didn't understand that mission until recently.

What I did learn came after years of reflection on haunting personal experiences. The sense of mission at the hospital was intense, and our performance as corpsmen went beyond what anyone could expect from our twelve weeks of formal training. Those without the stamina to handle the daily stress sometimes made irrational decisions to get out.

When I got to NSAH the wards were staffed with a handful of nurses who went about their typical supervisory roles in starched white uniforms. I am not certain when they arrived, but I believe it was about the time I did, as there were corpsmen working the wards who had preceded the nurses. My recollection is that they were all at least lieutenant in rank. Most were lieutenant commanders, and they were led by a Commander Cannon, who later made captain.

Their role was largely symbolic, and there was an uneasy truce between the nurses and the doctors, with the corpsmen often caught between. The areas of the hospital where corpsmen had most freedom in treating patients—Receiving I and II—were not staffed by nurses, and in fact they almost never made an appearance in either place. There was one nurse in the OR however, who may have been an anesthetist. She was always in scrub greens when we saw her, usually in the pre-op area just above the triage across from X-ray. But I am getting ahead of myself.

Staffing for the large, open bay wards was short. A single night corpsman often had to handle a ward with sixty or more patients. I remember making the temperature rounds at 0200 with a ward full of malaria patients, giving them the standard drill when their fevers were excessive: Sit under a cold shower and drink a recycled IV bottle full of cold water after swallowing five aspirins. Sometimes short on bedside manner, the wards provided real hot chow, showers and flushing toilets, and excellent medical care. To the grunt marines, the majority of our patients, they were paradise. Transferring from the wards was nearly impossible; it took an insubordinate encounter with a nurse to get me out.

Weekly sick call for Vietnamese civilians at the orphanage near China Beach, a few miles north of us, provided rare civilian exposure. The whole area was off limits, particularly the city of Da Nang. The doctor who organized these Medical Civic Action Program (MEDCAP) visits, a firm believer in winning hearts and minds, was senior physician on my ward. A lieutenant commander, he was also a devout Catholic, and I assume he had made contact with the Vietnamese Catholic nuns who ran the orphanage through the church. Their convent was next door to the orphanage.

The doctor had full trust in the ability of his corpsmen to treat what they could and refer what they could not, so we had total freedom on these visits, broadening our range of experience in disease and exposing us to the appalling local conditions. All this temporarily ended when the Tet Offensive made the MEDCAP visits too dangerous.

The medical ward was intensely busy, overflowing with malaria patients, most with *P. Falciparum*, which can lead to cerebral malaria and death. The lab was overextended, and samples sometimes sat unexamined for days. A lab tech showed me how to stain a slide with a drop of blood and examine it for parasites. The doctor had a microscope in his office and let me use it, encouraging me to take blood when a patient began the cycle of chills and fever. The nurse did not think I should be doing this duty, since it was the responsibility of the lab. This led to a shouting match one day, when I was examining a slide instead of mopping the floor.

In essence, I was fired. I was pretty certain that a captain's mast would be next, but I believe the doctor interceded, and I was transferred to Receiving I. That was a blessing.

The whole area of Receiving I was intimidating. Large signs in the covered outdoor triage beside the main walkway shouted in red OFF LIMITS and USE OF CAMERAS PROHIBITED. This was the first overflow triage. The main Receiving I Quonset hut was beside it.

At the door to the main Receiving I Quonset, OFF LIMITS greeted you in red. Inside, the place was all business. On either side of the hut near the rounded ceiling, pipes extended the length of the room suspending bottles of Ringer's lactate, ready for use. Pairs of sawhorses lined both sides below the pipes, pulled out to support stretchers bearing casualties as they arrived. Jelkos and other equipment filled bins along the walls, and there was a cardiac board that doubled as a pinochle table. Along the front wall, near the door, hung Unit Ones, flak jackets, and helmets. The wall was lined with suction machines for chest tubes. The floor was concrete, stained brownish red, a drain in the center. The room was incredibly cold, and a sickly green light from bare overhead fluorescent tubes bathed the grayish interior.

A complement of corpsmen and stretcher bearers was assigned to Receiving I. The bearers, mainly Seabees or seamen from the fleet, kept the triage clean, moved the patients from the chopper to triage to X-ray and pre-op, and sometimes performed medical procedures we taught them in case we were overloaded.

Receiving I corpsmen were at the top of the pecking order, a special bunch. But you had to prove yourself to them, and they doubted new personnel, especially those who had served on a medical ward. It was mostly learning by doing, and the corpsmen who had served on surgery wards had a shorter learning curve.

Only one MD oversaw Receiving I, a junior surgeon on twenty-four-hour duty, who called the duty senior physician if surgery was required. There were no nurses, no anesthetists, and the doctor was not on premises until needed. When casualties arrived, the corpsmen assessed the situation and began IVs using 14-gauge Jelkos, usually one in each arm and one in the neck. Corpsmen did venous cutdowns, inserted chest tubes, inserted tracheal tubes, and performed other emergency surgery. They were also on call to handle emergency ambulance runs and occasional chopper runs.

There were three triage areas. The main one was the Quonset hut. The first open unit outside was set up much as the Quonset hut: sawhorses below pipes suspending bottles of Ringer's lactate ready for use. As with the Quonset, vials of emergency fluids, mainly for those in cardiac arrest, were also at hand, but I believe the sterile pack with chest knife was only kept inside.

Across the walkway, the third area was full of sawhorses and pipes, but IVs were not kept ready. This was for overflow mass casualties, and when it was needed personnel from other areas, like the laundry or pharmacy, would be brought in to set up IVs and help haul stretchers. During the Tet Offensive the three areas were full most of the time, and stretchers were lined upon the walkway waiting for X-ray or to get into the pre-op, which was also full.

The drill with wounded was pretty well worked out. Corpsmen and stretcher bearers ran to meet the chopper, with the bearers carrying empty stretchers in case the wounded were just stacked up on the floor of the chopper—which often happened, particularly with the CH-46—or if the wounded were on tanks or amtracks. Sometimes a CH-46 would be so loaded with wounded you wondered why those on the bottom didn't suffocate.

The wounded were brought in and their stretchers placed on the sawhorses. Clothes and boots were cut off, blood pressure and pulse taken and written on bare chests in black marker. Three IVs with Ringer's lactate were started and blood taken for cross-matching at the blood bank, though sometimes this was difficult when the pressure was so low blood wouldn't flow. I remember seeing corpsmen do femoral sticks to find blood and start an IV, only later to have to restart it when pressure would build up enough to force the blood back into the bottle, having hit the artery and not the vein. Sometimes what flowed from wounds was Ringer's lactate. Seeing chests with 0/0 and 0 in black marker was not uncommon.

Circling above the room in my mind's eye, I can see the concrete floor covered with clotting blood like great mounds of liver, naked young men littering the room on blood-stained green stretchers while desperate corpsmen shout at them: "Make a fist!" starting an IV in the forearm, or "Bear down like you have to take a shit," trying to force up the vein in the neck.

During mortar and rocket attacks we stayed with the wounded and hoped for the best. There were enough hits on the chopper pad just outside the triage that the Seabees finally put up a pair of blockades of stacked railroad ties in front of the main Quonset hut and the outdoor triage to stop shrapnel. Fortunately, none of the triages ever took a direct hit, though wards and an OR did.

After I left, I buried my personal experience, studying mathematics, then working in industry. It was a number of years before I really learned about where I had been and its mission. After three decades ignoring my past, I decided I needed to go back. I searched the web and wrote organizations, but didn't get any information. It seemed the place had been forgotten. Then one day I got a hit; I found the abstract of a paper written by some navy physicians about a study done at the hospital and wrote for a copy of the paper.

Between January and June 1968, a study followed wounded patients from initial resuscitation through final disposition. Part of this study took place during my OWl triage service. The study was shelved for decades. Published in March 1988 in *Military Medicine*, the paper is entitled "Naval Support Activity Hospital, Da Nang, Combat Casualty Study." The authors were Captain B. G. McCaughey, MC, USN; J. Garrick, M.D.; L. C. Carey, M.D.; and J. B. Kelley, B.A. It had remained in the archives of the Naval Medical Research Institute for twenty years, though Dr. Garrick did analyze the data initially and describe the results in a lecture in 1969.

The paper backs up my memory of the personnel staffing the triage-surgical theater. There were three anesthesiologists, and only two nurse anesthetists, and as I told the former army nurse, those two nurses did not work the triage. In fact, on the rare occasion when there was a particularly difficult intubation to be performed (as on one occasion when a child blew open his mouth chewing a blasting cap), an anesthesiologist handled it, but usually the corpsmen did.

The statistics from the study make for interesting comparison. According to *The Vietnam War Almanac*, by Harry G. Summers, a former army infantry colonel, the mortality rate for wounded army personnel was nearly .036, while for marines it was about .028. The NSAH study indicates that the mortality rate at the hospital was about .021, a significant improvement. Even if one includes the number considered DOA at NSAH, the figures are about .027. Of course, many factors affect these figures, only one of which is emergency unit effectiveness, but the fact that the Marine Corps bore the brunt, the fighting in the I Corps—where the enemy was better equipped and trained than in other sectors—seems to indicate that navy corpsmen and physicians who served as medical personnel for the Marine Corps offered better service for their wounded.

A few comments in the study make these numbers even more impressive. "The types of casualties sent to NSAH were not representative of all those occurring in Vietnam, because the NSAH was staffed by a large variety of specialists and thus more capable of handling difficult medical problems." When I talk to marines who served in the area from Chu Lai to Hue, including all the hill country around Da Nang, and such hot spots as An Hoa, many of them remark on the NSA Hospital, particularly those who were wounded. I recall a retired gunnery sergeant, who had spent time with the MPs who provided security for the hospital, saying it was the best emergency hospital in the world at the time. He was probably right. Staffed with experienced and senior medical personnel, the hospital mission was to handle the most difficult cases.

As with most of the hospitals in Vietnam, the bulk of the casualties came directly out of the field without first passing through aid stations. The helicopter made this possible, and it saved an incredible number of lives by shortening the time between being wounded and receiving care. This was also noted in the study: "Combat casualties were generally taken to NSAH via helicopter and without primary definitive care." This can explain how the number of Marine Corps KIA in Vietnam was so much smaller than for the marines in World War II, even though the number of wounded was comparable. In World War II, transit time was generally six to twelve hours, while in Vietnam it was more like two to four hours.

The study does mention that the mean transit time was about five hours, suggesting that there were large outliers affecting this average. The authors wonder whether it might be the result of transfer of casualties from other units, but my experience is closer to that of Dr. Garrick, who recalls the difficulty of getting choppers into hot areas, particularly at night. The Marine Corps was using CH-46s, much larger and slower than the army's Hueys, which were more effective at getting into tight spots. I recall getting huge loads of casualties on '46s who had clearly been lying in the field for some time, covered with mud and leaches, and often dragged out of inaccessible areas on ponchos and sometimes carried on stretchers fashioned from bamboo poles and ponchos. These men were outside the norm of the transit time of two to four hours because of the vicissitudes of combat.

This article showed me clearly what I had known intuitively all those years: NSA Hospital was a special field hospital, staffed with specialists and stocked with all the medical supplies required to be a modern emergency hospital. The spirit of the place was dedicated and proud. We would have been hard pressed to provide better service to our wounded.

Two return trips to Vietnam within the last few years, along with discussions with former marines on the internet, by phone, and in person, have helped me rediscover the special unit where I served, and also perhaps a bit about myself.

It's easy to find the former hospital site. Before you get to the Marble Mountains heading south, you pass a pagoda set back off the road, hidden by trees. This is the Khuy Bach Pagoda, part of the Bac My An Village. The village consists of the My Da, My Thi, and Daman hamlets. The Daman hamlet was on the hospital's rear perimeter, and the Khuy Bach Pagoda was on its northern perimeter.

The village has since spread over the whole area where the hospital once stood. The pagoda sat just outside the concertina, as did the hamlet, and when I first arrived at the hospital there was a little footpath running along the concertina to the hamlet. Later it became more of a dirt road. Now it is paved. Facing the road and the old hospital grounds is a large red building, a museum to what was called Secret Area K20. That was the Viet Cong code name for the Bac My An village, an active area of Viet Cong resistance. Inside the museum is a model of the area, showing the tunnels by the river where VC hid. The former marine "gunny" on security for the hospital told me that they knew about the activities of the village. It is no surprise, since inside the museum is a map detailing the October 1965 attack on MAG-16 in which the hospital was also overrun. However, there is no indication of the hospital on either the map or the model.

Nonetheless, two old pictures of the pagoda, taken from the hospital grounds, hang under the gaze of a statue of Ho Chi Minh. I donated them to the museum on my first trip back. The curator of the museum was very excited by my old pictures, as they had none from that period. I also was able to speak to villagers who remembered the hospital and, in one case, had worked there.

NSA's withdrawal from the area began in May 1969, with the goal of handing over its extensive facilities to the Vietnamese military. The hospital was completely turned over to Vietnamese army control in May 1970, about a year after I left. I learned from the curator of the K20 Museum that it was dismantled some time after that, when the army pulled out of the area. You can still see parts of the hospital in the old part of the hamlet: gate posts of felled telephone poles, cut in half, and concrete walkways cut up into paving stones.

A great irony for me is that it was not until my trips back that I got to know anything about the area. I had been to the village of Binh Ky, birthplace of the author Le Ly Hayslip, in 1969, while on a road sweep with a squad from Golf Company, 2nd Battalion, 5th Marine Regiment. It was part of a sleepover, an invitation from their corpsman and the squad leader, and the closest I ever came to field duty. We spent the night at Tower Three, at the intersection of the Main Supply Road and Binh Ky road, in hostile territory south of the Marble Mountains.

But visits to the city of Da Nang were only made on official business. I made many of these trips, usually at night in ambulances, with wounded or sick civilians or Vietnamese military. Sometimes the trips took us to the civilian hospital downtown, a horrible place with shared beds and animals wandering the open wards. Sometimes the trips took us to the Vietnamese army hospital in Cam Le, where during the day you could see numbers of soldiers and children on crude crutches, amputees.

At night these trips were particularly eerie, the streets deserted. In fact, even in the day you saw no Americans in the crowds of Vietnamese on the streets. The city was off limits to all but a handful of Americans. Those few had to carry special passes allowing them to be in Da Nang. Nearly all of the navy personnel in the Da Nang area lived at the large Tien Sha base, and those who worked in the Da Nang area were transported to and from work in what we termed cattle cars. There were no open apartments you could rent. Any quarters in the area were guarded. There were no bars to visit except those on your base, and at night you stayed on your base unless you were on official business.

This flies in the face of the stories in Hayslip's *When Heaven and Earth Changed Places* and *Child of War, Woman of Peace*, which became the Oliver Stone potboiler *Heaven and Earth*. Hayslip tells of working at a navy hospital in Da Nang city, guarded by Vietnamese military personnel, that catered to Vietnamese civilians.

There was no such hospital. NSA Station Hospital, which she refers to as My Till Hospital, was the navy hospital in the area, and there were never Vietnamese military guarding it while I was there. She claims to have had an affair with a pot-smoking navy corpsman named Red, who had an apartment across the street from the hospital where women came and went at will. Red supposedly tried to force her to work in a strip joint frequented by military personnel. Since Hayslip is writing about the period when I was there, from 1967 until 1969, I have to say that is pure fiction. It may be that something like that came to pass after the navy gave the hospital to the Vietnamese military, as they were withdrawing, but I have yet to meet anyone who can verify it.

We treated numerous Vietnamese civilian and military patients at the hospital. However, Hayslip also claims she was treated at a military hospital as a civilian, in a dependent's clinic. That is far-fetched, since military personnel did not have dependents with them unless the dependents also happened to be working in Vietnam in some capacity like press or Red Cross. We certainly had no dependent units, and treating women was a special problem, since most of the wards were completely open with only a few private rooms and no segregated bathing or toilet facilities. There was no officer's ward, as I recall.

Marriage to Vietnamese nationals was simply not permitted except under very extreme circumstances. One interesting story is that of Duong Van Mai Elliot, author of *The Sacred Willow*, who married an American army sergeant she had gone to college with, while he was working as a translator and she for the Rand Corporation in Saigon. He lost his security clearance as a result.

We could walk or hitchhike the Main Supply Road to China Beach, north of the hospital, during the day, but we were not permitted to enter any buildings along the way. The short road from the Main Supply Road to the China Beach USO went off limits about six months after I arrived, as it bordered a squatter's village we called

Cabbage Patch, harboring young thieves who would steal from those afoot.

For me, one memorable evening on my second return visit was sitting in a restaurant north of the Old American Bridge. Out over the water, eating a hot pot with eel and plenty of seafood, I just looked at the lights on the other side of the river, on the strip that was East Da Nang, and knew this was a formerly forbidden pleasure.

I broke another old taboo when I met a man a few years my junior on the flight to Da Nang from Saigon. He spoke good English and we hit it off when I tried my Vietnamese on him. He could barely control his laughter. He invited me to his home, near the Furama, in what had been Cabbage Patch. He had built it himself, and he worked in a rubber factory as a manager. One night we went to dinner at a seafood restaurant at My Khe, the beach north of China Beach where the 95th Evac Hospital (the subject of the series *China Beach*) had been established some time in early 1969.

Near the northeast intersection of the Main Supply Road and the road to China Beach is a set of government buildings, where the Catholic orphanage had stood. The orphanage has been moved to Hoi An as a government facility, and the only reminder of our old MED-CAPs is the convent, where a handful of Vietnamese Catholic nuns are spending their last days.

At the end of the road to China Beach, near where the China Beach USO had stood, is the Furama Hotel. The Marble Mountains, which had once dominated the skyline, are now hidden behind buildings and billboards. The hospital has been gone for over thirty years now, a place whose physical existence lasted only about four years, but which has lived for decades in memory.

My own memories have lingered, though details have dulled. I recall how one night we got a marine, his neck blasted with shrapnel, with a perfect tracheotomy already performed, the metal tube neatly tucked in between scores of hemostats cutting off the bleeders. His corpsman had accompanied him to the hospital on the chopper to make certain the airway stayed open. The corpsman had been an OR tech who had seen dozens of tracheotomies performed, and besides his Unit One, he also carried a surgical kit. He had performed the surgery by flare light, while under fire, and the doctor on duty was amazed enough that he spread the word and his colleagues came to see the marvel. We put the corpsman up for the night, gave him a bottle of Scotch and some fresh surgical supplies, and he went back the following morning to his duty.

Amid deeper, sometimes painful memories, I also remember taking leeches we had removed from wounded marines to the outdoor triage, injecting them with acetone and lighting them, watching them explode. Thirty years ago wasn't a time I wanted to remember, but now I cherish the memories. I was part of something acting in the world, making a difference at a time when no one wanted to hear about it. That makes it all the more special.

Some time after my second revisit to Vietnam, I found a message posted by a former navy FMF corpsman on the internet. He described our triage and pre-op area from the casualty point of view. I wrote him an e-mail and he responded. We had a discussion by e-mail and he left me a phone number. I called him. He had come through our triage during my tour, though I probably did not work on him. The circumstances are special enough, however, that I believe I remember my good friend Bob Garrison talking about it.

The corpsman had stepped on a booby trap while treating a wounded marine. He sustained the following wounds: traumatic amputation of his left leg below the knee; deep shrapnel wounds to the left thigh; massive shrapnel wounds to the right ankle; multiple shrapnel wounds to the groin, including both testicles, with half the left testicle removed; massive shrapnel wounds to the left arm including a severed radial artery; shrapnel to the right eye, still there. He says he regained consciousness after we got an IV going, yelling at someone to cut the damned leg off, not aware that it was gone until he sat bolt upright and looked down at the mangled remains.

He probably would have died had there not been a Huey gunship in the area that picked him up and got him to us within minutes. He lived. In fact, he has lived a very productive, full life, with a family, a career, and a mission as counselor for a church.

Our conversation was not long, but it moved me. After thirty years I had found someone who lived because of us. It was always in the back of our minds, just how those who were horribly mutilated would consider us, those who had saved them? This former patient and fellow navy hospital corpsman remembers the Station Hospital and was glad we were there.

A DAY IN HELL
Doc Hoppy
South Vietnam, March–June 1969

Doc Hoppy preferred to be remembered by the name he had among the men he served with, rather than his full name.

On April 13th, 1969, we left LZ Alpine, and went north into the mountains. We traveled the same trail that the patrol had traveled when Coker and Playford were killed back on the 24th of March. I remember going by the headless corpse of one of the NVA that had been left at the trailside as a warning to others. The body was very aromatic by this time, and you became aware of its presence long before you saw it. We humped on up the mountain near a stream cascading down. It was really beautiful. At one point, a waterfall cascaded into a large pool, and looked really inviting. However, we kept humping up the hills, over the rocks and vines, and through the trees. My memory is very foggy at this juncture, concerning the events of the next few weeks. We were out there in the bush humping; hills blurred into only more hills, days blurred into weeks.

In latter April and most of May, we humped all over Mutter's Ridge area, I believe. At one point we were sent to run security for a downed helicopter. It was in a forested area, the main rotor mangled from its landing. Our demo guys blew trees down with C-4 explosives, and cleared an area for the repairs to be made, and the chopper to be able to take off once repaired.

It was in this area of operations that the entire company was stricken with dysentery. I made a request to the rear (no pun intended) for bulk (again no pun intended) medications to be helicoptered out to us forthwith. They sent out a mount-out box full of Kaopectate, and numerous other medications. Within a day or two, all seemed to be under control again. It amazes me we did not have more problems with dysentery, considering the sources of our water. We got it from streams, ponds, old rice paddy irrigation ditches, bomb craters . . . wherever we could. Some of it had creatures in it, and some was so black you couldn't see through it.

The company was back on its feet, so to speak, and off we went to our next objective. Some days later, the company was to be choppered up to Dong Ha Mountain, for a few days, and then to Qua Viet for a brief R&R. The night before we were picked up, good ol' Doc finally was bitten by the dysentery bug! I lost about twenty pounds overnight. By the next morning I was dehydrated and semidelirious, and my corpsmen wanted to medevac me. I refused, saying I just needed some rest, and we were going to be on the mountain a few days, so that would work out.

I reeked. I was, shall we say, extremely aromatic, and it seems that much room was made for me on the chopper ride up to the mountain. Arriving there, my guys went to the senior corpsman on the hill; he took one look at me, and said, "You're going out!" By this time, I had to concur. I could hardly walk or focus on anything. So, back on the chopper I went, and off to 3rd Medical Battalion.

At 3rd [Medical Battalion], I was treated for malaria! And, I truly believe, because I was a corpsman, the next day they sent me on down to Da Nang. There I was put in an air-conditioned hootch, and they like to have froze me to death. I eventually told the duty corpsman that dammit, I was an HM2, had dysentery, not malaria, and was going to catch pneumonia if I didn't get some covers! My fever had lowered considerably, so I was given a sheet, and shortly moved to another hootch, more like quarters. I can't remember how long I was in Da Nang (but I'm sure it was no more than three days or so) or how I got back to Mike Company. I did go see a psychiatrist while I was there, due to the nagging guilt syndrome over losing DiMilio. He listened to me, and basically said that I was not God, was not a doctor, and had to go on my instincts. That I had many people relying on me, and that I should get back to them and do the best I could. This was not very consoling to me, but back to the bush I did go!

I think I caught up with the company at Cua Viet, but I really don't know for sure. A lot of self-imposed guilt was upon me, and I was beginning to lose any semblance of awareness. Responsibility and the conflict were taking their toll. Self-doubt was setting in.

Not a good sign. You lose your edge, people get hurt. Still got a job to do. Keep it together!

June 17, 1969: Hell Day

On June 16th, if my memory is not totally out of whack, we were at Vandergrift Combat Base (VCB), having been choppered in there the day before. They had been hit in an ammo dump by rockets the day before we got there, as I remember. I know we were uneasy, even though it was a relatively "secure" area. It seems like I held a sick call there, but it is really a blur.

We were put on 6x6s, and convoyed into Dong Ha. We passed the Razorback and the Rockpile on the way, and I remember the steep hills to the south side of the road as we barreled eastward. I remember hills and dusty roads. We got into Dong Ha, and were shuffled into tents. We then had a grand meal of real steaks, vegetables, potatoes, *ice cream*, sodas . . . maybe even cold beer. (You'd think I'd remember that, wouldn't you?) Then we were herded back to the tents, and told to sit on our gear, and instructed "Do not leave this tent." The platoon honchos were called into a meeting, but no word got out what was going on; at least it didn't filter down to me. But there was an air of foreboding.

That night, it seemed late, maybe 2200 to 2300 hours, we were loaded back up on trucks. (At night ... nobody moves in trucks at night. Oh, crap!) We were driven out toward Gio Linh (although I had no idea where we were at the time), [where we] debarked and formed up for movement in a westerly direction at company strength.

There was some slight starlight, if memory serves me, just enough to keep from running into each other but not so much as to really be able to be fully aware of the terrain, and we moved inland for an hour or two, and then moved again, as I recall. Eventually, we sat on our gear for a couple of hours or so of "rest." Then about sunrise, we headed off again, still westerly bound. Then at some point we turned north, and a scraggly, sparsely treed area was in front of us. Further on, a hedgerow blocked the view. It was around 0800 hours.

The company was split out, and M79s and small arms prepped and teased the area. No response. I was with the CP [command post] group, and it seems like we went up the center with another platoon, maybe mortars.

All of a sudden, all hell broke loose.

I had never heard so much firing. We surged forward to an area with a few scraggly trees and bomb craters, more or less in the center of everything. I had no idea what the hell was happening, and couldn't seem to pinpoint where all it was coming from. It seemed to be right ... left ... and ahead.

The time frame now leaves me. We were in the middle of everything with the CP: Captain Riley, Gary Burnett the radioman, and a lot of other guys. Captain Riley seemed to disappear every so often . .. he was running the lines, making sure ammo was distributed where needed, reassuring his men, and doing a thousand other duties too. Many will remember that damn red bandana neckerchief he wore on his neck.

I knew the chaplain was with us, a hell of a day for that, but didn't know exactly where he was until later. He was out on the lines with our marines too.

I remember someone saying, "Doc, you gotta get him down!"

"What, who?"

"Doc Roth!"

I looked to my right rear where they pointed, and there was Tim, kneeling in the grass, exposed as hell. I ran low, then virtually crawled, to get to him, pushed him down, and told him to keep down. He was with Joseph "Frenchy" Fournier, an M79 man, who had been hit. They were close pals, but Frenchy was already dead by then. About that time a call for "Corpsman" came from north of us, and I said, "Tim, get him!" And off he went.

I scurried back to my post, after grabbing Frenchy's 45, since I hadn't had one since returning to the bush from my infamous medevac.

Then there was a call for "Corpsman " from north of me. Since I didn't know where my docs were, I headed up across and around small bomb craters to the hedge line. The marine was hit in the thigh, so I whipped a battle dressing on it.

Then someone said "Oh shit, Doc," and I turned to my left to see two Marines going down, as they crossed a clear space in the hedgerow about fifty to one-hundred feet away. The first one never moved, but the second one was moving. Someone hollered for him to lie still, but rounds were landing all around him, and he was trying to move to cover, but seemed disoriented.

Somebody arose and was on the move to get to them. I screamed at him to "keep your ass down, I already got two down over there, I don't need a third!" (Later I realized I was screaming at Chaplain John Dologhan.) Then I turned to the marines just in front of me, and told them to throw a grenade to make some dust to cover the retrieval. I got a brief argument, that the gooks would know where they were if they did that.

I told them to "give me a f***ing grenade, I'll throw it!" Well motivated, they were ready to pull the pin and toss, when the sky exploded as a jet screamed in just in front of us. It dumped napalm, and I remember the heat, and that smell. Then the air went black in front of us. I signaled the chaplain. He already had grabbed three marines and retrieved those two wounded.

We heard a resupply chopper coming in, so a marine and I grabbed the kid I was tending and dragged him by his flak jacket back toward the chopper. About the time we reached the CP area, someone took my place and got him on over to the chopper. The first of the two [who had gone down] in the clearing was KIA, I'm pretty sure; I heard they were FOs [forward observers].

A couple of years ago I discovered who the second one was. It was Carmen "Rick" Hazelwood, a Canadian, whom I have gotten to correspond frequently with since. He still has many complications from his injuries that day. The napalm bomb blew him over, injuring his back, and burned him some also. He was hit in the thigh, and has had problems ever since. The other FO, Private First Class Witty, was burned more severely. [Hazelwood] is the only [one] of the wounded from that day that I am positive I have had contact with. (This is no longer fact, since I have had contact in the last few years with many of my marines and corpsmen.)

I didn't know that many of my marines very well, because I stayed rather aloof, knowing that I could not bear to see a friend dying. But that was lost effort, due to the death of Lieutenant Kolter on this day. While I did not know him well, he always seemed to be pretty cool. I featured him as a schoolteacher for some reason.

Anyway, it was back to the CP area, and then, some time later, a round of WP [white phosphorous] went off about a click, or closer, to the east. Shortly, a freight train started coming in; at least it sounded like one. I never saw where the round landed, an eight- or sixteen-inch round from off the coast.

I was tucked inside my flak jacket and helmet, in a basin-sized hole in front of me. I was attempting to get as low as possible to the terrain, and my upper torso was indeed two or three inches lower in that slight depression. It seems all the firing quit momentarily, then the damn thing landed danger-close, in the middle of us just to the east of me.

I do not recall hearing the explosion. I remember bouncing, and large chunks of shrapnel whizzing past me—zshhhhhoooooffff . . . whoof-whoof—and sure as hell, the dirt that was blown up hadn't even finished landing, it seems, when I heard "Corpsman" around thirty to fifty feet away to my northeast.

I ran to the call, and here was a BNG [Brand New Guy], in a small depression, with his left foot severed, and his right shoulder all out of whack. I tourniqueted his leg; his foot was still connected by part of his Achilles tendon, cut cleanly off right at the boot top. Then I got a battle dressing under his flak jacket and shirt, on that area of damage. All this time, the battle was intensive, but we were several yards away from the hedgerow, and in that small depression, so it was relatively secure. I talked to him, and he was getting shocky. I gave him some morphine, and another one of those angels, a chopper, was on its way with resupply. We got him in a poncho, and I was still BSing him, when he asked for his mother. I about lost it right then.

I laid his boot, with his foot in it, in the poncho hoping beyond hope that it might be reattached, and with some help we got him on the chopper. I had the opportunity to talk with this marine in 2003; he did survive although they were not able to save his foot.

My memory from that point on is really fuzzy. Sergeant Roy Hoatland said the contact lasted three hours forty-five minutes. I pretty much went south later on when all the remaining KIAs were gathered, laid side by side, and I had to tag them. I don't remember who assisted with the IDs, but that was the most difficult thing I have ever done.

There were nine of our boys, no, our MEN, lying there, all looking blankly ahead to the heavens. (I still see those faces daily and nightly.)

With the weight of the world on my shoulders, and a heavy heart, I tagged Core, Dawson, Fournier, Granberry, Kolter, Revell, Rosenberger, Steele, and Stone. Witty, as well as Sergeant Neer, had apparently gone out already on earlier chopper runs. I now know we had at least twenty-six WIAs that day besides the eleven KIAs. Of the WIAs, fourteen were medevaced to 3rd Medical Battalion . . . and beyond possibly back to the States for recovery. The other eleven, I just know who they were, and were WIANE (treated in the field, not requiring medevac).

EPILOGUE: THE WAR ON TERROR

MEDICINE IN THE WAR ON TERROR
Captain John P. Feerick and
Captain Stephen S. Frost
Washington, D.C., September 11, 2001

*Captain John P. Feerick and Captain Stephen S. Frost were at
the Pentagon to attend a meeting when the building was struck
by hijacked American Airlines Flight 77.*

Feerick felt a rumble near the subway entrance—nothing particularly unusual. He thought it was a subway train. . . .

Frost: We were right outside the Reserve Affairs Office for the
Assistant Secretary of Defense. We followed the people out of the
building and saw a policeman outside directing people. We went over
to him and said we were physicians and that we would stand by if
needed. He called his command center and directed us to the area
where some injured lay on the front lawn by the impacted area near
the helipad. We were the only physicians there at the time.

Feerick: There were still some walking wounded stumbling
around, and parts of the building still caving. There were still small
pockets of what I presume was aviation fuel flaring up. There were
windows popping, and glass and particles in the air. Captain Frost
immediately entered this maelstrom and started triaging and
ministering to victims.

Frost: We saw many blast injuries, people with swollen faces and reddened skin and severe burns. The burns were the worst part. We really did not have much equipment. One of the emergency medical service trucks had their stuff out there, so we had a limited number of IVs for introducing intravenous solutions into bloodstream and bags. And that is basically what we were doing—starting IVs and just evaluating the injured for the severity. It was actually Captain Feerick who was able to get the EMS people to start transporting the people out of the area.

Feerick: Our heads were down when we hit the deck, but when I got to look up after stabilizing the patients that stumbled into me, there were ambulances coming all along that line. We had many, many people on-site. Who was medical and who was not was impossible to say at that point. Civilians and military were helping people. Those who had skills helped, and those who did not stood by and helped where they could with transport and carrying patients.

We saw about two dozen major injuries. I am sure there were more than that, but we did not manage more than six to nine hard cases and half a dozen other "maybes"—people that could develop respiratory problems or who might have spinal injuries.

Frost: After working near the impact point and evacuating those patients, we moved back to an area where the civilian EMS had set up a triage area.

Feerick: It was on the "knoll," about a couple of hundred yards on the other side where the tunnel goes into the South Parking Lot. But with multiple aviation threats—people calling in "Everyone get out. There is another air strike coming in,"—all this was disestablishing and scattering people. At that point I thought it was essential to get people under cover, so that we could have a fixed base.

There were a lot of people telling other people what to do, and my concern was that the chain of command was not being followed. My training was that the civilian on-site command medical officer was the director of all military and civilian activities. And I identified him as Dr. Jim Vayfier, an emergency room physician attached to the Alexandria Fire Department. He was superb; he was excellent. He was the best of the best, providing command support and assistance at all levels in reasonable, effective management.

I thought the underpass was a safe, secure place. It was cool, out of the sun, and there was good ventilation. Even though there was smoke all over the place, we had a wind blowing through there that cleared what did come in. We had the curb, two lanes, a middle island, two lanes, and another curb. We set up our medical supplies along the curb. Dr. Frost set up his triage area in the center, and I had the ambulances lined up on the other side. Fortuitously, also, it was close to the helicopter landing spot, which was just outside.

When we were setting up teams on that site, Captain Frost and I discovered Major Michael Moore, an air force officer who has experience in triage and disaster management. I put him in control of the triage program.

I made the decision early on to designate the civilian medical director to tell us what he wanted with us and to keep the military team together to form the backbone of the major medical supply. Civilian response was basically EMT—ambulances. The major casualty care was going to come from the military teams, with many attending civilians. I made the decision early in the process that we would use the EMS system and not bypass to go to military hospitals. I triaged and transported. I did not identify who was in what service, their serial number, and to what unit they belonged.

Frost: In our fullest capability we had seven teams ready to treat people. We saw maybe a dozen people the first few hours after the disaster. There was a team from the Navy Yard Clinic that responded on their own. They brought corpsmen, a couple of physician's assistants, a couple of docs, and some nurses. There were actually a fair number of civilian nurses, and I do not have their names. There was a nearby civilian pediatric physician who closed his office and came over. There must have been fifty to one hundred people that were there just to help with logistical problems.

Feerick: We probably had 150 medical personnel on the site at one time. Before we were through, Captain Frost had built himself a fleet hospital down in that underpass. You could have done open heart surgery. Later on, I brought the EMS director who was then in charge down to see what we had. He looked at what Frost had set up and said, "There is no way I am going to change this. Leave it as it is." He agreed with me that it was safe and secure, totally well organized. Had we actually had livable casualties, it would have been the busiest place in town.

Initially, supplies were available but there was a maldistribution. However, nothing affected patient care. We had more than enough for the few casualties we saw.

Frost: Initially, we had some supplies, perhaps a dozen IV setups and bandages. We did not have a lot of splinting material. We were concerned at first that we were going to have a big influx of patients, which never occurred. Nevertheless, we got those supplies within the next hour or two.

Feerick: As for the burn patients, they were pretty much evacuated from the site. Maintain an airway, get a line entry for shock, and get them out.

Frost: The worst burns were the ones we saw initially at the helipad area. And after that, the burns we saw were just minor. The major injuries were the ones that came out the first twenty minutes to half hour.

People commented on how well organized the people from the Navy Yard were. They stayed on until about four o'clock in the afternoon, when we were consolidating the medical assets. When it became obvious that they were not needed, half stayed anyway as a reserve in case of a catastrophe with the fire crews.

Feerick: Throughout the evening I had been cutting back our forces to basically just one team from Walter Reed. The navy assets finally went home in the morning when they reported to their clinic. Captain Frost and I remained on scene until relieved by Rear Admiral Mateczun. And it was pretty much twenty-four hours, at which time we went back to BUMED [Bureau of Medicine and Surgery] headquarters in Washington, D.C.

This was not a navy action. This was army, air force, navy. It was also civilian. We had civilian and military personnel with no medical training at all on-site who, instead of running in the other direction, ran to where they were needed, and in the face of hideously wounded and burned people. They showed the courage necessary to stand by and do what they could. Everybody acted up to their level of skill and far beyond it. At that point, rank did not matter. The people who knew the job and had a job did their job. Other people assisted them. It was the natural selection process. Many senior officers took a back seat to someone who was a better organizer. Many officers took direction from senior enlisted people who happened to have medical training when they did not. I had a marine— a colonel or a brigadier general—show up in the tunnel and say, "Show me how to carry stretchers, show me how to start IVs. Give me a job." People did not care about rank, and they did not care if they were trained or not. When everybody was running away, they went toward.

RECOLLECTIONS
Captain Ralph Bally
New York City, September 14, 2001

Operation Noble Eagle involved navy medical people helping at the destruction site of the World Trade Center on September 11, 2001. Captain Ralph Bally is a staff psychologist at the National Naval Medical Center and was the head of the mental health team on board USNS Comfort *(T-AH 20) during Operation Noble Eagle.*

September 14, 2001, turned out to be a tough day. We all got to National Naval Medical Center at Bethesda, Maryland early in the morning and boarded the buses for the four-hour ride up to Earle, New Jersey. Eventually, we all got unloaded, checked aboard, got our rooms, unpacked our sea bags, and checked into our workstations. Then, within an hour of arriving, there was an announcement that there had been a change in the mission. The hospital ship USNS *Comfort* was going to be used to provide comfort (meaning living spaces), food spaces, and showers, for the rescue workers at Ground Zero, the site of the World Trade Center, in Manhattan. And except for a very core crew, everybody else was told to pack their sea bags to go home.

I can remember being very disappointed because I thought there was going to be a big mental health portion of this. And I was ready to go. When anything this terrible happens to our country, we all want to pitch in and help. Then, all of a sudden, you were being told to go home.

Then, Commander Terry Dwyer, who is in charge of sick call operations, pointed his finger at me. I looked at myself and looked beside me as if to say, "Who is he pointing at?" He then said, "We need you and the rest of the mental health folks. You are going to be a part of this mission."

We were not actually on the ship as a Special Psychiatric Rapid Intervention team (SPRINT). When the ship goes out configured as a 250-bed hospital, it goes with dedicated mental health assets. I and one of the psychiatrists are part of the mental health assets. The unit is composed of myself as a psychologist, Lieutenant James Reeve, a psychiatrist, and a psych tech. We actually work in the trauma area. When patients come in and they have psychiatric problems, they will be triaged to us. And if they need further acute kind of treatment, they are actually moved onto the medical wards awaiting transfer off the ship.

It just so happens that on the 250-bed configuration there is also a psychiatric nurse, but she actually works on the medical wards. If the ship was going out in the 500-bed configuration, there is an extra psychiatrist and another psych tech that comes along. I asked for both of them to come out with the ship. What we actually had as mental health assets were myself, two psychiatrists, a psych nurse, and three psychiatric technicians. It also turned out that both of the chaplains who were out there were also trained in responding to disasters.

As for the mental health people aboard the ship, I saw a dual mission. Part of that mission was to take care of the rescuers, and part of the mission was to remember to watch the staff to make sure they were also taking care of themselves as they provided care for these folks.

I had a lot of mixed feelings as we neared our objective. There was a somberness and a pride. As we crossed the bay from Earle, New Jersey, we could see the smoke in the distance, and that gave me a very somber feeling. We knew where we were headed. But as we went under the Verrazano-Narrows Bridge . . . it is interesting. I am actually a little bit sad about this. Cars and trucks would slow down and you could see people wave and they would be beeping. Right away, you knew the ship was a tremendous symbol of comfort and hope coming to the people. The navy was coming to really help out in this disaster. So I had a sense of pride that I was a part of this tremendous operation.

We were still far enough back so you could see the skyline of New York with some smoke. Unless you had a picture in your hand that showed you where the two towers stood, you would not know that something was missing.

We did not park right there by the World Trade Center. Our berth was about two miles further up the river. Immediately, we were interested in getting down and seeing Ground Zero, and starting to make connections. The master chief came in and said, "Would you like to go down? I have made arrangements." And I said, "Absolutely." So I, the chaplain, the commanding officer, the executive officer, and the deputy mayor went down to see this firsthand.

What I found rather striking was this tremendous sense of camaraderie. I am used to going to New York City and it is always a hustle and bustle of cars. Everybody is beeping horns. Everybody is impatient. And lots of people are rude. And all of a sudden there are people handing out fruit and water at the different checkpoints and people applauding you as you are driving down because you are coming to help. It was just incredible!

We got down to the Battery, unloaded at the Coast Guard Station, and walked into the site. The first thing that struck me was a large group of folks who had lost people in the disaster. They all carried pictures with the names, looking for them. Has anybody seen them wandering around the city, in a hospital somewhere? And they were in shock and grieving at the loss.

Then we walked into the site. There were two huge five-story piles of rubble. One cannot grasp the immensity without standing there. You see a picture of the Grand Canyon and then you stand on the South Rim. Seeing the picture and then seeing it for real, you understand the immensity. The same thing applied at Ground Zero. You saw the pictures on television, but standing there amidst this huge amount of devastation and destruction . . .

Thousands of policemen, firemen, and rescue workers with a bucket brigade were trying to take this pile apart, bucket by bucket, and continuing to look for survivors and bodies. As you looked in their faces there was that determined focus that they were going to find someone alive, and they needed to get through the pile and get out the bodies of their comrades. But at the same time, there was a tremendous camaraderie and bonding taking place. People were talking and, in my view, this was very important. To get through these kinds of events, it is very important that people talk it out and percolate internally what has happened, and put the story together for themselves—to make some kind of sense out of the idiocy of it all.

We asked ourselves what we could do aboard the ship. We knew that policemen, firemen, emergency medical technicians (EMTs), and other rescue workers from Ground Zero would be coming aboard. So we decided to offer formal debriefings, and advertised all over the ship. Anybody who was interested could come and see us. We advertised as people came up the ramp. When you checked aboard there was a sign-up sheet for those who wanted to be part of this. We also had signs in the chow hall.

There was also a more informal approach. We provided one-page handouts on how to take care of yourself. "This is an upsetting event. It is upsetting for normal folks. These are the kinds of symptoms that normal folks have: loss of sleep, loss of appetite, nausea, feeling depressed, unsafe, angry, etc." And what to do to take care of it.

We looked for people sitting by themselves. We knew that one of the things that can help a person normalize what they have experienced is to have a support group. This is generally your friends. For those people who came from Idaho or Oklahoma or wherever to help out and came by themselves, they might not have a support group. In the chow hall, we gave them an opportunity to talk with us. We could both see how they were doing, and reinforce those kinds of things they needed to be doing to take care of themselves.

Therefore, the initial focus was working with individuals, but we also worked with groups. We also worked in sick call. Often, when patients were being treated for minor injuries in sick call, a corpsman would engage them in conversation. And if the corpsman saw the need, we would come in and talk to the patient. This is where the majority of our interventions were done, informally in the chow hall and in sick call.

As the days went by, we began seeing fewer people coming to the ship. We then began talking to some of the policemen and learned that they were making the transition from search and rescue to recovery. Even though it was not formally announced, you could see it was becoming more and more like a construction site. People who had previously been working seventeen and eighteen hours a day and were unable to drive home ended up eating and sleeping on the ship. Now they were starting to go home and be with their families. So fewer people were coming aboard.

At that time, we were able to contact a group of psychiatrists who respond to disasters. They were needing some help down at Ground Zero so we tied up with them and went down there on Friday and Saturday to do the same kind of informal talking with people. As I walked around Ground Zero and talked to the other mental health folks, I learned that much of what they were doing was just walking around and seeing how folks were doing and handing out information on anxiety reactions and Post Traumatic Stress Disorder (PTSD).

One night I was down at Ground Zero talking to a worker. I was not there more than sixty seconds when a man and woman walked up and introduced themselves to me. Clearly they were friends with the other man. At first I thought they all did the same thing, but when I started talking to the woman, it turned out she was a nurse. The other man was an administrator who worked for the police department. The common bond between all of them was that they had been there from the very beginning as rescue workers and had been part of the bucket brigade. They had seen parts of bodies and other things. They had formed a bond, and had been doing a lot of talking with each other, which was a very healthy kind of thing. I asked about their sleep and appetite and, after a while got the impression that here, at week two after the incident, they appeared to be coming through it. As they walked away, the man from the police department lingered behind. He told me he had some concerns that his experiences might turn into PTSD. He was eager for some information. I explained the usual anxiety responses normal people have to abnormal situations, and we talked about his symptoms. I assured him that because of what he had already done to take care of himself, it was unlikely he would experience PTSD.

Back at the ship, one of the ship's officers heard one of the folks talking about some of what he had seen and that he was having a lot of difficulty sleeping. The officer suggested that he come talk to me. He was an administrator who worked in disaster preparedness in one of the buildings near Ground Zero. He was at the base of the building when the first plane hit and debris began raining down. But then, as he told me, people came out and said things would be okay; people needed to go back to their offices. He was on the 53rd floor of his building looking out the window and saw the second plane hit. Later he saw some of the people jumping from the building and watched them hit the ground. Needless to say, he was having intrusive thoughts, losing sleep, and having nightmares.

In his case he did not have a lot of people to talk to. He lived in an apartment by himself. There was a next-door neighbor he helped take care of, an elderly woman, not someone he could talk to about this. So I was really the first person he had an opportunity to sit with and be able to tell his story to.

There is something else worth mentioning. Sick call is right below the flight deck. There were people with carts taking supplies across the flight deck and a few times there was a rumbling noise. As I talked with the administrator, I could see the fear on his face as he looked up. I reassured him that they were just moving supplies. And he said, "That is the sound the building made when it came down."

On another occasion, some policemen were providing supplies to the ship. One was very badly dehydrated and fainted. As his buddy went to grab him, he twisted his knee. We got them both up to sick bay. The one who fainted was in one bed and his buddy in another. As we took care of them, we learned they had lost one of their bosses in the collapse of the towers. And they had been working tremendously long hours: eighteen, nineteen, twenty hours. They were not getting to go home. And now both were feeling very guilty. "I am not out working but maybe after a couple of hours I'll get back to work." Here was this man with a splint from his hip down his leg taking care of his knee saying, "Gee, I will be back to work in a couple of hours." And here is his buddy, terribly dehydrated, saying, "I need to get back."

While all this was transpiring, five or six of their comrades showed up. We got them to talk about their loss. It was almost as though we were having an intervention with them right there—with the two buddies in bed and them. Part of the reason we could do this was because of the existence of this close-knit group.

When the two were well enough to go, we would not let them leave the ship until they ate. The whole group went to the chow hall, accompanied by two of our officers. We watched them from a distance and could see them getting back together as a group, joking and talking.

The departure from New York was a tremendous experience. We were all out on the flight deck on either side, all lined up at parade rest. I was facing up toward the George Washington Bridge. The Office of Emergency Management pier was right there. There were cars parked on top and you could see a couple of police cars and a few reporters with TV cameras. It was 11 a.m. on Monday, October 1. The tugs come in and the untying began. As we pulled away from the pier, we all saluted and held the salute. And people on the pier began to applaud, wave, and yell, "Thanks a lot." It was a very emotional experience.

As we went down the Hudson River, we all moved to the port side of the ship to salute the World Trade Center and the people there as we went by. But just before we got there, a fireboat pulled up on either side and let loose a huge spray—their way of saluting us! Then, as we approached directly across from the World Trade Center, we all stood at attention and saluted. As we did so, police boats put color in the water: red, white, and blue. It was just phenomenal and very moving.

I do not think anyone could say that sending the *Comfort* to New York was not the right thing to do. I spent a lot of time in the Casualty Receiving area where people arrived and departed, and talked to hundreds of them. To a person, they were all extremely grateful for the comfort we provided in terms of the navy being there, not only providing them with a place to get away, and a place to sleep in quiet, but a place where they could get regenerated before going back down to Ground Zero. But the one thing they all commented on was the tremendous care and hospitality that all the staff on the ship showed them. No matter what they wanted, people would go out of their way to get it for them or help any way they could.

As I was getting ready to go on the mission, and even after I had gone, many neighbors asked my wife how she felt about my being away. And her response was, "That is what they are trained to do. And he has an opportunity to do what he should be doing."

FIREFIGHT AT THE HADITHAH DAM
Andrew D. Davis
Iraq, March 29–April 10, 2003

Andrew D. Davis served in the U.S. Army during both Operation Enduring Freedom and Operation Iraqi Freedom.

The Hadithah Dam sits near the mouth of the Euphrates River in north-central Iraq, at the Persian Gulf end of the Fertile Crescent, the rumored location of the Garden of Eden. At the same time I realized the beauty of the scene in front of me, I realized it was the perfect combination of heaven and hell.

As we drove toward the dam, I noticed the first paved road for miles and stepped on the gas pedal of the Humvee. The vehicle is not like the luxury Hummer on the commercial market; it is big and boxy, makes a lot of noise, and, at 4,300 pounds, only accelerates to sixty-five kilometers per hour [forty miles per hour] in desert conditions. The vehicle was caked with fine dust particles—a texture that reminded me of the powdered sugar my mom uses to make cookies at Christmastime—which also stuck to the faces of the four Rangers who traveled with me. Though caked with dust, their faces teemed with anticipation, fingers on the trigger. Ready and alert, we had trained for this mission.

There were five small battles surrounding the western side of the dam. Each of these units needed fire support from my mortar section because we had the biggest guns on the battlefield—a pair of 120mm indirect-fire weapons capable of sending shrapnel in a hundred-meter radius upon impact. Ten rocketlike rounds have the capability of clearing a square kilometer.

By the sixth day, we sunk into a sense of quasicomfort with our surroundings. All of the enemy personnel within rifle and grenade range had been killed or captured. Our main threats were the enemy artillery pieces and the anti-aircraft guns, both of which could reach us from miles away. If fired upon by them, we would usually call in jets to take care of them, so we felt at ease. We took off our blouses and helmets and wore only our t-shirts and body armor. Instead of sleeping behind the concrete walls that afforded us cover, we started sleeping on top of the dam.

On the morning of the seventh day we dove into our daily routines, including taking turns with watch, filling sandbags, and cleaning weapons. We heard bouts of fire in the distance, but still considered ourselves relatively safe because it seemed that the enemy thought we encompassed the entire surface of the dam.

Around noon, we started making shelters to protect us from the midday sun. We placed our rain ponchos on the wall of the dam, secured them with rocks, and stretched them to the ground, creating a little tent. I made mine and lay down. Jeremy, one of the grunts, stood up to fix his shelter.

We didn't hear the usual whistle associated with an incoming artillery round, but we immediately recognized the unexpected explosion and cloud of dust. When the smoke cleared, Jeremy was lying on the ground twitching, bleeding from his face, hit by shrapnel from a 155mm howitzer. Blood poured out of his eyes and formed a puddle around his head. Justin ran to his side, while I called for the medic.

"We got a man down," I said with a raised voice. "You need to get your ass down here." The thirty seconds it took the medic to arrive seemed like an hour.

The medic arrived, checked Jeremy's vitals, and prepared him for transport. It visibly pained the medic to signal to us, stroking his fingers across his neck, that he didn't think Jeremy would make it. More than likely, the medic felt he had failed. Justin and two of the other men lifted Jeremy's limp body into the Humvee, which transported him to the center of the dam for evacuation—if he lived that long.

Our platoon sergeant accompanied Jeremy. As we awaited his return and a report on Jeremy's condition, we moved the guns to avoid enemy fire and cleaned the blood off our clothes. After three hours, the Sergeant First Class returned.

"The medics stabilized Jeremy for medevac, but he's in bad shape," he reported. When the Humvee reached the center of the dam, the Battalion's lead medic found Jeremy still alive, but in a lot of pain. The medic gave him morphine, which stimulated Jeremy to return to consciousness.

"Where are the guys?" Jeremy asked. "I want to go back and fight."

"Calm down," the medic said as he assessed Jeremy's injuries.

Jeremy started reciting the Ranger Creed: "Recognizing that I volunteered as a Ranger, fully knowing the hazards of my chosen profession, I will always endeavor to uphold the prestige, honor, and high esprit de corps of the Rangers. . . ."

The Battalion medics needed to evacuate Jeremy to a medical facility better equipped to handle his injuries. Later that day, we cleared a zone for the medevac helicopter to land, even though it was against better judgment to do this during the day. As a direct result of the quick action and thorough attention provided by the medics, Jeremy survived the attack.

APPENDIX A:
THE U.S. ARMY MEDICAL DEPARTMENT REGIMENT

The Continental Congress authorized a Medical Service for an army of twenty thousand men on July 27, 1775, effectively forming the U.S. Army Medical Department. It created the Hospital Department and named Dr. Benjamin Church of Boston as Director General and Chief Physician. On April 14, 1818, Congress passed an Act which reorganized the staff departments of the Army and provided for a Medical Department to be headed by a Surgeon General. Dr. Joseph Lovell, appointed Surgeon General of the United States Army in April 1818, was the first to hold this position in the new organization. The passage of this law marks the beginning of the modern Medical Department of the United States Army.

Throughout its early history, the size and mission of the U.S. Army Medical Department would wax and wane in response to military events around the world. There was, however, no formal regimental organization until World War I. Then, in the late 1950s, the brigade replaced the regiment as a tactical unit. In the reorganization that followed, some Army units lost their identity, their lineage, and their history. This loss did not go unnoticed, and the

U.S. Army Regimental System was created in 1981 to provide soldiers with continuous identification with a single regiment.

The mission of the regiment is to enhance combat effectiveness through a framework that provides the opportunity for affiliation, develops loyalty and commitment, fosters a sense of belonging, improves unit esprit, and institutionalizes the war-fighting ethos. The U.S. Army Medical Department Regiment was activated on July 28, 1986, during ceremonies at Fort Sam Houston, in San Antonio, Texas, the "home of Army medicine." Lieutenant General Quinn H. Becker, the U.S. Army Surgeon General and AMEDD Regimental Commander, was the reviewing officer. He was joined by general officers of the U.S. Army Reserves and the Army National Guard, representing the significant contributions and manpower of the reserve forces in the Total Army concept.

APPENDIX B:
THE U.S. NAVY HOSPITAL CORPS
HMCS (FMF) Mark T. Hacala, USNR

The first direction given to the organization of navy medicine consisted of only one article in the *Rules for the Regulation of the Navy of the United Colonies of North America* of 1775. Article 16 stated that "a convenient place shall be set apart for sick or hurt men, to be removed with their hammocks and bedding when the surgeon shall advise the same to be necessary: and some of the crew shall be appointed to attend to and serve them and to keep the place clean. The cooper shall make buckets with covers and cradles if necessary for their use."

In the late nineteenth century, the imminent danger of combat in the Spanish-American War spurred Congress to authorize a professional, well-trained group of individuals to provide medical care for the navy. Within a bill aimed at building the armed forces, one section provided for the navy's long-needed Hospital Corps. It was approved by President William McKinley on June 17, 1898. From that date to the present, either generically or by rating title, medical sailors have been called "hospital corpsmen."

By the end of 1918, the massive war increase in Hospital Corps strength to about seventeen thousand men necessitated additional schools to train the newcomers. Hospital corpsmen were assigned to the multitude of duty types and locations needed to support a navy involved in a world war. Naval training facilities and shore establishments needed hospital corpsmen as well as did occupation forces in Haiti and other bases around the world. But World War I provided the Hospital Corps a role that would afford it some of the most gruesome and dangerous challenges it would ever face: duty with the Marine Corps.

World War II became the period of Hospital Corps' greatest manpower, diversity of duty, and instance of sacrifice. Between 1941 and 1945, the ranks of this small organization swelled from its pre-war levels of near 4,000 to over 132,000 personnel. This increase came to fulfill new responsibilities with new technologies at new duty stations. In the face of great adversity, the Hospital Corps would cement its reputation for effectiveness and bravery.

Of all the hospital corpsmen in World War II, Fleet Marine Force personnel endured, perhaps, the most grueling side of war. As they swarmed numerous beaches in the Pacific, they became targets themselves as they braved fire to reach downed comrades. At Guadalcanal, Tarawa, Peleliu, Saipan, Tinian, Kwajalein, Iwo Jima, and Okinawa, hospital corpsmen bled and died, often in greater numbers than the Marines for whom they cared. Hospital Corps casualties in the 4th Marine Division at Iwo Jima, for example, were 38 percent.

Massive reorganization of the armed forces took place after World War II. A new Department of Defense was established, and the Army-Navy Medical Service Corps Act removed commissioned allied health and medical administration officers from the Hospital Corps. This law also provided for a separate Dental Technician rating, which remained a component of the Hospital Corps until 1972. New legislation permitted women, previously WAVES, members of the Women's Reserve, to enlist in the Regular Navy, and HM1 Ruth Flora became the first hospital corpsman to do so on July 12, 1948.

Hospital Corpsmen in Korea

As part of a United Nations force, Marines were committed to the Korean peninsula when South Korea was invaded by its northern neighbor in the summer of 1950. Within the first year, hospital corpsmen had participated in the dramatic landing at Inchon and the frigid retreat from the Chosin Reservoir. By the summer of 1951, a stalemated line of opposing forces took static positions. For the next two years, the war would be reminiscent of World War I, with bunkers, trenches, raids and artillery fire. The slow war of attrition was nonetheless lethal. In late March 1953, 3,500 Chinese Communist Forces soldiers attacked three outposts—Reno, Vegas, and Carson—of 40 Marines and one hospital corpsmen each. Out of this fighting came two Medals of Honor and numerous other decorations. In the Nevada Cities Outpost battles, most of the hospital corpsmen who were involved at the small unit level were either killed or wounded.

Although only one Marine division was involved in the war, the Hospital Corps lost 108 killed in action. Disproportionate to their numbers was their heroism. In Korea, hospital corpsmen earned 281 Bronze Star Medals, 113 Silver Star Medals, and 23 Navy Crosses. All 5 enlisted Navy Medals of Honor were awarded to Navy Hospital Corpsmen serving with the Marines.

Hospital Corpsmen in Vietnam

American military commitment in Southeast Asia grew in the decades following World War II. As early as 1959, a few hospital corpsmen provided medical support for U.S. military personnel as part of the American Dispensary at the U.S. Embassy. Four years later, in 1963, Navy Station Hospital, Saigon, was created. Ninety hospital corpsmen would staff the facility, which provided care for U.S. and allied (Australian, New Zealand, Filipino, and South Korean) military, as well as South Vietnamese civilians. These medical personnel conducted routine medical care and treated the victims of combat and terrorist actions until the hospital was transferred to the Army in 1966.

A new hospital was constructed in 1965 at Naval Support Activity Da Nang. A staff of 485 hospital corpsmen worked with doctors and nurses to care for combat casualties. The hospital, which was designed primarily to care for Marines in the I Corps sector, treated 23,467 patients in 1968 alone. Although not on the front lines, the hospital corpsmen here were subjected to routine rocket and mortar attacks.

Hospital corpsmen were assigned aboard ships of various kinds, providing off-shore medical support to U.S. forces. The largest commitment here was on the hospital ships USS *Repose* and USS *Sanctuary*. Some two hundred hospital corpsmen, representing the gamut of technical specialties, worked on each ship. Teams of twenty hospital corpsmen served on LPH class amphibious ships. Others supported the riverine force on APB class base ships.

U.S. State Department initiatives and the Medical Civic Action Program (MEDCAP) provided medical support for Vietnamese civilians. Beyond routine aid and treatment, the hospital corpsmen working through these programs provided guidance in sanitation and preventive medicine throughout South Vietnam.

By far the Hospital Corps' largest contribution in Vietnam was with Marine Corps units. Starting with the 50 who landed with the Marines at Da Nang in 1965, the enlisted medical component would grow to 2,700 hospital corpsmen assigned to 1st and 3d Marine Divisions, 1st Marine Air Wing, and other combat support units. Two medical battalions and two hospital companies operated field hospitals, collecting and clearing units, and dispensaries which treated the flow of combat casualties from the field. Closer support was provided at the battalion aid station (BAS) level, where casualties could be stabilized before evacuation to more definitive care. The BAS was often bypassed because of the exceptional medical evacuation capabilities of helicopter medical evacuation (MEDEVAC).

Hospital Corpsmen Today

In its first century, the Hospital Corps has compiled a truly honorable legacy of valor and sacrifice. In addition to the wars and conflicts recounted here, hospital corpsmen have responded to natural disasters, military accidents, and other peacetime emergencies. Moreover, they have maintained the regular health of their sailors and marines, giving immunizations, conducting preventive medicine efforts, and holding sick call. Today, the 23,000 regular and 6,000 reserve members of the Navy Hospital Corps continue to serve around the globe. They are assigned to naval hospitals and clinics, to surface ships and submarines. They fly search and rescue missions and deploy with Seabees. They maintain constant battle readiness with Marine Corps units and SEAL teams.

Hospital corpsmen have always had the job of maintaining the health of their shipmates. Their innumerable instances of heroism, of consciously exposing themselves to danger to save lives, are not spectacular because they were required to act. Their displays of courage have been noteworthy because these men and women cared about their shipmates.

ACKNOWLEDGMENTS

I would like to thank the following people for being involved in this project. First, to Chuck Wright for asking me to be part of it. He is the singular force behind the Medical Memorial and deserves much credit for not giving up on it in the face of many problems.

Jerry Jolly has been a great encouragement throughout this process. So have many of the men and women who served in the medical corps and sent me their stories. Thanks for your commitment. Much credit goes to you not only as war heroes, but as people who are willing to share the darkness of those terrible times.

Thanks to my wife Jeanette for encouraging me along the way.

Much thanks to the editors and personnel at MBI Publishing, most notably to Steve Gansen who first believed in this project and got it moving in the publishing house. Many others have been involved, whose names I don't even know. Thanks to you all.

Finally, great thanks to our God and Father for giving me the writing abilities I have and for guiding me to this project. He is the ultimate mover and shaker behind it (and I hope he is pleased with the outcome).

—Mark Littleton

Acknowledgments

I thank Jerry Jolly, the first person we were able to reunite with his corpsman. Jerry first encouraged me to think about putting together a "thank you book" where people could express their thanks and appreciation for the help rendered for them in wartime.

Much thanks to Bob Ashcroft for encouraging me to continue to work on finding the stories for this book and with the overall project.

Thanks to Richard Ritter, our webmaster, who assisted in obtaining stories through the internet.

Thanks to Bob and Earlene McClure who helped with the stories and getting people to send them in.

Thanks to Don "Doc" Ballard who also helped with finding stories.

—Chuck Wright

The Combat Medic Prayer

Oh, Lord I ask for the divine strength to meet the demands of my profession. Help me to be the finest medic, both technically and tactically. If I am called to the battlefield, give me the courage to conserve our fighting forces by providing medical care to all who are in need. If I am called to a mission of peace, give me the strength to lead by caring for those who need my assistance. Finally, Lord, help me to take care of my own spiritual, physical and emotional needs. Teach me to trust in your presence and never-failing love.

AMEN

If you have heard a heroic story of a medic, corpsman, or surgeon in combat, or if you have your own story of being wounded and helped by one, we would like to see it.

Please send your stories to:

Mlittleton@earthlink.net

Or to:
The National Combat Medical Memorial and Youth Education Center
1776 Parkview Avenue
Kansas City KS 66104
(816) 452-0606 (phone)
(816) 454-0897 (fax)
www.medicalwarmemorial.org